Intermediate Italian

FOR

DUMMIES®

by Daniela Gobetti
Cristiana Mora Thielmann
Chiara Marchelli

WILEY

Wiley Publishing, Inc.

Intermediate Italian For Dummies®

Published by
Wiley Publishing, Inc.
111 River St.
Hoboken, NJ 07030-5774
www.wiley.com

Copyright © 2008 by Wiley Publishing, Inc., Indianapolis, Indiana

Published simultaneously in Canada

For general information on our other products and services, please contact our Customer Care Department within the U.S. at 800-762-2974, outside the U.S. at 317-572-3993, or fax 317-572-4002.

For technical support, please visit www.wiley.com/techsupport.

Wiley also publishes its books in a variety of electronic formats. Some content that appears in print may not be available in electronic books.

Library of Congress Control Number: 2008930825

ISBN: 978-0-470-24794-5

Manufactured in the United States of America

10 9 8 7 6 5 4 3 2 1

WILEY

About the Author

Daniela Gobetti is a native of Italy who has lived in the United States for the last 30 years. She holds a *Laurea in Lettere e Filosofia* from the University of Turin, Italy, and a PhD in Political Science from Columbia University. She has taught political theory for several years and has helped build the European Union Center at the University of Michigan. She's one of the founders of PROXIMA — Global Education Consulting Training (www.proxima-gect.com), a consulting firm in the field of the internationalization of higher education and of cultural training.

Since coming to the United States, one of Daniela's goals has been to become as proficient as possible in English without losing her own mother tongue. To this end, she has taught Italian, translated books from Italian into English and from English into Italian, published peer-reviewed articles in both languages, and authored several books on learning Italian. She has revised *2001 Italian and English Idioms* and *Italian Idioms,* and she has published *Dictionary of Italian Slang* with Barron's Educational Series, *Better Reading Italian, Italian Pronouns and Prepositions, Must-Know Italian,* and *Italian Vocabulary* with McGraw-Hill.

Author's Acknowledgments

Thanks to my agent, Grace Freedson, who has trusted and helped me over many years. And thanks to my editors, Kristin DeMint and Elizabeth Rea, who have helped me work with the *For Dummies* approach to writing books.

Publisher's Acknowledgments

We're proud of this book; please send us your comments through our Dummies online registration form located at www.dummies.com/register/.

Some of the people who helped bring this book to market include the following:

Acquisitions, Editorial, and Media Development

Project Editor: Kristin DeMint

Acquisitions Editor: Michael Lewis

Senior Copy Editor: Elizabeth Rea

Copy Editor: Jessica Smith

Editorial Program Coordinator: Erin Calligan Mooney

Technical Editor: Cristiana Mora Thielmann

Editorial Manager: Michelle Hacker

Editorial Assistants: Joe Niesen, Jennette ElNaggar, David Lutton

Cartoons: Rich Tennant (www.the5thwave.com)

Composition Services

Project Coordinator: Katie Key

Layout and Graphics: Nikki Gately, Stephanie D. Jumper

Proofreaders: Laura Albert, Reuben W. Davis, John Greenough, Jessica Kramer, Mildred Rosenzweig

Indexer: Potomac Indexing, LLC

Special Help

Danielle Voirol, Alicia B. South

Publishing and Editorial for Consumer Dummies

Diane Graves Steele, Vice President and Publisher, Consumer Dummies

Joyce Pepple, Acquisitions Director, Consumer Dummies

Kristin A. Cocks, Product Development Director, Consumer Dummies

Michael Spring, Vice President and Publisher, Travel

Kelly Regan, Editorial Director, Travel

Publishing for Technology Dummies

Andy Cummings, Vice President and Publisher, Dummies Technology/General User

Composition Services

Gerry Fahey, Vice President of Production Services

Debbie Stailey, Director of Composition Services

Contents at a Glance

Table of Contents

Introduction

You may like Italian because it's the language of art, design, good (and healthy) food, icy mountains and deep blue seas, music, and of course great literature. As you get to know it better, you'll discover it's also the language of great scientists, traders, explorers, and emigrants. Italian is spoken by the 60 million inhabitants of Italy and by many people of Italian descent in foreign countries (about 16 million in the United States alone). And the number of Americans of non-Italian descent who want to learn Italian is growing.

Italian was established as the language of high culture in the thirteenth century thanks to the works of many poets and storytellers (the most important one being Dante and his *Divine Comedy*). Since then, one shared language has dominated high culture despite continued political fragmentation, while at the local level people spoke local languages and dialects also derived from Latin.

Italian, like any language, is a living thing that has changed remarkably over time and especially in the last 100 years, as modern society and the arrival of mass media have introduced a simpler, more direct way of speaking. Thanks to universal public education, TV, newspapers, and movies, Italians now all speak the same language, with only some variations in vocabulary and pronunciation. Still, a lot of people, especially those who don't live in big cities, continue to speak their local dialects, which after a phase of neglect are now popular again.

About This Book

The language I present in *Intermediate Italian For Dummies* is the language of everyday life in today's Italy. You'll find it used in newspapers, on TV, in modern novels, in instruction booklets, on the Internet, and so forth. At any given point in time, there are good ways and bad ways of expressing yourself, so I give you the correct version of the language and usage. But don't be surprised if you go to Italy and hear or read something different from what you find in this book. Over time you'll develop your own sensibility for expressions that are interesting variations on the language rather than merely mistakes.

As the title suggests, *Intermediate Italian For Dummies* is a reference book for people who have some familiarity with the language. You may find information that you're already aware of, in which case you can skip it and move on. You also can choose where to start and consult only the chapters that interest you. But keep in mind that the book does proceed logically from simpler matters to more complex ones. The Cheat Sheet and the appendixes provide you with some quick-reference tools to check basic things like unfamiliar words but especially pronouns and verb conjugations, which are two of the least intuitive aspects of Italian for English speakers.

The first part of the book is devoted to nouns, adjectives, and various pronouns. They share the fact that they vary in gender and number and require users to learn how to coordinate them when they're used together. I devote the middle part to verbs, both to their conjugations and to the way you use them in context. In the latter part I introduce topics that help you figure out how to put sentences together, either when asking questions or giving answers or when linking together sentences to convey complex information.

In each chapter you have the opportunity to practice what you've just read. You may be asked to come up with one word, craft an entire sentence, or select the best word or phrase to complete a sentence. The bottom line is that it's important to test your skills and be able to find information stored in your mind. The Answer Key at the end of each chapter allows you to check your progress.

Conventions Used in This Book

To make this book as easy to use as possible, I used certain conventions throughout:

- ✔ I **bold** all the Italian words so they stand out in the text; English translations are in *italics*.
- ✔ When a practice exercise has more than one correct answer, I provide both the more and the less common answers.
- ✔ I use some technical grammar terms. Every subject matter has its jargon, and it's much more convenient to learn the difference between *mood* and *tense,* or *coordination* and *subordination,* than to engage in verbose explanations of what those words define. The more you use these terms, the more familiar they become — trust me.

Foolish Assumptions

I made the following assumptions about you (my reader) and your Italian when writing this book:

- ✔ You're proficient enough in Italian to consider yourself an intermediate-level writer or speaker. You're already aware that even the simplest sentence in Italian requires an understanding of gender and number options, ability to coordinate endings, and memorization of strange verbal forms, to say the least.
- ✔ You understand basic concepts of English grammar. I define them, but I expect you to have encountered the terms before and to be able to apply them to any language. From a grammatical point of view, Italian and English are often substantively different, but with a few exceptions, the grammarians who systematized the two languages used the same concepts: A verb is a verb in both languages, as is a pronoun, a subordinate clause, and so on.
- ✔ You want to become more precise when using verbs, pronouns, and other parts of speech. Sure, Italians will understand you if you say **volere Coca-Cola** (*to want Coca-Cola*) instead of **Vorrei una Coca-Cola** (*I'd like a Coca-Cola*), but the pleasure of speaking a foreign language comes with proficiency in it.

> ✔ You want to use your Italian to read novels, travel to Italy, do business with Italians, or possibly pursue a degree in Italian.
>
> ✔ You want to know everyday Italian rather than the language of a special field, such as economics or medicine.

I do hope that you're the reader I had in mind when I was writing this book. If you find it too hard to use, perhaps a more elementary text can help you reach the point where this book becomes useful for you — it should be challenging, but approachable.

How This Book Is Organized

I divided this book into parts, starting with the building blocks of Italian and ending with the appendixes. Each part has several chapters that deal in detail with that part's subject matter. Here's a breakdown of the six parts.

Part 1: Getting Your Bearings: Reviewing the Basics

In this part, I explain the basic grammatical structures of Italian (and English), parts of speech, and the main differences between Italian and English grammar; the definite and indefinite articles; masculine, feminine, singular, and plural nouns; and numbers, including how to handle expressions of time and the calendar.

Part II: A Close Look at Parts of Speech

In this part, I guide you through the maze of Italian pronouns, which are numerous and complicated. I talk about adjectives and how to coordinate them with nouns; and how to form short phrases made of a preposition and a noun (called *complements*), which you need when the noun by itself can't carry your meaning. I also cover words like *this* and *that,* indefinites such as *some* and *a little,* and how to say that something belongs to you. I end this part with a chapter about relative pronouns and conjunctions — little words such a **e** (*and*), **ma** (*but*), **quando** (*when*), and **che** (*that*) that enable you to link sentences together.

Part III: What Would You Do without Verbs and Tenses?

Verbs are the core of any language because they convey so much meaning. All you need is one word — well, perhaps two or three in compound tenses — to give people a sense of time, the emotion you're feeling, whether you're talking about yourself or someone else, and whether you're doing something or you're the recipient of someone else's action. Italian verbs are more varied and more complicated than English verbs. They're conjugated (as the verb *to be* still is in English: *I am, you are, he is, we are, you are, they are*). I give you guidelines about how to conjugate verbs.

With the regular ones, well, they're regular, so you pick up the pattern and you apply it. With the irregular ones, you have to expect surprises. (Sometimes I still find myself surprised!)

Part IV: Adding Nuances to Moods and Tenses

More verbs, more nuances. This part explores how to give commands and how to convey possibility, hope, and uncertainty. Italian has very specific verbal forms for those concepts. This part also tells you how to use various moods (indicative, conditional, and subjunctive) in sentence combinations and how to do it when talking about the present, the past, and the future.

In addition, this part revolves around the idea that language is a public good in that you share it with others. You use it mostly to interact, and languages wouldn't exist if people weren't in the company of other human beings. So you ask questions and give answers in Italian, and you use different constructions to say that you're acting in the world, you're the object of your own actions, or you're experiencing something being done to you.

Part V: The Part of Tens

When you're talking with someone, you have the chance to clarify what you're saying, or the other person can give you a useful suggestion about how to express yourself better. But if you're writing, you're on you own. This part includes a list of *false friends,* words that look similar but mean different things. I also list ten ways of expressing yourself that will make your Italian richer and more idiomatic — in writing or speaking.

Part VI: Appendixes

The appendixes include a verb chart that summarizes conjugations of regular and irregular Italian verbs, an English-Italian dictionary to help you find the right words in Italian, and an Italian-English dictionary so that you can figure out the meaning of unfamiliar words.

Icons Used in This Book

As in all *For Dummies* books, icons tag information that's unique in some way. I used the following icons throughout this book (you can spot them in the left-hand margin):

This icon highlights advice that can help you use or remember the information at hand as well as emphasizes minor variations in the topic.

This icon alerts you to grammar rules, special cases, or points about meaning that you should pay particular attention to.

This icon highlights points where Italian and English differ in important ways.

Every language has rules . . . and a lot of exceptions! I point them out with this icon in order to make you aware that when you encounter an exception you have to trust your memory more than your deductive reasoning skills.

You see this icon at the start of each practice exercise.

Where to Go from Here

In *Intermediate Italian For Dummies,* I think of my readers as highly motivated people who are self-starters and have the patience to work through training exercises as if they were at the gym. Learning a language isn't easy, but you can make it more enjoyable by varying your approach. Perhaps you want to team up with a friend to quiz each other, write to an Italian pen pal who wants to improve his or her English in exchange for helping you with your Italian, pick up some Italian-language films to watch (without subtitles!), or start exploring Italian Web sites and message boards.

You can start with any chapter, so browse all you want. You may want to scan the table of contents or index first, or just pick a chapter and dive in. In each chapter I refer to other chapters when the subject matter requires it; I recommend that you follow the thread, as it were, because all pieces ultimately are tied together in a language. **Buon lavoro!**

Part I
Getting Your Bearings: Reviewing the Basics

The 5th Wave   By Rich Tennant

"Wait! Wait! I want to find out what gender 'eggplant' is so I know how to pick it up."

In this part . . .

Before you plunge into the maze of Italian verbs and
come out at the other end congratulating yourself for
your great sense of direction, I invite you to review some
basic information. In this part, you're likely to encounter
many things you already know about using the language,
but it's always good to refresh one's memory and integrate
new and old information. With that in mind, I go over the
parts of speech, all the possible endings of articles and
nouns, how to move from singular to plural and vice versa,
and how to count.

Chapter 1

What Do You Know?
Parts of Speech and Then Some

. . . .

In This Chapter

▶ Revisiting some grammar basics

▶ Understanding parts of speech

▶ Working with dictionaries of all sorts

. . . .

*I*talian is a *Romance language,* derived from Latin. It shares features with its parent language, including variation in the endings of nouns and adjectives, depending on the grammatical group they belong to; a sometimes maddening array of verbal forms that vary in person, tense, and mood (conjugation); and a weakness for linking sentences together by adding one or more dependent clauses to an independent clause.

In other words, Italian has a lot of markers, and gender, number, person, mood, and tense are just the main ones. The advantage of markers is that they enable you to see that two words are related even if they're far away from one another in a sentence. Therefore, the word order is less strict in Italian than in English, where at times position alone tells you a word's function. Because all the pieces can be tied and clustered together, writers can build long, fluid paragraphs. Hence the beautiful, flowing nature of the language.

The main disadvantage of all those markers is that Italian grammar is complex even at the beginner level. You need a lot of rules at your fingertips to say or write even the simplest sentence. This book aims to help you acquire that skill.

If Italian grammar is complex, its phonetics is easy. I say a few words about pronunciation in the section I devote to *phonology,* the part of grammar that studies sounds and spelling; but the long and short of it is that a one-to-one correspondence between what you write and how you say it makes Italian oral comprehension much easier and frees you from spelling nightmares!

Getting a Grip on Italian Grammar Terms and Nuances

Italian grammar has a long history, dating back to — guess what — Latin. Latin grammarians are the source of most of the terms used in European languages, including English. Grammatical terms do what mathematical terms do for you: They allow you to understand what object you're dealing with. Is 8 + 8 an addition or a subtraction? Is

¾ a fraction or an equation? These aren't just labels; rather, they're concepts that allow you to perform the correct operation with those numbers. Grammatical concepts do the same for languages, and you discover many of them in the upcoming sections.

When you consider a language, you can look at many different aspects of it:

✔ **Phonology:** The study of a language's sounds; for example, the difference between **ce** (the sound *cha*ir in English) and **che** (the sound *ke*ttle in English).

✔ **Morphology:** The study of the form words can take — are they singular (**gatto** [*cat*]) or plural (**gatti** [*cats*])? Masculine (**leone** [*lion*]) or feminine (**leonessa** [*lioness*])? First-person singular (**io** [*I*]) or third-person plural (**loro** [*they*])? Do they convey the present (**lui va** [*he goes*]) or the past (**lui andava** [*he used to go*])? Is the mood conditional (**vorrei** [*I'd like*]) or imperative (**alzati!** [*stand up!*])?

✔ **Syntax:** The study of the rules that tell you how you can form full sentences and link them together, as in **Vorrei un tè freddo perché fa così caldo** (*The lake is frozen because it's very cold*).

✔ **Semantics:** The study of the meanings of what people say; for example, if you say **È caldo** (*It's hot*), what are you talking about? The weather? The roast beef on your plate?

In this section (and in this book), I talk a little bit about phonology and a lot about morphology and syntax. And even without saying that I'm doing it, I talk about semantics throughout the book.

Phonology: Saying and spelling words correctly

If you're reading this book, I assume you already know the basics of Italian spelling and pronunciation. So with this section, I only want to remind you of some differences you may experience when listening (or speaking) and reading (or writing).

As in English, the letters **c** and **g** can have a hard sound ([c] as in *cat* and [g] as in *go*) or a soft sound ([s] as in *city* and [j] as in *gin*). Here's how the spelling affects pronunciation:

✔ **c** and **g** have a hard sound before **a, o,** and **u: casa** (*house*), **cosa** (*thing*), **cubo** (*cube*); **gamba** (*leg*), **gola** (*throat*), **gusto** (*taste*). They also have a hard sound when followed by **h,** as in **che** (*that*) and **ghiaccio** (*ice*).

✔ **c** and **g** have a soft sound before **e** and **i: cera** (*wax*), **cinema** (*cinema*); **gelo** (*freeze*), **giro** (*turn*).

Adding an **i** before **a, o,** or **u** makes the sound soft, as in **ciao** (*hello*) and **gioia** (*joy*). Adding an **h** before **e** and **i** makes the sound hard, as in **che** (*that*) and **chi** (*who*).

In Romance languages, accents can make a big difference. In Italian, you write the accent only on vowels, and only in the following cases:

✔ The accent falls on the vowel at the end of the last syllable, as in **città** (*city*) and **virtù** (*virtue*).

✔ Adding an accent helps avoid confusion with other words, as with **la** (*the, her*) and **là** (*there*); **da** (*from, by*) and **dà** (*he gives*).

Morphology: Word structure and variations in word forms

In Italian and English, morphology is the study of the inner structure of words, the forms they can take, and the functions they can serve when you use them in speech or writing. But language has thousands of words! Are you supposed to study their form, structure, and function one by one? Your work would never end! Luckily, grammarians have clustered words according to the basic function they play in the language. So before telling you a bit more about forms and functions of words, I tell you how they're grouped into the *parts of speech*.

Identifying the nine parts of speech

English has eight parts of speech, and Italian has nine, as listed in Table 1-1.

Table 1-1	Parts of Speech		
Part of Speech	*Definition*	*Examples*	*Notes*
articolo (*article*) (Note: This isn't listed as a separate part of speech in English, which handles articles with adjectives [also called determiners])	A special qualifier that modifies a noun by "determining" it	**il, lo, la** (*the* singular) **i, gli, le** (*the* plural) **un, un', uno, una** (*a, an*)	When referring to a specific object, you use a definite article. To point to an object among many like objects, you use an indefinite article. The article and the noun it refers to share the same gender and number.
nome (*noun*)	A word that indicates a person, animal, thing, or idea; it can be accompanied by an article	**uomo** (*man*) **cane** (*dog*) **penisola** (*peninsula*) **amore** (*love*)	In Italian, *all* nouns are either masculine, such as **il tavolo** (*table*), or feminine, such as **la sedia** (*chair*).
aggettivo (*adjective*)	A word that describes a noun, a name, or a pronoun	**piccolo** (*small*) **grande** (*large*)	Adjectives must match the word they refer to in gender and number.

(continued)

Table 1-1 *(continued)*

Part of Speech	Definition	Examples	Notes
pronome (*pronoun*)	A word that substitutes for a noun, name, or a phrase already mentioned; the replaced word or phrase is the *antecedent* of the pronoun; the pronouns **io** (*I*), **tu** (*you*), **noi** (*we*), and **voi** (*you*) are not replacements but rather identify speakers/listeners	**io** (*I*) **tu** (*you* singular) **lui** (*he*) **lei** (*she*) **esso, essa** (*it*) **noi** (*we*) **voi** (*you* plural) **loro, essi, esse** (*they*)	In the preceding column I list the subject pronouns. Italian is so rich in pronouns that it's not possible to list them all here. See Chapters 4, 7, and 17.
verbo (*verb*)	A word that shows an action, an event, or a state of being	**andare** (*to go*) **brillare** (*to shine*) **soffrire** (*to suffer*)	In Italian, verbs take different endings for each of the six subjects. See the chapters in Part III.
avverbio (*adverb*)	A word that qualifies a verb, adjective, noun, another adverb, or a sentence	**velocemente** (*quickly*) **bene** (*well*) **male** (*badly*)	Adverbs are invariable. Some are original words, but many others can be derived from adjectives by adding the ending **-mente,** which corresponds to the ending *-ly* in English (see Chapter 5).
preposizione (*preposition*)	A word that identifies a prepositional phrase or introduces nouns, names, and pronouns, linking them to the rest of the sentence	**di** (*of, from*) **a** (*at, to*) **da** (*from, by*) **in** (*in*) **su** (*on*) **con** (*with*) **per** (*for*) **fra/tra** (*between, among*)	Prepositions are invariable. Italian has eight basic prepositions that are often combined with the definite article (see Chapter 6).
congiunzione (*conjunction*)	A word that connects two words, phrases, or clauses	**e** (*and*) **ma** (*but*) **o** (*or*) **che** (*that*) **quando** (*when*) **perché** (*because, why*)	Conjunctions are invariable. You use coordinating conjunctions to link independent clauses together; you use subordinating conjunctions to tie a dependent clause to an independent clause.

Part of Speech	Definition	Examples	Notes
interiezione (*interjection*)	A word used to express strong feeling or sudden emotion; generally placed at the beginning of the sentence and followed by an exclamation point	**ahah!** (*ah!*) **ahi!** (*ouch!*) **uau!** (*wow!*)	Besides words that are only interjections (which are invariable), in both Italian and English you can use a lot of words to the same effect, as in **Bene!** (*Well!*) or **Davvero?** (*Indeed?, Really?*).

The terms of agreement: A few more details about word forms

When you know what part of speech a word is, you can ask questions regarding its form, structure, and function. The answers to those questions enable you to start using those words correctly with one another.

To start, you can ask questions about

- **Gender:** Does the word you're looking at have a gender or not? And which one? In both English and Italian, names used for people and animals have gender (**Paolo** [*Paul*] or **Anna** [*Anna*]), as do pronouns (**lui** [*he*] and **lei** [*she*]).

  But in Italian, a lot of other words have a gender, too, either masculine or feminine:

  - Nouns and articles, as in **il gatto** (*the male cat*) or **la gatta** (*the female cat*)

  - Adjectives, as in **bello** (*beautiful*) or **bella** (*beautiful*)

  - Past participles, as in **andato** (*gone,* referring to a singular masculine noun) or **andata** (*gone,* referring to a singular feminine noun)

- **Number:** Is the word singular or plural? In other words, does it vary in number? Examples of number change include **il gatto** (*the cat*) → **i gatti** (*the cats*); **la ragazza** (*the girl*) → **le ragazze** (*the girls*).

- **Person:** What's the grammatical person of the agent performing the action — the speaker (first person), the one spoken to (second person), or someone else (third person)? Italian and English have six grammatical persons: three singular and three plural.

In the sentences that follow, identify the underlined part of speech and write it next to the sentence. Then translate the sentence into English.

0. Mauro e Giovanna <u>ballano</u> il tango.

A. **Verbo;** *Mauro and Giovanna dance the tango.*

1. <u>Ah</u>! Ci hai fatto una bella sorpresa! _____

2. Luigi non si sente <u>bene</u>. _____

3. Non mi è piaciuto <u>il</u> film. _____

4. Vado <u>con</u> lei <u>in</u> montagna. _____

5. Bianca mangia il pesce, <u>ma</u> non mangia la carne. _____

6. Hai comprato <u>le</u> uova? _____

7. <u>Siete partiti</u> in orario? _____

8. Mi hanno dato una buona <u>ricetta</u>. _____

9. Non <u>ci</u> hanno ascoltato. _____

Conjugating verbs

In Italian, verbs take a lot of different forms. A verb can change according to

- ✔ Which one of the six grammatical persons is performing the action

- ✔ When that action occurs (time)

- ✔ What feeling the action conveys (mood)

- ✔ Whether the subject is performing the action (active voice), is being acted upon (passive voice), or is acting upon itself (reflexive voice)

- ✔ Whether the verbal form is finite (such as indicative or subjunctive), meaning that it conveys a specific subject; or nonfinite (such as infinitive or gerund), meaning that it doesn't convey a specific subject

Italian verbs take different forms depending on all the criteria in the preceding list. When you change the ending of the verb according to those criteria, you *conjugate* the verb. The families of verbs that behave in the same way are called *conjugations*. When it comes to Italian verb conjugations, you encounter the following:

- ✔ Three regular conjugations with the infinitive form of the verbs ending in

  - **-are: guardare** (*to look at*)

  - **-ere: temere** (*to fear*)

  - **-ire: sentire** (*to hear, to feel*)

- ✔ Regular verbs that change spelling: **giocare** (*to play*) → **giochiamo** (*we play*)

- ✔ Irregular verbs, which may change

  - Stem: **andare** (*to go*) → **vado** (*I go*)

  - Ending (when you compare it to the endings of regular forms): **cadere** (*to fall*) → **caddi** (*I fell*), not **cadei** or **cadetti**

  - Both stem and ending: **vivere** (*to live*) → **vissi** (*I lived*)

You need to know all the verb forms in order to convey time and mood correctly and to match the verb with the subject. When the verbal form includes a past participle, you have to decide whether you can leave it in its default form, which is the masculine singular (as in **amato** [*loved*]), or you have to coordinate its ending with the subject or the object of the sentence, choosing among **amato, amata, amati,** and **amate** (*loved*). See Chapter 10 for details.

If you want to acquire full command of verb conjugations, learn them by heart. Choose mood and tense, and then conjugate a verb in the three persons (in both singular and plural), with or without the subject pronouns. Repeat the conjugation in a singsong manner on the treadmill, while you're driving, or before falling asleep. For example, the simple or historic past of **essere** is **[io] fui, [tu] fosti, [lui] fu** (*[I] was, [you] were, [he] was*); **[noi] fummo, [voi] foste, [loro] furono** (*[we] were, [you] were, [they] were*) — and remember to breathe! You need to *say* the verbal forms, not just repeat them in your mind in order for them to stick. With practice, you may find yourself pleasantly surprised when you need the Italian counterpart of *we were* and it just pops into your mind: **noi fummo!**

Table 1-2 gives you a sense of how many moods and tenses Italian verbs can take and gives you their English counterparts. I also provide short examples of how you use that tense and mood in context, and I refer you to the chapters in this book that I devote specifically to the tense in question.

Table 1-2		A Lineup of Tenses and Moods		
Tense/Mood (Italian)	*Tense/Mood (Translation)*	*Example*	*Translation*	*Chapter(s) Containing More Information*
Indicativo (Indicative Mood)				
presente	present	**Vado all'università a Milano.**	*I go to college in Milan.*	9
presente progressivo	present progressive	**Sto andando all' università.**	*I'm going to college.*	9
passato prossimo	present perfect	**Sono andato all' università in Spagna.**	*I went to college in Spain.*	10
imperfetto	simple past/ imperfect	**Quando ero giovane andavo all'università.**	*When I was young I went to college.*	11
imperfetto progressivo	past/imperfect progressive	**Stavo andando a lezione quando l'ho incontrato.**	*I was going to class when I met him.*	11
trapassato prossimo	past perfect	**Ero andato all' università prima che ci andasse Marisa.**	*I had gone to school before Marisa did.*	11
preterit	simple/histor- ical past	**Andai all'università a Roma.**	*I went to college in Rome.*	10
trapassato remoto	pluperfect	**Dopo che fui andato all'università incontrai Marisa.**	*After I had gone to college I met Marisa.*	
indicative futuro	future indicative	**Andrò all'università l'anno prossimo.**	*I'll go to college next year.*	12

(continued)

Table 1-2 *(continued)*

Tense/Mood (Italian)	Tense/Mood (Translation)	Example	Translation	Chapter(s) Containing More Information
Indicativo (Indicative Mood)				
futuro anteriore	future perfect	**Sarò andato all'università prima che tu ritorni dal servizio militare.**	*I'll have gone to college by the time you're back from your tour of duty in the military.*	12
Modo Congiuntivo (Subjunctive Mood)				
present	present	**La mamma crede che io vada all'università.**	*Mom thinks I'm going to college.*	14, 15
passato	past	**La mamma crede che io sia andato all' università.**	*Mom thinks I have gone/ went to college.*	14, 15
imperfetto	imperfect	**La mamma credeva che io andassi all' università.**	*Mom thought I was going to college.*	14, 15
trapassato	past perfect	**La mamma credeva che io fossi andato all'università.**	*Mom believed I had gone/ went to college.*	14, 15
Modo Condizionale (Conditional Mood)				
presente	present	**Vorrei andare all' università.**	*I would like to go to college.*	14, 15
passato	past	**Avrei voluto andare all'università.**	*I would have liked to go to college.*	14, 15
Modo Imperativo (Imperative Mood)				
presente	present	**Vai all'università!**	*Go to college!*	13
futuro	future	**Andrai all'università!**	*You will go to college!*	13
Modo Infinito (Infinitive Mood)				
presente	present	**Andare all'università è importante.**	*It's important to go to college.*	9
passato	past	**Essere andato all' università è stata una esperienza positiva.**	*To have gone to college has been a positive experience.*	
Modo Participio (Participle Mood)				
presente	present	**andante** (used as a noun)	*going* (used in the pro-gressive forms)	
passato	past	**andato** (used to form compound tenses)	*gone*	

Syntax: Putting words in order

Syntax tells how you can put words together to form phrases, sentences, and groups of sentences in a meaningful way. In this section, you go through some syntax-related terminology and review some basic rules of syntax.

Syntax lingo

This section presents some terms related to syntax so you that can choose the appropriate form and structure for your words, phrases, and sentences. A *phrase* is a group of words without a subject or a verb that forms a unit of meaning within a sentence. The term is often used to describe a prepositional phrase, such as **per caso** (*by chance*).

A *clause* is a group of words that includes a verb, such as **noi preghiamo** (*we pray*). In Italian, you rarely use subject pronouns because the verb ending already tells you which person is doing the action, so even the single word **preghiamo** (*we pray*) is a clause. Usually the verb is in a *finite form* — in other words, in one of the moods and tenses that can take a specific subject.

Clauses can be independent or dependent:

- ✔ They're *independent* when they're meaningful by themselves, as in **noi preghiamo** (*we pray*).

- ✔ They're *dependent* when they need to lean on an independent clause to convey a complete meaning. For example, **. . . che le piace il gelato** (*. . . that she likes ice cream*) needs an introduction — **So che le piace il gelato** (*I know that she likes ice cream*).

When you add dependent clauses to an independent one, you can classify the clauses on the basis of the meaning they convey:

- ✔ Declarative clauses introduced by **che** (*that*)
- ✔ Hypothetical clauses introduced by **se** (*if, whether*)
- ✔ Causal clauses introduced by **perché** (*because*)

Chapter 8 covers coordinating and subordinating conjunctions and relative clauses in detail, and Chapter 15 addresses declarative and *if . . . then* clauses.

A *sentence* is a group of words that convey a complete thought, and it's made up of one or more clauses and punctuation. One word may be enough, such as when you say, **Vai!** (*Go!*). In Italian, the subject is understood thanks to the form the verb takes, but the exclamation mark is essential, because if you take it away and leave **vai** (*you go*), you're no longer issuing an order; rather, you're making a statement of fact.

Sentences can be simple, compound, or complex:

- ✔ A *simple sentence* is a single independent clause: **Lei gioca a palla.** (*She's playing ball.*)

- ✔ A *compound sentence* consists of multiple independent clauses joined together using coordinating conjunctions (see Chapter 8): **Vanno in Russia ma non vanno a San Pietroburgo.** (*They're going to Russia, but they're not going to St. Petersburg.*)

✔ A *complex sentence* consists of one or more independent clauses with at least one dependent clause linked to the main one through subordinating conjunctions (see Chapter 8): **Se ti piace il pesce, quel ristorante è molto buono.**
(*If you like fish, that is an excellent restaurant.*)

The clauses also may be joined by a relative pronoun.

Basic syntax rules

Knowing syntax enables you to put words together so that you can say what you want to say. Italian and English share some basic syntax rules:

✔ To build a sentence you put words in sequence in four basic ways:

- Subject + verb: **Anna dorme.** (*Anna is sleeping.*)

- Subject + verb + qualifier of the subject: **Lisa è professoressa di storia.** (*Lisa is professor of history.*); **Ugo è astuto.** (*Ugo is cunning.*)

- Subject + verb + object: **Mario compra un libro.** (*Mario is buying a book.*)

- Subject + verb + prepositional phrase(s): **Lucia viene al cinema con noi.** (*Lucia will come to the movies with us.*)

✔ The crucial syntactical distinction is the distinction between independent clauses and dependent clauses. For instance, **io vado** (*I'm going*) is an independent clause; **se vuoi** (*if you want*) is not. The tense and mood of the independent clause determines the tense and mood of the dependent clause. For example, it's meaningless to say **Sono andato al mercato perché ne ho voglia** (*I went to the farmers' market because I wish to*). You have to say either **Sono andato al mercato perché ne avevo voglia** (*I went to the farmers' market because I wished to*) or **Vado al mercato perché ne ho voglia** (*I'm going to the farmers' market because I wish to*).

Italian and English differ in the following ways:

✔ English uses the progressive form (*I'm going, I was going, I will be going,* and so on) much more than Italian, which uses only **Io sto andando** (*I'm going*), **Io stavo andando** (*I was going*), and **Staranno andando** (*They're likely to be going*).

✔ In the past tense, English doesn't distinguish between the **imperfetto** (*imperfect*) and the **preterit** (*past definite*), as in **Io leggevo il libro/Io lessi il libro** (*I read the book*).

✔ In the past tense, Italian uses the **passato prossimo** (*present perfect*) in most cases when English uses the simple past.

✔ English no longer uses the subjunctive, except in set phrases such as **Esigo che lui mi risponda** (*I demand that he answer me*). Italian uses it quite a lot (see Chapters 14 and 15).

✔ English changes the word order and uses auxiliaries (helping verbs) to ask questions; Italian doesn't. For example, **Lei andava all'università** (*She went to college*) becomes a question in Italian: **Lei andava all'università?** (*Did she go to college?*).

✔ English uses auxiliaries to modify verb tenses, such as in the future and the conditional; Italian doesn't. For example, **Venderanno la barca** (*They'll sell the boat*); **Mi impresteresti la moto?** (*Would you lend me your motorbike?*).

> ✔ English favors the active voice over the passive voice more than Italian. For example, in Italian you may say **La forma passiva sarà studiata dagli studenti** (*The passive form will be studied by the boys and girls*), but English prefers **I ragazzi studieranno la forma passiva** (*The boys and girls will study the passive form*).

The following sentences have been scrambled. Reorder them to make sense again. Capitalized words and punctuation marks help you find the beginning and the end of each sentence.

O. a con noi? sciare venire Volete

A. **Volete venire a sciare con noi?** (*Do you want to come skiing with us?*)

10. a bambini giardino. giocano I in palla.

_____

11. bicicletta e faccio forma i in in Per pesi. restare vado

_____

12. dal del finestrino salutandoti Stanno treno.

_____

13. arrestati ieri I ladri mattina. sono stati

_____

14. andare Avrei Cina, ho in ma potuto rinunciato.

_____

15. che credo Enrico. lasci lei lo Non per sposare con

_____

Getting the Most Out of Dictionaries

If you don't know how to translate a word, you can look it up in a bilingual dictionary, but even in simple cases, you have to be careful to get the right word. Suppose you want to know how to say *cat* in Italian. You find **gatto** (*male cat*) in your dictionary, but you need to be aware that you also can use **gatta** (*female cat*). Here's another example: Suppose you're translating a recipe. You need to be aware that in Italian, *celery* has a sort of *leg* — **un gambo di sedano** (*a stalk of celery,* masculine noun) — just as flowers do (*stem*). But a human or table leg is **la gamba** (feminine noun).

In electronic dictionaries, you can find a word by entering only a few letters, triggering the program to list all the possible combinations. But remember that if you look for **facessero,** for example, you may not find it. You see similar forms, making it easier to understand that **facessero** is a form of the verb **fare.** Of course, you can enter entire words and check dictionaries online. A lot of results pop up based on your entry, which helps you see the word in context. Such tools also help you check your grammar. For example, do you say **Me piace?** or **Mi piace?** (*Do I like it?*) Many more entries surface under **mi piace,** which is likely to be correct. But beware that the majority answer isn't always correct.

Use online translations only to acquire a general idea of the topic in question, not to find a reliable translation.

Navigating a monolingual Italian dictionary

Here are some points to remember when you check an entry in an Italian dictionary:

- ✔ **All verbs are listed in the infinitive.** To find the infinitive when the verb is in another mood and tense, you need to distinguish between the stem of the verb and its possible endings. For help in this area, consult Parts III and IV for regular and irregular endings and Chapter 17 for reflexive verbs.

- ✔ **The masculine singular is the default gender.** In an Italian dictionary, adjectives and other qualifiers that can vary in gender and/or number are listed in the masculine singular (unless they exist only in the feminine, such as **la spia** [*spy*]). For example, *no/no one* is listed under **nessuno.** Only the examples in the entry indicate (if you don't know it already) that you can use **nessuna** (feminine singular). Similarly, *red* is listed as **rosso** (*red*), even though it can become **rossa, rossi,** and **rosse.**

  In an Italian dictionary, you find both **gatto** and **gatta,** but if you check only **gatto,** you get no warning that an entry for **gatta** exists. When in doubt, check for a feminine version of a masculine noun (or vice versa) and its meaning (as in the case of **il gambo** [*stalk, stem*] and **la gamba** [*leg*]).

- ✔ **A dictionary tells you whether a verb is transitive, intransitive, or reflexive.** This information is crucial because it affects most aspects of verb conjugation and use, as you see in Chapters 10 and 17.

- ✔ **In a complete Italian dictionary, all irregular verbal forms are listed in any mood and tense only in the first person that carries that irregularity.** If you look up **facessi** (*that I did*), the dictionary sends you to the verb **fare** (*to do, to make*). But it doesn't do so for **facessero** (*that they did*). On the other hand, you find both **feci** (*I did*), which is first-person singular, simple past of the indicative, and **facesti** (*you did*), which is second-person singular, because they're the first instances of two different irregular patterns. But you don't find **facemmo** (*we did*).

- ✔ **You only find entries of present and past participles that are also used as adjectives or nouns.** For example, you find **cantante** (*singer*) but not **guardante** (*looking*), **amato** (*loved*) but not **ballato** (*danced*).

Navigating a bilingual Italian-English/ English-Italian dictionary

Here follow two (shortened) entries for the verb **parlare** (*to speak*) from a sizeable English-Italian/Italian-English dictionary, such as you might use at this stage of your knowledge of the language. The English entry for *to speak* comes first, followed by the Italian entry for **parlare:**

> **speak** [spi:k]. *v.* (*pret.* **spoke**, *p.p.* **spoken**) **I.** *v.i.* **1** parlare: *to learn to speak*: imparare a parlare; **2** (*to converse*) parlare (*to, with* con, a) conversare (con), discorrere (con); (*to communicate vocally*) parlare a. **3** (*to make a speech*) parlare, tenere un discorso **II** v.t. **1** dire, pronunciare, esprimere **2** (*of a language*) parlare, sapere, conoscere: *to ~ six languages*, parlare sei lingue **3** (*to reveal*) esprimere, dire, rivelare. [idioms] *to ~ for*, parlare a nome di, *to ~ of* parlare di: *he spoke of his problems* parlò dei suoi problemi; *to ~ out* parlar chiaro

> **parlare** I *v.i.* (*aus.* avere) **1** to speak, to talk: *chi ha parlato?* who spoke? **2** (*avere un colloquio*) to speak (*con* with, to), to talk (to), **3** (*tenere un discorso*) to speak, to make a speech, **4** (*fare oggetto di chiacchiere*) to talk, to gossip **II** *v.t.* to speak: *parla bene il tedesco* he speaks German well **parlarsi** *v.r. (recipr.)* **1** to speak to e.o. **2** (*pop*) (*amoreggiare*) to go together, to go steady [idioms] *~ chiaro* to speak clearly; *~ di fare una cosa* to talk about doing something

Both entries tell you that the verbs in question are used first of all intransitively, **v.i.** (meaning by themselves or with an indirect object), but also transitively, **v.t.** (meaning by themselves or with a direct object), and that the Italian verb can take the reflexive (**v.r.**) form with a reciprocal meaning. They tell you what prepositions you need (**a, con,** *to, with*) when you want to convey the person you're addressing. They give you variations on the basic meaning of the verb and some idiomatic expressions, in particular phrasal verbs in English (verbs whose meaning is modified by a preposition that always follows them, such as *to speak out*), which in Italian you have to convey with a turn of phrase.

Two points about these entries are worth noting:

- ✔ The two entries don't match one another exactly. In the English entry, you find out that *to speak out* is **parlar chiaro,** but in the Italian entry you find out that the translation of **parlare chiaro** is *to speak clearly.* Why? Because the English part of the dictionary was written by linguist A and the Italian part of the dictionary was written by linguist B, and no one reconciled the two. Don't conclude that this is a poorly written dictionary. It's a very good one. You'll find inconsistencies or incomplete entries in any dictionary. (Trust me.)

- ✔ The English side tells you what form the strong verb *to speak* takes in the past tense and the past participle, but it doesn't tell you what auxiliary the Italian verb **parlare** needs, a crucial piece of information for using verbs in Italian. The Italian side does the opposite.

Keep in mind these five rules of thumb when using a bilingual dictionary:

- ✔ Use an English-Italian/Italian-English dictionary so that you can check entries from English into Italian and from Italian into English.

- ✔ A dictionary doesn't substitute for knowing what to do with the information you find. If you don't find a listing for the auxiliary of a verb, you need to know at least that.

- ✔ Use both a bilingual dictionary *and* two monolingual dictionaries to acquire a full picture of the word you're checking. That's heavy-duty, so the following is less ponderous and more effective: When you find a word you don't know, look at the context in which it's used. Then use that word often to fix it in your mind. For example, you say **Gioco a carte, a calcio, a tennis** (*I play cards, soccer, and tennis*) but **Suono il pianoforte** (*I play the piano*).

✔ Beware of *false friends,* which are words that look the same but have different meanings (see Chapter 18). A **galleria** is both a *tunnel* and an *art gallery* in Italian, so the road sign **Accendere i fari in galleria** (*Turn on beams in tunnel*) doesn't mean that you must turn on the lights if you go to the Museum of Modern Art!

✔ Languages are full of *idioms* — that is, phrases and sentences used figuratively that you may misunderstand or fail to understand even if you know all the words they use. For example, **prendere qualcuno per la gola** doesn't mean *to grab someone by his or her throat* but rather *to win over someone by feeding that person what he or she likes best*. **Gola** here translates to *gluttony,* not *throat*. Complete dictionaries help you sort out the most common idioms, as do specialized publications devoted both to idioms and false friends.

Answer Key

1 <u>Ah</u>! Ci hai fatto una bella sorpresa! **Interiezione**; *Ah! You prepared a nice surprise for us!*

2 Luigi non si sente <u>bene</u>. **Avverbio**; *Luigi doesn't feel well.*

3 Non mi è piaciuto <u>il</u> film. **Articolo**; *I didn't like the movie.*

4 Vado <u>con</u> lei <u>in</u> montagna. **Preposizione**; *I'm going to the mountains with her.*

5 Bianca mangia il pesce, <u>ma</u> non mangia la carne. **Congiunzione**; *Bianca eats fish but she doesn't eat meat.*

6 Hai comprato <u>le</u> uova? **Articolo**; *Did you buy eggs?*

7 <u>Siete partiti</u> in orario? **Verbo**; *Did you leave on time?*

8 Mi hanno dato una buona <u>ricetta</u>. **Nome**; *They gave me a good recipe.*

9 Non <u>ci</u> hanno ascoltato. **Pronome**; *They didn't listen to us.*

10 **I bambini giocano a palla in giardino.** (*The children are playing ball in the yard.*)

11 **Per restare in forma, vado in bicicletta e faccio i pesi.** (*To stay in shape, I ride a bike and lift weights.*)

12 **Stanno salutandoti dal finestrino del treno.** (*They're waving at you from the window of the train.*)

13 **I ladri sono stati arrestati ieri mattina.** (*The robbers were arrested yesterday morning.*)

14 **Avrei potuto andare in Cina, ma ho rinunciato.** (*I could've gone to China, but I passed on the opportunity.*)

15 **Non credo che lei lo lasci per sposare con Enrico.** (*I don't believe she's going to leave him to marry Enrico.*)

Chapter 2

Noun and Article Basics: Gender and Number

In This Chapter

▶ Sorting out definite and indefinite articles

▶ Drawing the line between masculine and feminine nouns

▶ Working with plural nouns and articles

Nouns serve similar purposes in English and Italian, but in English, nouns don't have a gender, whereas in Italian, they can be masculine or feminine. When Italian nouns refer to things or abstractions, their grammatical gender is merely a product of convention and usage: **sole** (*sun*) is masculine, but **luna** (*moon*) is feminine. At times nouns are masculine or feminine because they refer to a male or female person or animal. In this chapter, I show you how to distinguish between feminine and masculine nouns and how to move from the masculine to the feminine (and vice versa when changing gender is possible).

In many cases, you can make out the gender of a noun from its ending. But in a lot of cases, you can't. You have to know a noun's gender by heart or by looking at clues in other words that accompany the noun. Because the clearest indicator of gender is the definite article (corresponding to the English *the*), in this chapter, I start with articles and then introduce nouns.

As in English, Italian nouns can be singular or plural. Most follow regular patterns, but some behave irregularly or come only in the singular or the plural. I show you how to form the plural and how to reconstruct the singular masculine form of a noun. Because the masculine is usually the default gender in Italian, you find words listed in that gender in dictionaries.

A Primer on Articles

Looking at nouns out of context is useful for helping you understand the general rules that govern grammar, but because you need to know each noun's gender and because the most reliable indicator of a noun's gender is the definite article, I devote this first section to articles.

English has a definite and an indefinite article — *the* and *a/an* respectively — as does Italian. With the definite article, you point to a specific item, as in **Il bambino è caduto dall'altalena** (*The child fell off the swing*). With the indefinite article, you point to one thing among many like things, as in **Leggi un libro?** (*Are you reading a book?*).

Memorize new nouns with their articles to make sure you know their gender as well.

Dealing with the definite article "the"

In Italian, articles vary in gender, number, and spelling. English and Italian use the *definite article* to point to a specific thing or person:

> **Il libro è sul tavolo.** (*The book [we are/were talking about] is on the table.*)

> **I bambini stanno giocando in giardino.** (*The children are playing in the garden.*)

Table 2-1 provides the three forms of the definite article, **il, lo,** and **l',** which you use with singular masculine nouns. It also presents the two forms of the masculine plural definite article, **i** and **gli,** which you use with plural masculine nouns.

Table 2-1		**Masculine Definite Articles**		
Placement	*Singular*	*Singular Examples*	*Plural*	*Plural Examples*
Before most single consonants and groups of consonants	il	**il gioco** (*the game*) **il senatore** (*the senator*) **il treno** (*the train*)	i	**i giochi** (*the games*) **i senatori** (*the senators*) **i treni** (*the trains*)
Before **gn-, pn-, ps-, s** + another consonant, **x-, y-,** and **z-**	lo	**lo gnocco** (*the dumpling*) **lo psicologo** (*the psychologist*) **lo spettro** (*the ghost*) **lo yogurt** (*the yogurt*) **lo zaino** (*the backpack*)	gli	**gli gnocchi** (*the dumplings*) **gli psicologi** (*the psychologists*) **gli spettri** (*the ghosts*)
Before any vowel	l'	**l'uomo** (*the man*) **l'ufficio** (*the office*)	gli	**gli uomini** (*the men/ human beings*)

Table 2-2 lists the two forms of the definite article used with singular feminine nouns, **la** and **l',** as well as the plural feminine article, which has only one form: **le.**

Table 2-2		**Feminine Definite Articles**		
Placement	*Singular*	*Singular Examples*	*Plural*	*Plural Examples*
Before any consonant or group of consonants	la	**la casa** (*the house*) **la trappola** (*the trap*)	le	**le case** (*the houses*) **le trappole** (*the traps*)
Before any vowel	l'	**l'anima** (*the soul*) **l'ora** (*the hour*)	le	**le anime** (*the souls*) **le ore** (*the hours*)

The feminine **l'** is the same as **la** but with the **-a** replaced by an apostrophe. Likewise, the masculine **l'** is the same as **lo** but with the **-o** replaced by an apostrophe.

In Italian, the definite article can play the role the possessive adjective plays in English, as in **Cerco la borsa** (*I'm looking for my handbag*). (See Chapter 7 for more on possessive words.)

Saying "a" or "an" in Italian: Indefinite articles

Besides the definite article, Italian uses the indefinite articles **un, un', una,** and **uno,** which correspond to the English *a* or *an*. Because **un** means *one*, you can use it only with singular nouns, as in **una villa** (*a villa*) or **un paese** (*a country*). Table 2-3 lays out the forms of the indefinite article used with singular masculine nouns, and Table 2-4 does the same for the feminine article.

Table 2-3	Masculine Indefinite Articles	
Article	*Placement*	*Examples*
un	Before any vowel or consonant and most groups of consonants	**un ufficio** (*an office*) **un uomo** (*a man*) **un treno** (*a train*)
uno	Before **gn-, pn-, ps-, s** + another consonant, **x-, y-,** and **z-**	**uno psicologo** (*a psychologist*) **uno zaino** (*a backpack*)

Table 2-4	Feminine Indefinite Articles	
Article	*Placement*	*Examples*
una	Before any consonant or group of consonants	**una casa** (*a house*) **una trappola** (*a trap*) **una strega** (*a witch*)
un'	Before any vowel	**un'amica** (*a girlfriend*) **un'ora** (*an hour*)

Distinguishing between Masculine and Feminine Nouns

In most Indo-European languages (the family to which both Italian and English belong), nouns have a gender. In Italian, you deal with only two genders: masculine and feminine. Other parts of speech have a gender as well, and as you progress through this book, you discover how to match these other words to the gender of the noun.

This section focuses on nouns, discussing what word endings tell you about gender and which words can and should undergo a gender change.

Recognizing common noun endings

In Italian, most nouns are masculine or feminine. Grammatically, their endings in the singular help you figure out to which gender they belong. Masculine nouns often end in the following:

- ✔ **-o:** **letto** (*bed*), **libro** (*book*), **giorno** (*day*), **gatto** (*male cat*), **buco** (*hole*)
- ✔ **A consonant:** **autobus** (*bus*), **sport** (*sport*), **bar** (*bar*), **chef** (*chef, cook*), **zar** (*czar*)

However, some nouns ending in **-o** are feminine, such as **auto** (*automobile*), **radio** (*radio*), **mano** (*hand*), and **moto** (*motorbike*). So are some foreign words, especially when they translate an Italian word that has the same meaning, such as **star del cinema** (*film star*).

Feminine nouns often end in

- ✔ **-a:** **barca** (*boat*), **ora** (*hour*), **pianta** (*plant, tree*)
- ✔ **-i:** **analisi** (*analysis*), **crisi** (*crisis*), **tesi** (*thesis*), **diagnosi** (*diagnosis*)
- ✔ **-tà** or **-tù:** **bontà** (*goodness*), **virtù** (*virtue*), **verità** (*truth*)

Some nouns ending in **-a** are masculine because they derive from classical Greek: **problema** (*problem*), **tema** (*theme*), and **programma** (*program*).

Some words have a masculine and a feminine version, with different meanings. For example, **il buco** (*hole*), **la buca** (*pit, hole in golf*); **il foglio** (*sheet of paper*), **la foglia** (*leaf*); **il fine** (*aim, goal*), **la fine** (*end*); **il capitale** (*financial capital*), **la capitale** (*capital city*).

Both masculine and feminine nouns can end in **-e**, but I can't give you any general rule that explains why some are masculine and others feminine. For example, **sole** (*sun*) is masculine, and **notte** (*night*) is feminine — so just have a dictionary on-hand until you're more familiar with noun gender.

Decide whether the following nouns are masculine or feminine and mark an *M* or *F* on the corresponding blank lines.

Q. analisi

A. F

1. algebra: _____

2. biro: _____

3. corsa: _____

4. dialisi: _____

5. medicina: _____

6. colle: _____

7. pera: _____

8. pino: _____

9. sapienza: _____

10. pelle: _____

Sorting nouns into three classes

When it comes to gender, you find three classes of nouns in Italian:

- **Nouns that are gender-specific:** If the individual in question is male, you use one word: **il padre** (*father*); if it's female, use another word: **la madre** (*mother*).

- **Nouns that can move from masculine to feminine:** The masculine is the default gender, so you tend to look up a noun in the masculine and then see whether you make a feminine noun out of it: **Lo zio** (*uncle*) becomes **la zia** (*aunt*). In real life, of course, you may encounter a noun in the feminine first and then wonder whether it has a masculine version. It usually does, but the masculine may be really different from the feminine: **La dottoressa** (*female doctor/graduate*) doesn't become **il dottoresso** but rather **il dottore** (*male doctor/graduate*).

- **Nouns that are used for males and females but don't change:** **La guida** (*guide*) is feminine, but it's used for men, too; **il soprano** (*soprano*) is masculine, but it's used for women.

Gender-specific nouns

Some nouns are gender-specific — that is, you use different words to refer to masculine and feminine variations of the noun. See Table 2-5 for a sampling of these nouns.

Table 2-5	Nouns that Indicate the Gender of the Individual
Masculine Noun	*Feminine Noun*
il padre (*father*)	la madre (*mother*)
il papà (*dad*)	la mamma (*mom*)
il fratello (*brother*)	la sorella (*sister*)
il marito (*husband*)	la moglie (*wife*)
il genero (*son-in-law*)	la nuora (*daughter-in-law*)
l'uomo (*man*)	la donna (*woman*)
il porco (*pig, boar*)	la scrofa (*sow*)
il toro (*bull*)	la vacca (*cow*)

Universal nouns that change the article (and sometimes the ending) to switch gender

For nouns that aren't gender-specific, you take the masculine noun and change either the article alone or the article and the ending to make the noun feminine. This change can play out in several ways, depending on the spelling of the masculine noun. Table 2-6 breaks down the possibilities.

Table 2-6		Making Masculine Nouns Feminine	
Masculine Ending	**Ending Change**	**Masculine Noun**	**Feminine Noun**
-o	Change **-o** to **-a**	l'amic**o** (*boyfriend*) il figli**o** (*son*) lo zi**o** (*uncle*) il lup**o** (*male wolf*)	l'amic**a** (*girlfriend*) la figli**a** (*daughter*) la zi**a** (*aunt*) la lup**a** (*female wolf*)
-ista, -cida, sometimes **-e**	None; only article changes	il giornalista (*male journalist*) l'omicida (*male killer*) il nipote (*grandson, nephew*)	la giornalista (*female journalist*) l'omicida (*female killer*) la nipote (*granddaughter, niece*)
-tore	Change **-tore** to **-trice**	l'impera**tore** (*emperor*) l'at**tore** (*actor*) il pit**tore** (*male painter*)	l'impera**trice** (*empress*) l'at**trice** (*actress*) la pit**trice** (*female painter*)
-e (many professions, animals)	Change **-e** to **-essa**	il princip**e** (*prince*) lo student**e** (*male student*) il leon**e** (*lion*) l'elefant**e** (*male elephant*)	la princip**essa** (*princess*) la student**essa** (*female student*) la leon**essa** (*lioness*) l'elefant**essa** (*female elephant*)

Some names of professions or people's titles change the final **-e** to **-a: il cameriere** (*waiter*), **la cameriera** (*waitress*), **il signore** (*gentleman, Sir*), **la signora** (*lady, Madam, Ms.*). There's neither rhyme nor reason to why these nouns take **-a** instead of **-essa,** except, perhaps, ease of pronunciation: **Camerieressa** sounds horrible.

And newly invented words take either **-essa** or **-a: l'avvocato** (*male lawyer*), **l'avvocatessa** (*female lawyer*); **l'architetto** (*male architect*), **l'architetta** (*female architect*). How do you know whether a word is a new word? Practice and a dictionary.

Nouns used for both males and females

Some masculine nouns can refer to females, and some feminine nouns can refer to males. Nouns that are always masculine, regardless of the gender of the animal or person described include **il pavone** (*peacock*), **il serpente** (*snake*), and **il cicerone** (*tour guide*).

Some nouns that are always feminine, regardless of the gender of the animal or person described, are **la tigre** (*tiger*), **la volpe** (*fox*), and **la spia** (*spy*).

To distinguish between male and female animals, add the words **maschio** (*male*) and **femmina** (*female*) to the basic noun:

- **la volpe maschio** (*male fox*)
- **la volpe femmina** (*female fox*)

- **il serpente maschio** (*male snake*)
- **il serpente femmina** (*female snake*)

Turn the following nouns from masculine to feminine, and include the definite article.

Q. nemico

A. **la nemica**

11. artista: _____

12. cavallo: _____

13. cognato: _____

14. musicista: _____

15. parente: _____

16. pediatra: _____

17. traditore: _____

18. padrone: _____

19. infermiere: _____

20. presidente: _____

Moving from Singular to Plural: Basic Rules

As in English, Italian nouns can become plural by changing the ending, and the plural of nouns varies depending on the ending of the singular. Table 2-7 illustrates the regular patterns.

Table 2-7	Regular Plural Noun Endings		
Masculine Singular	*Masculine Plural*	*Feminine Singular*	*Feminine Plural*
-o: gatto (*cat*)	-i: gatti (*cats*)	-a: casa (*house, home*)	-e: case (*houses, homes*)
-e: pesce (*fish*)	-i: pesci (*fish[es]*)	-e: chiave (*key*)	-i: chiavi (*keys*)
-a: problema (*problem*)	-i: problemi (*problems*)		

Plural and singular nouns share some of the same endings, so it may be difficult to tell the number and gender of a noun such as **sere**; after all, **-e** is an ending for feminine plural nouns, masculine singular nouns, and feminine singular nouns. If the noun comes with the article, you know at once: **Le sere** is the feminine plural of **la sera** (*evening*). If the context doesn't help you, consult a dictionary (check out Appendix C for an Italian-English dictionary). Dictionaries list nouns in their default form, usually the masculine singular form. You can use trial and error until you find the right noun.

Some nouns have both a masculine and a feminine plural, but there's no rule establishing which meaning is associated with which gender. You pick up on these variations as you encounter them in context. Here are some examples:

Singular	Masculine Plural	Feminine Plural
il braccio	**i bracci** (_wings, branches_)	**le braccia** (_body arms_)
il membro	**i membri** (_members_)	**le membra** (_limbs_)
l'osso	**gli ossi** (_animal bones_)	**le ossa** (_human bones_)

Turn the following nouns from singular to plural, and include the article.

Q. l'orto

A. **gli orti**

21. l'albero: _____

22. l'altalena: _____

23. il cameriere: _____

24. la capitale: _____

25. il dottore: _____

26. l'impiegata : _____

27. la nipote: _____

28. la notte: _____

29. il ragazzo: _____

30. il signore: _____

Exceptions to the Basic Rules on Number

With language, nothing's ever quite as simple as it may seem. When you get a rule or pattern, you have to accept the fact that languages can't be rationalized beyond a certain point. This section contains the many exceptions to those rules.

Changing more than just the ending

Some groups of nouns don't change just the last vowel when you turn them into the plural but rather change the entire last syllable. Other nouns switch genders. Check out the following rules:

✔ Nouns ending in **-co, -go, -ca,** and **-ga,** which have a hard sound in the singular, add an **h** before the suffix of the plural to preserve it:

   cuoco (_cook_) → **cuochi** (_cooks_)

   fungo (_mushroom_) → **funghi** (_mushrooms_)

   barca (_boat_) → **barche** (_boats_)

   strega (_witch_) → **streghe** (_witches_)

The most important words that are exceptions to this rule are **medico** (*physician*) → **medici, amico** (*friend*) → **amici** (*friends*), and **nemico** (*enemy*) → **nemici** (*enemies*). However, the feminine versions — **amica** (*girlfriend*) and **nemica** (*female enemy*) — do become **amiche** (*girlfriends*) and **nemiche** (*female enemies*). Other words, such as **chirurgo** (*surgeon*) → **chirurghi/chirurgi** (*surgeons*) and **stomaco** (*stomach*) → **stomachi/stomaci** (*stomachs*), can have either ending.

✔ Nouns ending in **-cia** or **-gia** accented on a syllable that isn't the last one add **-e** if the last syllable is preceded by a consonant, and they add **-ie** if the last syllable is preceded by a vowel:

> **provincia** (*province*) → **province** (*provinces*)
>
> **spiaggia** (*beach*) → **spiagge** (*beaches*)
>
> **camicia** (*shirt*) → **camicie** (*shirts*)
>
> **valigia** (*suitcase*) → **valigie** (*suitcases*)

Nouns that end in **-cìa** or **-gìa**, accented on the **ì**, form the plural by adding **-ie**: **allergia** (*allergy*) → **allergie** (*allergies*). However, be aware that the accent isn't marked in Italian, so you have to figure out which nouns are accented on the **i** as you go along.

✔ Nouns ending in **-io** take **-ii** in the plural if the accent falls on the **ì** and take only one **-i** if the accent falls on a preceding syllable (the accent is not marked):

> **pendio** (*slope*) → **pendii** (*slopes*)
>
> **viaggio** (*trip*) → **viaggi** (*trips*)

If nouns end in **-ia,** the plural is regular: **biglia** (*pinball*) → **biglie** (*pinballs*).

✔ Some nouns change gender from the singular to the plural. The following words are among the most frequently used:

> **il dito** (*finger, toe*) → **le dita** (*fingers, toes*)
>
> **l'uovo** (*egg*) → **le uova** (*eggs*)
>
> **il ginocchio** (*knee*) → **le ginocchia** (*knees*)

Turn the following nouns from singular to plural, including the article. (I've added the accent when necessary to help you follow the rules outlined.)

Q. pediatra

A. **i pediatri, le pediatre**

31. albergo: _____

32. abbazìa: _____

33. bacio: _____

34. baco: _____

35. basilica: _____

36. boccia: _____

37. ciliegia: _____

38. coniglio: _____

39. figlio: _____

40. zìo: _____

Changing only the article

There are some names that are *invariable,* so you need to check the article to find out if they're used in the singular or in the plural form. Some common examples include the following:

✔ Masculine nouns: **cinema, brindisi, caffè, film**

✔ Feminine nouns: **radio, metropolis, città, spezie**

Assign the nouns to the following categories: masculine singular *(MS),* masculine plural *(MP),* feminine singular *(FS),* and feminine plural *(FP).*

Q. i caffè

A. MP

41. un albero: _____

42. un amante: _____

43. un'amante: _____

44. le analisi: _____

45. un artista: _____

46. le attrici: _____

47. i bar: _____

48. le biro: _____

49. i bit: _____

50. i cardiologi: _____

Using nouns only in the singular or the plural

You can use some nouns only in the singular or only in the plural. Following are some categories of singular nouns, along with some examples:

✔ Abstractions: **il coraggio** *(courage),* **la fede** *(faith)*

✔ Chemical elements and metals: **l'oro** *(gold),* **il rame** *(copper)*

✔ Some festivities: **il Natale** *(Christmas),* **la Pasqua** *(Easter)*

✔ Foods: **il grano** *(wheat),* **il vino** *(wine),* **l'acqua** *(water),* **il latte** *(milk)*

✔ Nouns such as **la fame** *(hunger),* **la sete** *(thirst),* **il sangue** *(blood)*

When used in the plural, nouns such as **i vini** and **le acque minerali** mean *kinds of wine* and *kinds of mineral water,* respectively; **le fedi** means *confessions.*

Following are some categories of nouns used in the plural, along with some examples:

✔ Objects that come in pairs: **i pantaloni** *(trousers),* **le forbici** *(scissors),* **gli occhiali** *(eyeglasses)*

✔ Sets: **i piatti** *(dishes, dinnerware),* **gli spiccioli** *(coins, change),* **le dimissioni** *(resignation)*

✔ Nouns that come in the plural from Latin: **le nozze** *(nuptials),* **le ferie** *(paid vacation days),* **le tenebre** *(darkness)*

Deciding When to Include an Article

When you're confident in your knowledge of nouns as they relate to gender and number, you can move on to when and how to use articles and nouns together. Deciding when to use the indefinite article is easier because people use it in similar ways in English and Italian. Also, all you need to know is that you're singling out one item among many: **Un cane abbaia** (*A dog is barking*).

Becoming confident in using the definite article is more challenging than choosing when to use the indefinite. In the sections that follow, I indicate the instances when the use of each type of article is correct and the few when it's definitely incorrect.

When (and when not) to use a definite article

Deciding when and when not to use the definite article is a tricky topic in both Italian and English. One rule of thumb is that Italian uses the definite article much more than English. For example, Italian uses articles before foods (**il pane**, *bread;* **la mela**, *apple*), before body parts (**il braccio**, *arm;* **le dita**, *finger*), before dates (**il 25 aprile**, *April 25*), before titles (**il professor Baldini**, *Professor Baldini*) and before abstract nouns (**la forza**, *strength*). It also uses the article before possessive adjectives (**la mia borsa**, *my handbag*) and family members when referred to in the plural (**le mie sorelle**, *my sister*).

People

Articles are used when referring to a professional (il Dott. Cecconi) or before a female name to express affection and familiarity (La Elena), but they're not used in direct address. For example, you use the article when you say **Ho visto il Dott. Cecconi martedì sera** (*I saw Dr. Cecconi on Tuesday evening*), but you don't use it when you say **Buon giorno, Dott. Cecconi** (*Good morning, Dr. Cecconi*).

Places

You use the Italian definite article with the following geographical features:

- Mountains, rivers, and lakes: **le Alpi** (*the Alps*), **il Monte Bianco** (*Mont Blanc*), **il Po** (*the Po River*), **il [lago di] Garda** (*Lake Garda*), **il lago Michigan** (*Lake Michigan*)

- Many large islands and archipelagos: **la Sicilia** (*Sicily*), **l'Inghilterra** (*England*), **le Bahamas** (*the Bahamas*); but skip the article for **Long Island** (*Long Island*) and **Cuba** (*Cuba*)

- Regions and states: **il Lazio** (*the Lazio region*), **la Puglia** (*Apulia*), **la California** (*California*)

- Nations (singular or plural) and continents: **l'Italia** (*Italy*), **gli Stati Uniti** (*the United States*), **l'Asia** (*Asia*)

Italian doesn't use the definite article before names of cities and most small islands: **Bologna, Roma** (*Rome*), **New York, Capri, Malta**.

The rules for articles change when prepositions and idiomatic expressions are used. With idiomatic usage, you don't use an article with a preposition unless the object of the preposition is modified and then the preposition is contracted. For example, you don't use an article when you say **Vado in Italia** (*I'm going to Italy*), but you do use an article when you say **Vado nell'Italia centrale** (*I'm going to central Italy*).

Things

Use the definite article with the following things:

- Countable plural nouns: **Le scimmie e le mucche sono mammiferi.** (literally: *Monkeys and cows are mammals.*)

- Uncountable nouns: **il sale** (*salt*), **lo zucchero** (*sugar*), **l'acqua** (*water*)

  In English, uncountable nouns take the definite article only when you mean a type of or a portion of something, as in **Mi passi il sale, per favore?** (*Can I have the salt, please?*); but when you talk (in English) about salt, sugar, water, and so on in general, you use neither the definite nor the indefinite article. In Italian, you have to use the definite article.

- Possessive adjectives and pronouns: **La nostra macchina è rossa** (*Our car is red*); **La macchina rossa è la nostra** (*The red car is ours*).

- Firms, institutions, and clubs: **la General Motors** (*General Motors*), **la Chiesa** (*the Church*), **la Roma** (*Roma Football Club*).

- Abstractions: **La tolleranza è fondamentale in democrazia.** (*Toleration is fundamental in democracies.*)

When (and when not) to use an indefinite article

Although Italian uses the indefinite article much the same as English does, in some situations where an indefinite article is appropriate in English, Italian leaves it out. Consider the following situations where you'd leave out the indefinite article:

- When using a noun as a qualifier of the subject after the verbs **essere** (*to be*): **Mia madre è vedova** (*My mother is a widow*); **Suo fratello è medico** (*Her brother is a physician*).

- In exclamations introduced by **che** and **quanto** (*how*): **Che uomo coraggioso!** (*What a courageous man!*)

Fill in the appropriate definite or indefinite article (if any) in the following sentences.

Q. ____ Africa è un continente antichissimo.

A. L'Africa è un continente antichissimo.

51. Amano ____ gatti.

52. ____ dinosauri e ____ uccelli hanno molte caratteristiche simili.

53. _____ Francia produce molti vini.

54. "Hai bisogno di _____ vite?" "No, ho bisogno di due viti."

55. "Prendi _____ mia bicicletta?" "No, prendo la sua."

56. Mi passi _____ zucchero, per favore?

57. "Qual è il fiume più lungo del mondo?" "_____ Nilo."

58. _____ Trentino si trova nell'Italia settentrionale.

59. A loro piace molto _____ Long Island.

Answer Key

1 algebra: **F** (*algebra*)

2 biro: **F** (*ballpoint pen*)

3 corsa: **F** (*run*)

4 dialisi: **F** (*dialysis*)

5 medicina: **F** (*medicine*)

6 colle: **M** (*pass, hill*)

7 pera: **F** (*pear*)

8 pino: **M** (*pine tree*)

9 sapienza: **F** (*wisdom*)

10 pelle: **F** (*skin*)

11 **l'artista** (*female artist*)

12 **la cavalla** (*mare*)

13 **la cognata** (*sister-in-law*)

14 **la musicista** (*female musician*)

15 **la parente** (*female relative*)

16 **la pediatra** (*female pediatrician*)

17 **la traditrice** (*female traitor*)

18 **la padrona** (*mistress, boss, owner*)

19 **l'infermiera** (*female nurse*)

20 **la presidentessa** (*female president*)

21 **gli alberi** (*trees*)

22 **le altalene** (*swings*)

23 **i camerieri** (*waiters*)

24 **le capitali** (*capitols*)

25 **i dottori** (*male doctors*)

26 **le impiegate** (*female office workers*)

27 **le nipoti** (*granddaughters, nieces*)

28 **le notti** (*nights*)

29 **i ragazzi** (*boys*)

30 **i signori** (*gentlemen*)

31 **gli alberghi** (*hotels*)

32 **le abbazie** (*abbeys*)

33 **i baci** (*kisses*)

34 **i bachi** (*silkworms*)

35 **le basiliche** (*basilicas*)

36 **le bocce** (*bocce balls*)

37 **le ciliegie** (*cherries*)

38 **i conigli** (*rabbits*)

39 **i figli** (*sons*)

40 **gli zii** (*uncles*)

41 un albero: **MS** (*a tree*)

42 un amante: **MS** (*a male lover*)

43 un'amante: **FS** (*a female lover*)

44 le analisi: **FP** (*analyses*)

45 un artista: **MS** (*an artist*)

46 le attrici: **FP** (*actresses*)

47 i bar: **MP** (*bars*)

48 le biro: **FP** (*ballpoint pens*)

49 i bit: **MP** (*bits*)

50 i cardiologi: **MP** (*cardiologists*)

51 Amano **i** gatti. (*They love cats.*)

52 **I** dinoasuri e **gli** uccelli hanno molte caratteristiche simili. (*Dinosaurs and birds have many similar features.*)

53 **La** Francia produce molti vini. (*France produces a lot of wines.*)

54 "Hai bisogno di **una** vite?" "No, ho bisogno di due viti." (*"Do you need one screw?" "No, I need two screws."*)

55 "Prendi **la** mia bicicletta?" "No, prendo la sua." (*"Are you taking my bike?" "No, I'm taking his."*)

56 Mi passi **lo** zucchero, per favore? (*Will you pass the sugar, please?*)

57 "Qual è il fiume più lungo del mondo?" "**Il** Nilo." (*"What's the longest river in the world?" "The Nile."*)

58 **Il** Trentino si trova nell'Italia settentrionale. (*The Trentino region is in northern Italy.*)

59 A loro piace molto Long Island. (*They like Long Island a lot.*)

Chapter 3

Numbers, Dates, and Time

• •

In This Chapter

▶ Counting and establishing numbered order

▶ Making accurate references to the calendar and the clock

• •

*Y*ou count the calories you eat and the minutes spent on the treadmill. You check appointments ten times a day and celebrate anniversaries. Numbers are a central part of your life, and fortunately, numerals are used all over the world these days. But when you spell out numbers or talk about them, you use different words, and each language has its own words and conventions to separate integers and decimals, to talk about centuries, and to tell the time.

In this chapter, I help you express quantities such as 25, 149, and even 2,689,365.00! You also find out how to set things in numerical order — first, second, third, and so on — and how to manage time and dates (or at least write about them).

Counting Items with Cardinal Numbers

If you say that you've seen ten movies, you're using a *cardinal number* — that is, a number that conveys an absolute quantity. When written in full, numbers are invariable in Italian, and you form them more or less as you form numbers in English. The first ten each have their own names. Those between 11 and 19 add the suffix **-dici** or the prefix **dici[a]-,** which both mean *ten.* Starting with 21, you encounter the pattern that you repeat from 30 to 99. Following are the numbers from 0 through 29.

✔ **zero** (*0*)	✔ **dieci** (*10*)	✔ **venti** (*20*)
✔ **uno** (*1*)	✔ **undici** (*11*)	✔ **ventuno** (*21*)
✔ **due** (*2*)	✔ **dodici** (*12*)	✔ **ventidue** (*22*)
✔ **tre** (*3*)	✔ **tredici** (*13*)	✔ **ventitré** (*23*)
✔ **quattro** (*4*)	✔ **quattordici** (*14*)	✔ **ventiquattro** (*24*)
✔ **cinque** (*5*)	✔ **quindici** (*15*)	✔ **venticinque** (*25*)
✔ **sei** (*6*)	✔ **sedici** (*16*)	✔ **ventisei** (*26*)
✔ **sette** (*7*)	✔ **diciassette** (*17*)	✔ **ventisette** (*27*)
✔ **otto** (*8*)	✔ **diciotto** (*18*)	✔ **ventotto** (*28*)
✔ **nove** (*9*)	✔ **diciannove** (*19*)	✔ **ventinove** (*29*)

When you add 1, 2, 3, and so on to numbers from 20 to 29, you drop the **i** when the following number starts with another vowel; otherwise, you keep the vowel and simply add the number:

✔ **trenta + uno = trentuno** (*31*)

✔ **trenta + due = trentadue** (*32*)

✔ **quaranta + sette = quarantasette** (*47*)

✔ **quaranta + otto = quarantotto** (*48*)

✔ **cinquanta + uno = cinquantuno** (*51*)

✔ **cinquanta + quattro = cinquantaquattro** (*54*)

✔ **sessanta + otto = sessantotto** (*68*)

✔ **sessanta + nove = sessantanove** (*69*)

Except for **tre** (*3*), all numbers ending in **-tré** carry an accent, such as **trentatré** (*33*) and **settantatré** (*73*).

Table 3-1 lists multiples of 10 and 100. You build numbers from 200 to 900 as you do in English, by adding **-cento** to any of the first ten numbers, as in **duecento** (*200*). For numbers between 200 and 999, add any other number to the number you've just formed, as in **trecentoquarantatré** (*343*). You write them as one word.

Directly after the word **cento** (*100*), you add **-uno** and **-otto** without dropping any vowel, even if another vowel follows, as in **centouno** (*101*) and **centootto** (*108*). You add all the other numbers without modifying them: 117 is **centodiciassette,** and 148 is **centoquarantotto.**

Table 3-1	Cardinal Numbers with Double and Triple Digits	
Multiples of 10	*Multiples of 100*	*Numbers 101–909*
dieci (*10*)	cento (*100*)	centouno (*101*)
venti (*20*)	duecento (*200*)	duecentodue (*202*)
trenta (*30*)	trecento (*300*)	trecentotré (*303*)
quaranta (*40*)	quattrocento (*400*)	quattrocentoquattro (*404*)
cinquanta (*50*)	cinquecento (*500*)	cinquecentocinque (*505*)
sessanta (*60*)	seicento (*600*)	seicentosei (*606*)
settanta (*70*)	settecento (*700*)	settecentosette (*707*)
ottanta (*80*)	ottocento (*800*)	ottocentootto (*808*)
novanta (*90*)	novecento (*900*)	novecentonove (*909*)

In Italian, 1,000 is **mille.** For numbers between 1,000 and 1,999, you add hundreds to **mille-.** For example, to write 1,100, you add 100 to **mille-** and get **millecento.** To write 1,999, you add 999 to 1,000 and get **millenovencentonovantanove.**

To form higher numbers, you use **-mila** (*thousand*) as follows:

✔ To form thousands, you add units from 2 to 9: **duemila** (*2,000*), **cinquemila** (*5,000*)

✔ To form tens of thousands, you add tens, from 10 to 90: **undicimila** (*11,000*), **trentamila** (*30,000*), **sessantamila** (*60,000*)

✔ To form hundreds of thousands, you add hundreds, from 100 to 900: **duecentomila** (*200,000*), **settecentomila** (*700,000*)

When you write numbers as numerals, you use a period to separate thousands and a comma to separate integers from decimals — basically, the opposite of the punctuation in English. For example, **1.000.543,25** corresponds to *1,000,543.25*. When saying the number, you read the comma as **virgola,** as in **un milionecinquecentoquarantatremila virgola venticinque.**

When you get to **un milione** (*1,000,000*), you write it as two separate words, but you link all the lower numbers together and then to the word **milione,** as in 1.300.000: **un milionetrecentomila** (*1,300,000.00*).

Milione, bilione, and trilione take the plural, as in **quindici milioni di euro** (*fifteen million euros*).

When you use cardinal numbers to express a measurement you place them after the measurement symbols: **cm. 22** (*22 centimeters*), **kg. 84** (*84 kilos*).

In both numerals and when spelled out, write the cardinal numbers that come before and after the numbers listed.

Q. 141

A. **140: centoquaranta; 142: centoquarantadue**

1. 144

_____

2. 813

_____

3. 87

_____

4. 4.395.652

_____

5. 2.129.370.686

_____

6. 86.407,25

_____

7. 537,88

_____

8. 47,1

_____

9. 83,91

_____

10. 9.397.868,17

_____

Putting Items in Order with Ordinal Numbers

With *ordinal numbers,* you set things in order, using them to establish ranking. The first ten have special forms:

- **primo** (*1st*)
- **secondo** (*2nd*)
- **terzo** (*3rd*)
- **quarto** (*4th*)

- **quinto** (*5th*)
- **sesto** (*6th*)
- **settimo** (*7th*)
- **ottavo** (*8th*)

- **nono** (*9th*)
- **decimo** (*10th*)

In Italian, ordinal numbers behave like adjectives in that they need to match in gender and number with the nouns or pronouns they refer to. You form ordinal numbers above **decimo** by adding the ending **-esimo** (masculine singular), **-esima** (feminine singular), **-esimi** (masculine plural), or **-esime** (feminine plural) to the corresponding cardinal number (see the preceding section).

Following are some ordinal numbers from 11th to 100th, in the standard masculine singular form:

- **primo** (*1st*)
- **undicesimo** (*11th*)
- **dodicesimo** (*12th*)
- **tredicesimo** (*13th*)
- **quattordicesimo** (*14th*)
- **quindicesimo** (*15th*)
- **sedicesimo** (*16th*)

- **diciassettesimo** (*17th*)
- **diciottesimo** (*18th*)
- **diciannovesimo** (*19th*)
- **ventesimo** (*20th*)
- **trentesimo** (*30th*)
- **quarantesimo** (*40th*)
- **cinquantesimo** (*50th*)

- **sessantesimo** (*60th*)
- **settantesimo** (*70th*)
- **ottantesimo** (*80th*)
- **novantesimo** (*90th*)
- **centesimo** (*100th*)

When you use an ordinal number in the context of a sentence, you usually place it before the word it refers to, accompanied by the article; for example, **Le chiavi sono nel terzo cassetto** (*The keys are in the third drawer*).

You can write an ordinal number using numerals followed by a superscript letter related to the ordinal number's ending. That is, you use ° for **primo** (*first*) and ª for **prima** (*first*). For example, you write **il 1° maggio** (*May 1st*).

When you use a Roman numeral — for example, in a person's name or title (Pope John Paul II, Thurston Howell III) or when you talk about **il XVIII secolo** (*the *eighteenth century*) — you read that numeral as an ordinal number. For example, you'd say **Papa Giovanni Paolo Secondo** (*Pope John Paul the Second*).

Rewrite the cardinal number in parentheses using the corresponding ordinal number when appropriate. When the number doesn't indicate a date or a century, write it out in full.

Q. Colombo esplorò l'America centrale _____ secolo. (in, 15)

A. Colombo esplorò l'America centrale **nel XV** secolo. (*Columbus explored Central America in the fifteenth century.*)

11. Le colonie americane dichiararono l'indipendenza nel _____. (1776)

12. Il figlio di Marta è il _____ della classe. (1)

13. Le ragazze della staffetta 4 x 100 sono arrivate _____ai Campionati europei. (3)

14. I giocatori della squadra di basket della scuola sono arrivati _____ ai campionati regionali! (15)

15. Il secolo tra il 1600 e il 1700, che è il _____ secolo, viene anche chiamato il _____. (17, 600)

16. Massimo è arrivato solo _____ nella gara di sci. (48)

Managing Your Calendar and Your Time

You live in the age of digital planners, e-mail appointment reminders, cellular phones with calendars and flight schedules, and clocks on every possible gadget. That's why it's pretty important to know how to handle information about time, starting with centuries and proceeding to years, seasons, months, days of the week, hours, minutes, and seconds.

Il calendario: The calendar

The U.S. and Italy (and the entire world) share the same calendar. Here follows the vocabulary you use to talk about centuries, years, seasons, months, dates, and days of the week.

Secoli, anni e stagioni: Centuries, years, and seasons

In Italian as in English, you refer to a century with Roman numerals as opposed to ordinal numbers. The Italian word for *century* is **secolo,** so when speaking about a century, you say the Roman numeral as an ordinal number, followed by **secolo:** **Newton visse nel XVIII (diciottesimo) secolo** (*Newton lived in the eighteenth century*). See the earlier section on ordinal numbers for details on writing ordinal numbers.

If you're referring to a particular year, you add the definite article to the cardinal number indicating the year, as in **il 2000** (*the year 2000*); when you need a preposition, you use the form combined with the article (see Chapter 6), as in **nel 1945** (*in 1945*). You can say **il 1968/il millenovecentosessantotto** (*nineteen sixty-eight*) or **il '68/sessantotto** (*sixty-eight*), but you can't say **il diciannove sessantotto** (*nineteen sixty-eight*). And you only use **il 2008/duemilaotto** (*two thousand eight*), not **lo '08.**

The four seasons are **la primavera** (*spring*), **l(a)'estate** (*summer*), **l(o)'autunno** (*autumn*), and **l(o)'inverno** (*winter*).

Mesi e date: Months and dates

You don't capitalize the names of the months. They're all masculine and take **il** (*the*), except **agosto** (*August*), which takes **l'** (*the*) (see Chapter 2). Here are the months:

- **gennaio** (*January*)
- **febbraio** (*February*)
- **marzo** (*March*)
- **aprile** (*April*)

- **maggio** (*May*)
- **giugno** (*June*)
- **luglio** (*July*)
- **agosto** (*August*)

- **settembre** (*September*)
- **ottobre** (*October*)
- **novembre** (*November*)
- **dicembre** (*December*)

When mentioning a particular date, you use cardinal numbers, except for the first of the month, in which case you use the ordinal number **primo.** You write dates in the day-month-year format, without commas. For example, you say **Oggi è il primo maggio** (*Today is May 1st*), but you say **Partiamo il 15 aprile** (*We will leave on April 15th*).

If you want to know the specific day of the week that something occurred or occurs, you say **In che giorno . . .?** (*On what day . . .?*). If you ask for the date, you usually say **Che giorno è?,** which may mean *What's the date?* or *What's today?* If you need to be more precise, you can ask **Quanti ne abbiamo oggi?,** which literally means *What's today's number?* but is the same as asking **Qual è la data di oggi?** (*What's today's date?*). The answer is phrased **Oggi è il 29 febbraio** (*Today is February 29th*). And if you want to know the day of the week, you ask **Che giorno è della settimana?** (*What day is today?*), and the answer is phrased **Oggi è venerdì** (*Today is Friday*).

I giorni della settimana: Days of the week

Just as with months, you don't capitalize the days of the week in Italian. They're all masculine and take **il,** except for **la domenica** (*Sunday*). In Italian calendars, the week starts on Monday. The days from **lunedì** (*Monday*) through **venerdì** (*Friday*) are **i giorni feriali** (*weekdays*); **la domenica** and other holidays are **i giorni festivi** (*festivities*); **il sabato** (*Saturday*) and **la domenica** form **il fine settimana/il week-end** (*week-end*). Here are the days of the week:

- **lunedì** (*Monday*)
- **martedì** (*Tuesday*)
- **mercoledì** (*Wednesday*)

- **giovedì** (*Thursday*)
- **venerdì** (*Friday*)

- **sabato** (*Saturday*)
- **domenica** (*Sunday*)

L'ora: The time

If you want to catch a train or a plane, make sure the store is open, or check the movie theater's schedule, you need to know the right time. To ask the time, you say **Che ora è/sono?** (*What time is it?*).

When you answer, you can use the 24-hour system (which in the U.S. is usually associated with the military) or the 12-hour system:

✔ You find the 24-hour system printed on schedules and notebook pages, event programs, and so forth: for example, **Il treno parte alle [ore] 15,45/15:45** (*The train leaves at 1545 hours [3:45 p.m.]*). When you tell the time this way, you add minutes to the hour, as in **15:45**, which you read as **le quindici e quarantacinque.** You use this system in everyday life when you want to avoid misunderstandings or be very formal (for example, if you're someone's secretary setting an appointment for his or her boss).

✔ Otherwise, you use the 12-hour system. You say **Sono le tre e cinquantanove** (*It's 3:59*). You can add **di mattina** (*a.m., in the morning*) or **di pomeriggio/ di sera** (*p.m., in the afternoon/evening*) to avoid misunderstandings, as in

> **"Partono alle 4."** (*"They're leaving at 4."*)
>
> **"Di mattina?!"** (*"In the morning?!"*)
>
> **"No! Di pomeriggio."** (*"No! In the afternoon."*)

When expressing time, you add the definite article to the number: **l'una** (*1 a.m./p.m.*); **le tredici** (*1 p.m.*); **le ventuno** (*9 p.m.*). You use the indefinite article in the expression **un quarto a** (*a quarter to*). You coordinate the article with the gender and number of the hour you're talking about (see Chapter 2 on gender-number coordination).

You use the verb **essere** (*to be*) in the plural with all hours over **una** (*1 a.m.*), as in **Sono le tre meno cinque** (*It's five minutes to 3 a.m./p.m.*). Check out the following examples:

✔ **È l'una** (*1 a.m./p.m.*)

✔ **È mezzogiorno** (*12 p.m., noon*)

✔ **È un quarto a . . .** (*a quarter to . . .*)

✔ **È l'una e tre quarti** (*It's a quarter to 1 a.m./p.m.*) or **È un quarto alle due** (*1:45 a.m./p.m*).

Check out the following examples of ways in which you can convey fractions of the hour:

✔ **Sono le due e dieci** (*2:10 a.m/p.m.*)

✔ **Sono le otto meno un quarto** (*a quarter to 8 a.m./p.m.*)

✔ **Sono le dieci e un quarto** (*10:15 a.m./p.m.*)

✔ **È l'una e tre quarti**, or **è un quarto alle due** (*1:45 a.m./p.m*)

✔ **Sono le tre meno cinque** (*5 minutes to three a.m./p.m.*)

✔ **È mezzogiorno** (*noon, 12 p.m.*)

✔ **È mezzanotte** (*midnight, 12 a.m.*)

✔ **Sono le quattro e mezza/o** (*4:30 a.m./p.m.*)

What follows are the first entries in the travel plan of a young woman. Translate the words she left in English in her travel plan into Italian, using the 24-hour system. Use the prepositions indicated in parentheses. If you add the definite article, prepositions form one word with it (see Chapter 2). Rewrite dollar or euro amounts according to the Italian style (see "Counting Items with Cardinal Numbers" for details).

Q. **Saturday, June 15, 2008.** Partenza!

A. **Sabato, 15 giugno 2008.** Partenza! (*Saturday, June 15, 2008. Departure day!*)

17. Partenza **at 5:45 p.m.** Arrivo ad Amsterdam **at 7:30 a.m.** (a)

_____

18. Partenza per Roma **at 11:30 a.m.** Arrivo **at 1 p.m.** (a)

_____

19. Cambiare 500 dollari; probabilmente saranno solo **289.5** euro.

_____

20. Per prima cosa, il mattino dopo, **June 16,** colazione **at 9 a.m.** con caffè espresso e bombolone! (a)

_____

21. Visita del Pantheon **at 10 a.m.** (a)

_____

22. Pranzo da Tino **at 12:30 p.m.** (a)

_____

23. **Sunday at 12 noon** in Piazza San Pietro. (a)

_____

24. Al pomeriggio, visita ai giardini ed al museo di Villa Borghese **from 3 to 6 p.m.** (da, a)

_____

25. Cena sul Lungo Tevere **at 9:30 p.m.** (a)

_____

Answer Key

1   143: centoquarantatré; 145: centoquarantacinque

2   812: ottocentododici; 814: ottocentoquattordici

3   86: ottantasei; 88: ottantotto

4   4.395.651: quattromilionitrecentonovantacinquemilaseicentocinquantuno; 4.395.653: quattromilionitrecentonovantacinquemilaseicentocinquantatré

5   2.129.370.685: due miliardi centoventinovemilioni trecentosettantamilaseicentoottantac-inque; 2.129.370.687: due miliardi centoventinovemilioni trecentosettantamilaseicen-toottantanove

6   86.407,24: ottantaseimilaquattrocentosette virgola ventiquattro; 86.407,26: ottantaseim-ilaquattrocentosette virgola ventisei

7   537,87: cinquecentotrentasette virgola ottantasette; 537,89: cinquecentotrentasette virgola ottantanove

8   47: quarantasette; 47,2: quarantasette virgola due

9   83,90: ottantré virgola novanta; 83,92: ottantré virgola novantadue

10   9.397.868,16: novemilionitrecentonovantasettemilaottocentosessantotto virgola sedici; 9.397.868,18: novemilionitrecentonovantasettemilaottocentosessantotto virgola diciotto

11   Le colonie americane dichiararono l'indipendenza nel **1776.** (*The American colonies declared independence in 1776.*)

12   Il figlio di Marta è il **primo** della classe. (*Marta's son is the first in his class.*)

13   Le ragazze della staffetta 4 x 100 sono arrivate **terze** ai Campionati europei. (*The girls of the 4 x 100-meter relay came in third at the European Championship.*)

14   I giocatori della squadra di basket della scuola sono arrivati **quindicesimi** ai campionati region-ali! (*The players of the school's basketball team came in fifteenth at the regional championship!*)

15   Il secolo tra il 1600 e il 1700, che è il **XVII** secolo, viene anche chiamato il **Seicento.** (*The century between 1600 and 1700, which is the seventeenth century, is also called the Seicento.*)

16   Massimo è arrivato solo **quarantottesimo** nella gara di sci. (*Massimo came in only forty-eighth in the ski race.*)

17   Partenza **alle 17:45.** Arrivo ad Amsterdam **alle 7:30 di mattina.** (*Departure at 5:45 p.m. Arrival in Amsterdam at 7:30 a.m.*)

18   Partenza per Roma **alle 11:30.** Arrivo **alle 13.** (*Departure for Rome at 11:30 a.m. Arrival at 1 p.m.*)

19   Cambiare 500 dollari; probabilmente saranno solo **289,5** euro. (*Change 500 dollars; it will proba-bly be only 289.5 euros.*)

20 Per prima cosa, il mattino dopo, **16 giugno,** colazione **alle 9** con caffè espresso e bombolone! (*First thing, the following morning, June 16, breakfast at 9 a.m. with coffee and a donut!*)

21 Visita del Pantheon **alle 10:00 di mattina.** (*Visit to the Pantheon at 10 a.m.*)

22 Pranzo da Tino **alle 12:30.** (*Lunch at Tino's at 12:30 p.m.*)

23 **Domenica alle 12:00 (a mezzogiorno)** in Piazza San Pietro. (*Sunday at 12 [noon] in St. Peter's Square.*)

24 Al pomeriggio, visita ai giardini ed al museo di Villa Borghese **dalle 15 alle 18/dalle 3:00 alle 6:00.** (*In the afternoon, visit to Villa Borghese's gardens and museum, from 3 to 6 p.m.*)

25 Cena sul Lungo Tevere **alle 21:30 di sera.** (*Dinner on the Lungo Tevere at 9:30 p.m.*)

Part II
A Close Look at Parts of Speech

The 5th Wave   By Rich Tennant

"Mona's trying to form endings to Italian adjectives. This from a woman who can't form an ending to a conversation."

In this part . . .

*I*n this part, I guide you through the Italian parts of speech, starting with pronouns (which are both numerous and complicated). I talk about adjectives and how to coordinate them with nouns; about prepositions and how to combine them with the definite article; and how to form complements — that is, short phrases needed when the noun by itself can't carry your meaning. I also talk about *this* and *that,* indefinites such as *some* and *a little,* and how to say that something belongs to you.

Chapter 4

All About Pronouns

Italian has many types of pronouns, each with a special function. Most pronouns replace people, places, concepts, and quantities that have already been mentioned. *Subject pronouns* don't replace anything but rather they convey who's performing the action. Italian uses pronouns often because they allow you to avoid repetition and shorten sentences. Here's an example of a sentence without and with subject pronouns:

> **Io ho telefonato a Giovanna. Ho detto a Giovanna che ero stanca. Non credo di andare al cinema con Giovanna. Purtroppo, Giovanna ha già ordinato i biglietti e io ho già pagato i biglietti.** (*I called Giovanna. I told Giovanna that I was tired. I don't think I'll go to the movies with Giovanna. Unfortunately, Giovanna already ordered the tickets and I already paid for the tickets.*)

> **[Io] ho telefonato a Giovanna e le ho detto che ero stanca. Non credo di andare al cinema con lei. Purtroppo, Giovanna ha già ordinato i biglietti e io li ho pagati.** (*I called Giovanna and I told her that I was tired. I don't think I'll go to the movies with her. Unfortunately, she already ordered the tickets and I already paid for them.*)

Understanding and using Italian pronouns is challenging because they vary so much in form, positioning, and function, but they're indispensable, so you need to work through the tough stuff. In this chapter, I present the various pronouns and the functions they perform. They can be

✔ Subject pronouns, as in **Io ho telefonato a Giovanna** (*I called Giovanna*)

✔ Stressed pronouns, as in **Non credo di andare al cinema con lei** (*I don't think I'll go to the movies with her*)

✔ Direct object pronouns, as in **Li ha già ordinati** (*She already ordered the tickets*)

✔ Indirect objects pronouns, as in **Le ho detto che ero stanca** (*I told her that I was tired*)

I also talk about two other pronouns that perform a lot of functions in Italian: **ci** (*here, there, about this/that, of this/that, on this/that*) and **ne** (*of/about him/her/them, of/about this/that*). You also may use another set of pronouns, called *reflexive pronouns,* when the object of the sentence is the same as the subject. In English, it's translated with *myself, yourself,* and so on. Reflexive pronouns don't substitute already mentioned concepts, but they're conjugated directly with the verbs.

In most cases, Italian and English use pronouns in very similar ways, but there are also some differences:

- ✔ **Italian uses subject pronouns much less than English.** In Italian, you can omit subject pronouns because the verb conjugation indicates the person performing the action.

- ✔ **Italian has several sets of pronouns.** Even when they perform the same function, the object pronouns may change in form, depending on where they're placed in the sentence.

- ✔ **Italian conveys a direct object and an indirect object together by forming double pronouns.**

Reader, Meet the Subject Pronouns

Grammatically speaking, six persons can perform an action: the first, second, and third persons, singular and plural. But there are more pronouns than persons because the third person differentiates between masculine, feminine, and neuter forms (*it*).

Table 4-1 lists the subject pronouns. *Note:* In Italian, when animals are seen as possessing feelings and even a personality, you use pronouns once reserved for human beings: **lui** (*he*), **lei** (*she*), and **loro** (*they*).

Table 4-1	Subject Pronouns	
Person	*Singular*	*Plural*
First	**io** (*I*)	**noi** (*we*)
Second	**tu** (*you*)	**voi** (*you*)
Third	**lui** (*he*), **lei** (*she*), **esso/essa** (*it*)	**loro** (*they*), **essi/esse** (*they*)
Third (singular and plural, used to address people formally)	**Lei** (*you*)	**Loro** (*you*)

The traditional subject pronouns for people are **egli** (*he*), **ella** (*she*), and **essi/esse** (*they*). You may find them used in older writings and formal settings. Today, the third-person pronouns **lui, lei,** and **loro** are used as pronouns.

Knowing when to use them

Most of the time, you don't use subject pronouns in Italian because the verb conjugations indicate the subject. In the sentence **Guardano la televisione tutte le sere** (*They watch TV every night*), you know the subject is **loro** (*they*) because **guardano** is conjugated in the third-person plural form. I cover verb conjugation details in Part III.

At times, you do need subject pronouns. You should use them whenever you're

✔ Emphasizing what a particular person is doing: **Io darò le dimissioni.** (*I'm going to resign.*)

✔ Emphasizing one subject over another (often inverting the word order): **Decido io, non tu, a che ora devi tornare a casa!** (*I'm the one who decides what time you must come home, not you!*)

✔ Forming a sentence that may generate confusion about the subject: **Lui capisce cose che io non capisco.** (*He understands things that I don't understand.*)

Adapting subject pronouns for formal and informal usage

In addition, you can address people formally or informally in Italian, altering your pronoun and verb choice accordingly:

✔ Informally, you address people with the following pronoun-verb combinations:

  • **tu** (*you* singular) + the verb in the second-person singular: **[Tu] vieni alla partita, Andrea?** (*Are you coming to the game, Andrea?*)

  • **voi** (*you* plural) + the verb in the second-person plural: **[Voi] venite alla partita, Andrea e Giacomo?** (*Are you coming to the game, Andrea and Giacomo?*)

✔ Formally, you address people with the following pronoun-verb combinations:

  • **Lei** (*you*) with either a man or a woman + the verb in the third-person singular: **[Lei] viene alla partita, Signore/Signora?** (*Are you coming to the game, Sir/Madam?*)

  • **Loro** (*you*) + the verb in third-person plural: **[Loro] vengono alla partita Signori/Signore/Signori e Signore?** (*Are you coming to the game, Sir/Madam/Ladies and Gentlemen?*)

  • Nowadays you can use **voi** (*you* plural) to address more than one person informally or formally, as in **[Voi] venite alla partita Signori/Signore/Signori e Signore?** (*Are you coming to the soccer game, Sir/Madam/ladies and gentlemen?*)

When you address someone formally, you use his or her last name preceded by **Signor** (*Mr.*), **Signora** (*Mrs., Ms.*), **Signorina** (*Miss, Ms.*), **Dottor/Dottoressa** (*Dr.* for all those with a **laurea** or university degree), **Ingegner** (*Engineer*), **Avvocato** (*Counselor*), and so on with specific professional titles.

Read the following e-mail written to a friend. Taking clues from the verbs, fill in the blanks with the appropriate subject pronouns.

Q. Caro Marco, ti scrivo da Cortina. _____ sto bene. Come stai _____?

A. Caro Marco, ti scrivo da Cortina. **Io** sto bene. Come stai **tu**? (*Dear Marco, I'm writing you from Cortina. I'm well. How are you?*)

New Message

File   Edit   View   Insert   Format   Tools   Message   Help

Send   Cut   Copy   Paste   Undo | abc✔ Check

From: Marco
To: studio.branzini@visp.com
Cc:

Oggetto: Pratica Fratelli Letta

Cara Giulia,

ti scrivo da Cortina. Purtroppo, scrivo (1) _____ perché Elena
si è fatta male alla mano destra in un'ascensione e (2) _____
non potrà scrivere per un po'. A parte questo incidente, (3)
_____ stiamo tutti bene. Il tempo è splendido e il panorama,
come (4) _____ sai bene, magnifico. Lo scorso fine settimana i
miei suoceri sono venuti a trovarci. (5) _____ non sono dei
grandi camminatori, ma sono rimasti con i bambini e con Elena,
così (6) _____ sono andato a fare una bella scalata con i miei
amici. Li conosci anche (7) _____, vero? Spero che l'estate
prossima tutti (8) _____ potremo stare insieme.

Un abbraccio,

Marco

Stressed Pronouns

Stressed pronouns are most often placed after a preposition, as in **Vieni con me al mercato!** (*Come to the market with me!*). But you also can use them directly after a verb without a preposition for emphasis, as in **La mamma vuole te!** (*Mom wants you!*). At this stage, to make your life simpler, use the stressed pronoun only when you have a preposition. For example, **Qualcuno ha lasciato un messaggio per te** (*Someone left a message for you*).

Table 4-2 demonstrates the forms of the stressed pronouns. As you can see, the only forms that change from the subject projects are the forms for **io (me)** and **tu (te).** Although only four prepositions are shown here, any preposition can be combined with a stressed pronoun.

Table 4-2	Stressed Pronouns
Pronouns	*Translation*
me (*me*)	**a/con/di/per me** (*to/with/about/for me*)
te (*you,* singular informal)	**a/con/di/per te** (*to/with/about/for you*)
lui (*him*), **lei** (*her*), **esso, essa** (*it him/her/it*)	**a/con/di/per lui/lei/esso/essa** (*to/with/about/for him/her/it*)
Lei (*you,* singular formal)	**a/con/di/per Lei** (*to/with/about/for you*)
noi (*us*)	**a/con/di/per noi** (*to/with/about/for us*)
voi (*you,* plural informal)	**a/con/di/per voi** (*to/with/about/for you*)
loro (*them*)	**a/con/di/per loro** (*to/with/about/for them*)
Loro (*you,* plural formal)	**a/con/di/per Loro** (*to/with/about/for you*)

Fill in the blanks in the following sentences by substituting stressed pronouns for the words in parentheses.

0. Non mi piace lavorare con _____. (Gianluca)

A. Non mi piace lavorare con **lui**. (*I don't like working with him.*)

9. Volete venire con _____ a cena? (me e Mario)

10. Giovanni va con _____ al mare. (i figli)

11. Gioco a carte con _____. (te e i tuoi cugini)

12. Piero si fida totalmente di _____. (sua madre)

13. Chiamo _____? (tu)

14. Ho affidato tutti i miei affari a _____. (mio cognato)

Direct Object Pronouns

Whereas subject pronouns are sometimes optional, object pronouns aren't — you rely on object pronouns to replace objects or people who are recipients of that action — nice and straightforward. Here are a few key points about direct objects and direct object pronouns:

✔ Direct objects are those that follow transitive verbs and are called such because the action affects the object directly, as in **Vedo Angela** (*I see Angela*). If you replace **Angela** with a pronoun, the sentence becomes **La vedo** (*I see her*).

✔ Direct object pronouns usually answer the questions *who?* or *what?*. When you can answer those questions, you can replace the answer (the direct object) with a pronoun. For example, **Leggo il giornale la domenica** (*I read the paper on Sunday*): What do I read? The paper. **Lo leggo** (*I read it.*) Here's another example: **Ho invitato i nostri amici a cena** (*I invited our friends to dinner*). Who? Our friends. **Li ho invitati a cena** (*I invited them to dinner*).

✔ Direct object pronouns can replace people, animals, things, and abstractions. For example, **Il ragazzo accarezza il cucciolo** (*The boy is petting the puppy*), **[Lo] L'accarezza** (*He is petting it*); **Quell'uomo ha perso la libertà** (*That man lost his freedom*), **L'ha persa** (*He lost it*).

Table 4-3 shows the direct object pronouns.

Table 4-3	Direct Object Pronouns
Pronoun	*Translation*
mi	*me*
ti	*you*
lo (MS)	*him*
la (FS)	*her*
lo/la	*it*
La (MS/FS, formal)	*you* (singular formal)
ci	*us*
vi	*you*
li/le (MP/FP)	*them*
Li/Le (MP/FP, formal)	*you* (plural formal)

When you address someone formally in speech or writing, the direct object pronouns you use are **La** (*you* singular for a man or a woman), **Li** (*you* plural) for a group of men, **Le** for a group of women, or **Li** for a group of men and women:

> **Signore/Signora, La ringrazio di essere venuto/a.** (*Sir/Madam, thank you for coming.*)

> **Signori/Signore e Signori, Li ringrazio di essere venuti/e.** (*Gentlemen/Ladies and gentlemen, thank you for coming.*)

> **Signore, Le ringrazio di essere venute.** (*Ladies, thank you for coming.*)

In everyday life, the **voi** (*you* plural) form is much more commonly used (formally or informally), which simplifies things considerably. For example, **Signore e Signori, vi ringrazio di essere venuti** (*Ladies and gentlemen, thank you for coming*).

Placement of the direct object pronoun varies according to the verb form:

✔ The direct object pronoun often precedes the conjugated verb: **Quel ragazzo non dice mai la verità** (*That boy doesn't ever tell the truth*); **Non la dice mai** (*He never tells it*).

✔ If the verb is in the infinitive, imperative, or gerund form, you attach the pronoun to the verb. When attached to the infinitive, the final **-e** is dropped.

   • Infinitive: **"Ti piacerebbe comprare la borsa?" "Sì, mi piacerebbe comprarla."** (*"Would you like to buy the purse?" "Yes, I would like to buy it."*)

   • Imperative: **Porta i bambini al mare!** (*Take the children to the beach!*); **Portali al mare!** (*Take them to the beach!*)

   • Gerund: **Avendoli preparati [i panini], li ho portati al mare.** (*Having made the sandwiches, I took them to the beach.*)

✔ When using the direct object pronouns **lo** and **la** before a verb that begins with a vowel, **-o** or **-a** can be dropped and replaced with an apostrophe, or they can remain as they are, as in **Bianca lo/l'aspetta** (*Bianca's waiting for him*).

When using a direct object pronoun with a compound tense, the past participle agrees in gender and number with the pronoun.

   "Hanno ricevuto la lettera?" "No, non [la] l'hanno ancora ricevuta." (*"Did they receive the letter?" "No, they didn't receive it yet."*)

   "Avete fatto i compiti?" "Li abbiamo fatti!" (*"Did you do your homework?" "We did (it)!"*)

Fill in the blanks in the following sentences by replacing the underlined words with the appropriate direct object pronouns. (Use Table 4-3 for reference.)

Q. Cercano il dottore? (*Are they looking for the doctor?*)

A. Sì, **lo** cercano. (*They're looking for him.*)

15. Non capisco voi. Non _____ capisco.

16. Vedono spesso il fratello di Beppe. _____ vedono spesso.

17. Chiamate noi domani! Chiamate_____ domani!

18. Non mangiano la carne. Non _____ mangiano.

19. Ho comprato il vestito. _____ ho comprato.

20. Ha suonato la trombetta. _____ ha suonata.

21. Voglio dire la verità. _____ voglio dire. or Voglio dir_____.

22. Luigi mangiava gli spinaci quasi ogni giorno. Luigi _____ mangiava quasi ogni giorno.

23. Desidero pagare il caffé. Desidero pagar_____.

Fill in the blanks with the appropriate formal direct object pronouns. The context of the sentence should indicate when you're addressing a man, a woman, a group of men, a group of women, or a mixed group.

Q. Signora, _____ aiuto io a salire le scale.

A. Signora, **L'**aiuto io a salire le scale. (*Madam, I'll help you walk up the stairs.*)

24. Signore, _____ volevo avvisare che la squadra femminile è al completo. (plural)

25. Signori, _____ volevo avvisare che la squadra maschile è al completo.

26. Signora, _____ vorrei avvertire che la gonna che Lei ha ordinato è arrivata.

27. Signore, si è fatto male a una mano? _____ aiuto io.

Indirect Object Pronouns

Indirect object pronouns refer to living beings. They're used with transitive verbs and answer the question **a chi?** (*to whom?*). Prepositions used with indirect objects can include **a/per/con** (*to/for/with*) + a person or animal.

> **Scrivo a mia madre ogni giorno** (*I write to my mother every day*) becomes **Le scrivo ogni giorno** (*I write to her every day*)

> **Telefono a Luigi una volta alla settimana** (*I call Luigi once a week*) becomes **Gli telefono una volta alla settimana** (*I call him once a week*)

In Table 4-4 I list the indirect object pronouns that are generally placed before the verb or attached to it when the verb is an infinitive, an imperative, or a gerund. The **loro** form always follows the verb, as in **Ho detto loro quello che pensavo** (*I told them what I was thinking*).

Table 4-4	Indirect Object Pronouns
Pronoun	*Translation*
mi	*to/for me*
ti	*to/for you*
gli	*to/for him*
le	*to/for her*
Le (MS/FS, formal)	*you (MS/FS, formal)*
ci	*to/for us*
vi	*to/for you*
gli (or **loro** after the verb with or without a preposition)	*to/for them*
gli (or **Loro** after the verb with or without a preposition)	*you (plural formal)*

Note the following nuances of the indirect object pronouns:

✔ In the third-person plural form, **gli** is used for both masculine and feminine forms. **Compro un regalo per le mie figlie** (*I'm buying a gift for my daughters*) becomes **Gli compro un regalo** (*I'm buying a gift for them*). You also can use **gli** for only males or male and female combined, as in **"Cosa regali ai nonni per Natale?" "Gli regalo una radio"** (*"What are you giving our grandparents for Christmas?" "I'm giving them a radio"*).

✔ When you address people formally, you use the **Le** form in the third-person singular for both male and female, as in **Signore/Signora, Le apro io la porta** (*Sir/Madam, I'll open the door for you*).

✔ Note that the third-person plural form has two options that mean the same thing. The **gli** form is being used more frequently in modern spoken Italian, although the **loro** form is still acceptable. In the plural, you may use the pronoun **Loro** after the verb with or without a preposition, as in **Signori/Signore/Signore e Signori, apro Loro la porta/apro la porta per Loro** (*Gentlemen/Ladies/Ladies and gentlemen, I'll open the door for you*).

Contrary to the rules of direct object pronouns, the past participle in compound tenses doesn't agree in gender and number with the indirect object pronoun. Rather, the past participle remains unchanged: **"Avete telefonato ad Adriana?" "No, non le abbiamo telefonato"** (*"Did you call Adriana?" "No, we didn't call her"*).

Fill in the blanks in the following sentences by replacing the underlined words with the appropriate indirect object pronoun.

Q. Hanno fatto un grosso favore <u>a noi</u>. (*They did a big favor for us.*)

A. **Ci** hanno fatto un grosso favore. (*They did us a big favor.*)

28. Compriamo un gelato <u>per voi</u>. _____ compriamo un gelato.

29. Raccontano una storia <u>a Enzo</u>. _____ raccontano una storia.

30. Mando dei fiori <u>a Paola</u>. _____ mando dei fiori.

31. Ha offerto <u>a noi</u> il suo aiuto. _____ ha offerto il suo aiuto.

32. I genitori hanno dato la macchina <u>al figlio</u>. I genitori _____ hanno dato la macchina.

33. Tu hai scritto una cartolina <u>a me</u>? Tu _____ hai scritto una cartolina?

34. Hanno pagato il conto <u>per voi</u>? _____ hanno pagato il conto?

35. Ho preparato la cena <u>per gli amici</u>. _____ ho preparato la cena.

In the following sentences, fill in the blanks with the appropriate direct object pronouns or indirect object pronouns, using the words in parentheses as clues. (Don't forget that the preposition indicates that the object pronoun is indirect. Refer to the tables earlier in this chapter for help.)

Q. _____ do i biglietti. (a te)

A. **Ti** do i biglietti. (*I'll give you the tickets.*)

36. Io _____ scrivo una lettera. (a Tom)

37. Signora, posso pesar_____ per Lei? (i pomodori)

38. _____ desidero ordinare. (la pizza)

39. Noi _____ parliamo sempre di voi. (a Lei)

40. Mamma, _____ compri una Ferrari? (a me)

41. Vogliamo visitar_____ subito. (il museo)

42. _____ descrivo il mercato. (a te)

43. Voglio imparar_____ bene. (l'italiano)

Combining Direct and Indirect Object Pronouns to Form Double Pronouns

Italians say things quickly and take it for granted that the listener understands what they're talking about after they've mentioned something once. The language accommodates this through double pronouns, which, like the other pronouns covered in this chapter, are placed either before the verb or attached to the infinitive, imperative, or gerund. You form double pronouns by combining the indirect object pronouns (**mi, ti, gli, le, ci, vi,** and **gli**) with the direct object pronouns, usually in the third-person singular and plural (**lo, la, li,** and **le**). You use double pronouns when you want to convey both a direct object and an indirect object together.

When combining **gli** + **lo, la, li** or **le,** you connect them with an **e: glielo, gliela, glieli, gliele.**

The following examples show how to replace the direct object and the indirect object with pronouns. In the sentence **Regalo un libro al bambino** (*I give a book to the little boy*), **un libro** (*a book*) is the direct object, and **al bambino** (*to the little boy*) is the indirect object. Here are the ways to recast this sentence combining the direct and indirect object pronouns:

✔ Replace **al bambino** with the indirect object pronoun **gli: Gli regalo un libro.** (*I give him a book.*)

✔ Replace **un libro** with the direct object pronoun **lo: Lo regalo al bambino.** (*I give it to the little boy.*)

✔ Combine the two object pronouns, starting with the indirect object pronoun followed by the direct object pronoun: **Glielo** is the combination of **gli** meaning *to him* and **lo** meaning *the book*, so you get **Glielo regalo** (*I give it to him*).

When combining the two object pronouns in the third person, the indirect object pronoun is always **gli** even if the translation is *to her*. You know that the pronoun **le** means *to her,* but when combining pronouns, the indirect object pronoun will always be **gli.** In the same example **Regalo un libro al bambino,** substitute **al bambino** with **alla bambina.** Watch the transformation: Replace **alla bambina** with the indirect object pronoun **gli** (not **le**), and replace the direct object pronoun with **lo.** The combination is the same: **Glielo regalo.**

When using the combined pronouns and a compound tense, the past participle will agree in gender and number with the direct object pronoun. For example, **Ho regalato una bicicletta alla bambina** (*I gave a bicycle to the little girl*) becomes **Gliel'ho regalata** (*I gave it to her*). When **lo** and **la** precede the verb **avere,** the vowel can be dropped and replaced with an apostrophe, or they can remain as they are.

Table 4-5 lists pronoun combinations. **Mi, ti, ci,** and **vi** change to **me, te, ce,** and **ve** to ease pronunciation, and the third-person singular and plural becomes one word.

Table 4-5	Double Pronouns: Indirect + Direct Object Pronouns
Double Pronouns	*Translation*
me lo/la/li/le	*him/her/it/them/ to me*
te lo/la/li/le	*him/her/it/them to you* (singular informal)
glielo/gliela/glieli/gliele	*him/her/it/them to him* or *to her*
Glielo/Gliela/Glieli/Gliele	*him/her/it/them to you* (third-person singular, formal)
ce lo/la/li/le	*him/her/it/them to us*
ve lo/la/li/le	*him/her/it/them to you* (plural informal)
glielo/gliela/glieli/gliele	*him/her/it/them to them*
Glielo/Gliela/Glieli/Gliele	*him/her/it/them to you* (third-person plural, formal)

Note that in the third-person plural, **glielo** (in its various forms) can also be replaced by **loro** after the verb. For example, **Lo compro loro** (*I'll buy it for you/them*).

When using double pronouns with the imperative (see Chapter 13), one syllable commands (**da', fa', sta, di', va'**) followed by a direct, indirect, or combined pronoun double the initial consonant of the pronoun attached. For example, **Da' il conto a me!** becomes **Dammelo!** (*Give the bill to me!*).

Rewrite the following sentences, replacing the direct and indirect objects with a double pronoun.

Q. Scriverai una lettera allo zio? (*Will you write a letter to your uncle?*)

A. Sì, **gliela** scriverò. (*Yes, I'll write to him.*)

44. Porti le chiavi ad Elisa? _____

45. Dai quel portafoglio a me! _____

46. Restituisci il pallone a Roberto? _____

47. Mandano il libro a lei? _____

48. Compro il biglietto per te. _____

49. Mi prepari la torta? _____

50. Hanno visto l'opera? _____

51. Vi hanno spedito il CD? _____

But Wait — There's More! Special Italian Pronouns

Italian has two special pronouns: **ci** (*here, there*) and **ne** (*of this/that/him/her/them*). They're considered pronouns because they replace prepositional phrases. In the case of **ci**, it generally replaces the prepositions **a, in,** and **su** + a place or a thing. **Ne** generally replaces the prepositions **di** and **da** + a person or thing. When used idiomatically, both pronouns can refer to entire sentences or ideas, as you find out later in this section.

The adverbial pronoun ci

All languages have *homonyms* — that is, words that look and sound alike but that have different meanings. For example, *sound* may mean "noise" or "stretch of water." In Italian, the pronoun **ci** is similar: It can mean *us/to us,* but it's also an adverbial pronoun that can mean *here, there.*

For example, if someone says **Sei andatoagli Uffizi quest'estate?** (*Did you go to the Uffizi Museum this summer?*), you answer **No, ci sono andato l'estate scorsa** (*No, I went there last summer*). The **ci** stands for **agli Uffizi.**

Ci is also used with the verb **essere** to mean *there is* and *there are.*

You use **c'è** (*there is*) with a noun or name in the singular and **ci sono** (*there are*) with a noun or name in the plural. **C'è/ci sono** also can take the spelling **vi è/vi sono,** but it's used more in literature than in spoken language. However, if you do see **vi è/vi sono,** be careful not to confuse **vi** with the pronoun meaning *you.* Here are some examples of the adverbial pronouns at work:

> **C'è/Vi è molta neve in montagna.** (*There's a lot of snow in the mountains.*)

> **C'era una volta una bellissima principessa . . .** (*Once upon a time, there was a beautiful princess . . .*)

You also can use **ci** as a pronoun referring to

✔ Places already mentioned, with phrases such as **qui/lì** (*here*), **là, in quel posto** (*there, in/to that place*), **da/per/attraverso quel posto** (*through there/that place*)

> "Vieni spesso a Firenze?" "Sì, ci vengo ogni estate." (*"Do you come to Florence often?" "Yes, I come here every summer."*)

✔ With special verbs having idiomatic meaning, such as **pensarci, vederci, volerci,** and **crederci**

> "Hai pensato al tuo dilemma?" "Ci ho pensato." (*"Did you think about your dilemma?" "I thought about it."*)

✔ Things or situations already mentioned, with such phrases as **a questo, a quello, a ciò** (*of/about this/that*)

> "Tu credi a quello che ha detto?" "No, non ci credo." (*"Do you believe what he said?" "No, I don't believe it."*)

It may help you to think about **ci** like this: When you have a place introduced by the prepositions **a, in,** or **per** (*at, to, in, through*), you can use **ci** to refer to the preposition + noun combination in the sentence that follows. Some examples include the verbs **andare a/in** (*to go to*), **entrare a/in** (*to enter*), **passare per** (and also **di/da**) (*to go through*), **stare a/in** (*to stay at/in*), and others. For example, "Sei mai stato in Croazia?" "No, non ci sono mai stato." (*"Have you ever been to Croatia?" "No, I've never been there."*)

Some verbs associated with **ci** are idiomatic. The verb **volerci** is one of these. It means *to take, to need*. It's conjugated in the third-person singular and plural forms depending on the object of the sentence. For example, **Ci vogliono tre ore per andare a Roma da qui** (*It takes three hours to get to Rome from here*), but **Ci vuole un uovo per questa ricetta** (*You need one egg for this recipe*).

Translate the following sentences into Italian. You have to use **ci** in all its functions: as it's used in the expressions **c'è/ci sono** (*there is, there are*); as an adverbial pronoun meaning *here/there/about that;* and simply meaning *us/to us*. The conjugated verb forms are given if the verb used is not **essere**.

Q. There's a new film with George Clooney.

A. **C'è un nuovo film con George Clooney.**

52. "Are they going (vanno) to Germany?" "Yes, they're going (vanno) tomorrow."

_____

53. There are too many books on the table.

_____

54. They see (vedono) us from the street.

_____

55. "Will they go (vanno/andranno) to the theater tomorrow?" "Yes, they'll (vanno/andranno) go."

_____

56. He doesn't think (pensa) at all about it.

_____

The pronoun ne

Ne (*of this/that/him/them, from this/that place*) is a useful pronoun. It can refer to people, animals, things, individual objects, or entire sentences that have already been mentioned. You place **ne** before the verb or attached to it if the verb is an infinitive, imperative, or gerund.

Ne means *of this, of them,* and *from there* because it's used with verbs that are always followed by either **di** (*of, about*) or **da** (*by, from*). For example, if someone asks you **Avete fatto delle foto?** (*Did you take some pictures?*), you can answer **Ne abbiamo fatte molte** (*We took many of them*). If someone asks you **Ritorni adesso dal mercato?** (*Are you just now coming back from the market?*), you can answer **Ne ritorno adesso** (*I've just come back [from it]*) because the verb **ritornare** (*to return, to come back*) can be followed by the preposition **da**. Therefore, when you have a thing or a place introduced by the preposition **di** or **da** you can use **ne** to refer to the preposition + noun combination.

The following examples further illustrate the use of **ne** with a verb that takes **di** and one that takes **da**:

> **"Hai parlato di tua figlia con il medico?" "Gliene ho parlato."** (*"Did you speak to the doctor about your daughter?" "I spoke to him about her."*)

> **"Quando sei arrivato da Pisa?" "Ne sono arrivato mezz'ora fa."** (*"When did you get in from Pisa?" "I just got here half an hour ago."*)

Verbs with which **ne** is commonly used include **andare via da** (*to go away from, to leave*), **pensare bene/male di** (*to think well/badly of someone*), and **venire da** (*to come from*). For example, **"Dov'è Massimo?" "Si è arrabbiato e se n'è andato"** (*"Where's Massimo?" "He got mad and left"*).

Table 4-6 shows what **ne** can substitute.

Table 4-6	The Many Meanings of Ne
Phrases That Ne Can Replace	*Translation*
di lui, di lei, di loro	of/about him, of/about her, of/about them
da lui, da lei, da loro	by/from him, by/from her, by/from them
di ciò, di questo, da quello	of/about this, of/about that
da qui, da lì, da là, da questo/da quel posto	from here, from there, from this/that place

A couple of other uses of **ne** are as follows:

✔ You can pair **ne** with indirect object pronouns **(mi, ti, le, gli, ci, vi, gli)** to form double pronouns **(me ne, te ne, gliene, ce ne, ve ne, gliene, ne loro)**. A sentence such as **Ha parlato a te di quel problema?** (*Did he talk to you about that problem?*) can become **Te ne ha parlato?** (*Did he talk to you about it?*).

✔ **Ne** can substitute for words that indicate quantity, such as **molto, parecchio, tanto,** and **un po' di.** For example, **"Vorresti un po' d'acqua?" "Ne vorrei proprio un po', grazie"** (*"Would you like a little water?" "I'd like just a little, thanks"*).

✔ **Ne** is used idiomatically when asking the date: **Quanti ne abbiamo oggi?** (*What's the date?*)

When you address someone directly, you don't use **ne** but rather repeat the preposition + personal pronoun construction:

> **"Hai sentito parlare di me?" "Ho sentito parlare di te."** (*"Have you heard anything about me?" "Yes, I have [heard something about you]."*)

Ne can drop the **-e** when combined with the third-person present and imperfect forms of **essere**. For example, **È rimasto colpito da Bianca** (*He was struck by Bianca*); **N'è rimasto colpito** (*He was struck by her*).

When **ne** substitutes for a partitive, the past participle agrees in number and gender with the object it replaces, as in **"Hanno bevuto tanta birra?" "Sì, ne hanno bevuta tanta"** (*"Did they drink a lot of beer?" "Yes, they drank a lot [of it]"*).

Rewrite the following sentences, replacing the underlined words with the pronoun **ne** in the appropriate place.

Q. Avete letto <u>del nuovo presidente</u>? (*Did you read about the new president?*)

A. **Ne abbiamo letto.** (*We read about him.*)

57. Sono appena tornati <u>dalla Grecia</u>.

_____

58. Vengono adesso <u>dallo studio dell'avvocato</u>.

_____

59. Ho sentito parlare <u>di lei</u>.

_____

60. Pensiamo bene <u>di Anna</u>.

_____

61. Comprano <u>delle mele</u>?

_____

When the Subject Is Also the Object: Reflexive Pronouns

Reflexive pronouns convey that the subject is also the recipient of the action, as in **Mi lavo ogni mattina** (*I wash myself every morning*). You use these pronouns with reflexive verbs, which I cover in Chapter 17. Table 4-7 lists the pronouns.

Table 4-7	Reflexive Pronouns
Singular	*Plural*
mi (*myself*)	**ci** (*ourselves*)
ti (*yourself*)	**vi** (*yourselves,* informal)
si (*himself, herself, itself*)	**si** (*themselves*)
Si (*yourself,* third-person singular, formal)	**Si** (*yourselves,* third-person plural, formal)

When conjugating a reflexive verb, conjugate it exactly as you would a verb that's not reflexive, but place the reflexive pronoun in front of the conjugated verb:

Marco si sveglia ogni mattina alle 6:00 ma non si alza fino alle 6:30. Io mi sveglio alle 6:00 ma mi alzo subito. (*Marco wakes up every morning at 6:00 but he doesn't get out of bed until 6:30. I wake up every morning at 6:00 but I get up immediately.*)

Fill in the blanks in the following letter with the correct forms of the reflexive pronouns.

Q. **I ragazzi si annoiano d'estate?** (*Do the children get bored in the summer?*)

A. **No, non si annoiano mai.** (*No, they never get bored.*)

Cara Loredana,

ti scrivo per darti mie notizie. Io (62) _____ sento molto felice oggi perché Roberto mi ha

chiesto di sposarlo e noi (63) _____ sposiamo/sposeremo a giugno. Sai che noi (64) _____

divertiamo sempre insieme ed è un po' che usciamo. E tu (65) _____ senti di essere la mia

damigella? Volevo chiederti subito perché mia madre (66) _____ metterà) subito ad

organizzare tutto e mi è molto importante che tu ne faccia parte! Fammi sapere al più presto!

Un abbraccio,

Carla

Answer Key

1 – 8

📨 New Message

File   Edit   View   Insert   Format   Tools   Message   Help

✉️ Send   ✂️ Cut   📄 Copy   📋 Paste   ↩️ Undo   abc✔ Check

From:	Marco Baldini
To:	giulia@libero.it
Cc:	
Oggetto:	Saluti

Cara Giulia,

ti scrivo da Cortina. Purtroppo, scrivo (1) **io** perché Elena si è fatta male alla mano destra in un'ascensione e (2) **lei** non potrà scrivere per un po'. A parte questo incidente, (3) **noi** stiamo tutti bene. Il tempo è splendido e il panorama, come (4) **tu** sai bene, magnifico. Lo scorso fine settimana i miei suoceri sono venuti a trovarci. (5) **Loro** non sono dei grandi camminatori, ma sono rimasti con i bambini e con Elena, così (6) **io** sono andato a fare una bella scalata con i miei amici. Li conosci anche (7) **tu**, vero? Spero che l'estate prossima tutti (8) **noi** potremo stare insieme.

Un abbraccio,

Marco

Dear Giulia,

I'm writing from Cortina. Unfortunately, I'm writing because Elena hurt her right hand in a hike up a mountain and she won't be able to write for a bit. Except for this, we are all well. The weather is wonderful and the views, as you well know, are magnificent. Last weekend my inlaws came to visit us. They aren't big hikers but they stayed with the children and with Elena, so I was able to go on a beautiful hike with my friends. You know them, right? I hope next summer we will all be able to stay together.

Hugs,

Marco

9   Volete venire con **noi** a cena? (*Do you want to come to dinner with us?*)

10   Giovanni va con **loro** al mare. (*Giovanni goes with them to the seashore.*)

11   Gioco a carte con **voi**. (*I'll play cards with you.*)

12   Piero si fida totalmente di **lei**. (*Piero trusts her wholeheartedly.*)

13   Chiamo **te**! (*I'll call you!*)

14   Ho affidato tutti i miei affari a **lui**. (*I entrusted all my affairs to him.*)

15   Non **vi** capisco. (*I don't understand you.*)

16   **Lo** vedono spesso. (*They see him often.*)

17   Chiamate**ci** domani! (*Call us tomorrow!*)

18   Non **la** mangiano. (*They don't eat it.*)

19   **Lo/L'**ho comprato. (*I bought it.*)

20   **La/L'**ha suonata. (*He/she played it.*)

21   **La** voglio dire. or Voglio dir**la**. (*I want to tell it.*)

22   Luigi **li** mangiava quasi ogni giorno. (*Luigi ate it almost every day.*)

23   Desidero pagar**lo**. (*I want to pay for it.*)

24   Signore, **Le** volevo avvisare che la squadra femminile è al completo. (*Ladies, I wanted to inform you that the women's team is complete.*)

25   Signori, **Li** volevo avvisare che la squadra maschile è al completo. (*Gentlemen, I wanted to inform you that the men's team is complete.*)

26   Signora, **La** vorrei avvertire che la gonna che Lei ha ordinato è arrivata. (*Madam, I'd like to inform you that the skirt you ordered has arrived.*)

27   Signore, si è fatto male a una mano? **La/L'**aiuto io. (*Sir, did you hurt your hand? I'll help you.*)

28   **Vi** compriamo un gelato. (*We'll buy you an ice cream.*)

29   **Gli** raccontano una storia. (*They're telling him a story.*)

30   **Le** mando dei fiori. (*I'm sending her flowers.*)

31   **Ci** ha offerto il suo aiuto. (*He/She offered us his/her help.*)

32   I genitori **gli** hanno dato la macchina. (*His parents gave him a car.*)

33 Tu **mi** hai scritto una cartolina? (*Did you send me a postcard?*)

34 **Vi** hanno pagato il conto? (*Did they pay the bill for you?*)

35 **Gli** ho preparato la cena. (*I made dinner for them.*)

36 Io **gli** scrivo una lettera. (*I am writing him a letter.*)

37 Signora, posso pesar**li** per Lei? (*Can I weigh them for you?*)

38 **La** desidero ordinare. (*I'd like to order it.*)

39 Noi **le** parliamo sempre di voi. (*We always speak to her about you.*)

40 Mamma, **mi** compri una Ferrari? (*Mom, will you buy me a Ferrari?*)

41 Vogliamo visitar**lo** subito. (*We want to visit it right away.*)

42 **Ti** descrivo il mercato. (*I'll describe the market to you.*)

43 Voglio imparar**lo** bene. (*I want to learn it well.*)

44 **Gliele porti?** (*Are you going to take them to her?*)

45 **Dammelo!** (*Give it to me!*)

46 **Glielo restituisci?** (*Are you going to give it back to him?*)

47 **Glielo mandano?** (*Are they sending it to her?*)

48 **Te lo compro.** (*I'll buy it for you.*)

49 **Me la prepari?** (*Will you make it for me?*)

50 **L'hanno vista?** (*Did they see it?*)

51 **Ve l'hanno spedito?** (*Did they send it to you?*)

52 "Vanno/Andranno in Germania?" "Sì, ci vanno/andranno domani."

53 Ci sono troppi libri sul tavolo.

54 Ci vedono dalla strada.

55 "Vanno/Andranno a teatro domani?" "Sì, ci vanno/andranno."

56 Non ci pensa nemmeno.

57 **Ne sono appena tornati.** (*They just returned.*)

58 **Ne vengono adesso.** (*They're coming right now.*)

> 59 **Ne ho sentito parlare.** (*I heard about her.*)

> 60 **Ne pensiamo bene.** (*We think well of her.*)

> 61 **Ne comprano alcune.** (*He/She bought some of them.*)

> 62 – 66

Cara Loredana,   5 aprile 2009

ti scrivo per darti mie notizie. Io (62) **mi** sento molto felice oggi perché Roberto mi ha chiesto

di sposarlo e noi (63) **ci** sposiamo/sposeremo a giugno. Sai che noi (64) **ci** divertiamo sempre

insieme ed è un po' che usciamo. E tu (65) **ti** senti di essere la mia damigella? Volevo

chiederti subito perché mia madre (66) **si** metterà subito ad organizzare tutto e mi è molto

importante che tu ne faccia parte! Fammi sapere al più presto!

Un abbraccio,

Carla

Dear Loredana,   *April 5, 2009*

I'm writing with my news. I'm really happy today because Robert asked me to marry him

and we are going to get married in June. You know that we always have a great time

together and that we've been going out for a while. Would you like to be my bridesmaid? I

wanted to write right away because my mother is going to get started organizing

everything and it's really important for me that you be part of it. Let me know as soon as

you can.

Hugs,

Carla

Chapter 5

Adjectives, Adverbs, and Comparisons

If you say **Marina ha una casa grande** (*Marina has a big house*) or **Marina ha una casa piccola** (*Marina has a small house*), all you've changed is one word, but you've said two very different things. **Grande** (*big*) and **piccola** (*small*) are adjectives that convey qualities of people, animals, objects, and situations. In Italian, as in English, you employ adjectives with nouns, names, and pronouns.

Adverbs are another part of speech that helps you describe actions. In both Italian and English, adverbs are invariable, which means that you don't need to match them to the words they modify. You can add an adverb to qualify a verb, an adjective, a noun, a sentence, and even another adverb. For example, if you say **È molto presto** (*It's very early*), you're using two adverbs — **molto** and **presto** — together.

The final topics of this chapter are comparatives and superlatives because, in using adjectives and adverbs, you may want to establish comparisons and rankings between two or more things or people. Consider these examples: **Gianni è alto come Umberto** (*Gianni is as tall as Umberto*); **Pino è il più alto della classe** (*Pino is the tallest in his class*); and **È arrivata tardissimo!** (*She arrived very late!*).

In this chapter, I explain the various endings adjectives can have as well as the differences between masculine and feminine, singular and plural adjectives and how to match them to the words that they refer to. I also talk about where to place adjectives in the sentence. As for adverbs, I explain the difference between original and derived adverbs and how to form the latter. I also give you suggestions for their placement in sentences. I wrap up this chapter with coverage of comparatives and superlatives, helping you figure out how to use them to best express yourself.

Matching Adjectives to Nouns in Gender and Number

In Italian, you must match adjectives in gender and number to the nouns that they modify. You need a masculine singular adjective with a masculine singular noun, a feminine singular adjective with a feminine singular noun, and so forth. For example, **Maria + bello → Maria è bella** (*Maria is beautiful*).

A few adjectives are invariable; they only have one form. I list the most important ones in the later section, "Invariable adjectives."

When you match an adjective and a noun, remember that you may end up with two words with the same ending, as in **Il cavallo è piccolo** (*The horse is small*), or you may not, as in **Il cavallo è intelligente** (*The horse is smart*). If you check the possible endings of nouns listed in Chapter 2 and look at the possible endings of adjectives listed in this chapter, you can come up with several combinations. (This is a good exercise for you in order to practice your mastery of noun-adjective endings and combinations.)

In order to come up with the right match, you must consider the gender of the noun and then choose the gender of the adjective. For example, if you choose the noun **castello** (*castle*), which ends in **-o,** and the adjective **grande** (*huge*), which ends in **-e,** the right combination is **castello grande** (*huge castle*); if you choose the feminine noun **pena** (*sorrow*) and the adjective **grande** (*huge*), the right combination is **castello rinascimentale** (*renaissance castle*) because the adjective **grande** has one ending for both the masculine and feminine gender. If the noun is in the plural, you also have to choose the correct ending of the adjective in the plural, so **castelli** (*castles*) needs **grandi** (*huge*) to form **castelli grandi** (*huge castles*), just as **pene** needs **grandi** to form **grandi pene** (*great sorrows*) because, again, **grande** becomes **grandi** in the plural for both masculine and feminine nouns.

Adjectives fit into one of three categories, depending on how they change to match a noun's gender and number.

- ✔ **Regular adjectives** vary in their endings depending on gender (masculine or feminine) and number (singular or plural). Regular adjectives are clustered in three broad categories:

  - **Those with four endings** (masculine and feminine, singular and plural)

  - **Those with two endings** (singular and plural)

  - **Those with three endings,** one for the singular (masculine and feminine) and two for the plural

- ✔ **Irregular adjectives** change the spelling of several letters, not just the last one, especially when going from singular to plural (as seen for nouns; see Chapter 2).

- ✔ **Invariable adjectives** are few and far between, so you don't need to change their ending when you match them to the words they describe.

I've organized the following subsections according to the categories in the preceding list. When you finish this section, you should be able to take an adjective you've never seen before and place it in the proper group just by looking at its ending. When in doubt, as usual, consult a dictionary.

Regular adjectives

Regular adjectives are those that modify only the last letter to change either gender and number or only number. Table 5-1 shows the possible variations and some example adjectives.

Table 5-1	Variations of Regular Adjective Endings		
	Four endings: -o, -a, -i, -e	**Two endings:** -e, -i	**Three endings:** -a, -i, -e
Masculine singular (MS)	piccolo (*small, short*)	intelligente (*intelligent*)	egoista (*selfish*)
Feminine singular (FS)	piccola	intelligente	egoista
Masculine plural (MP)	piccoli	intelligenti	egoisti
Feminine plural (FP)	piccole	intelligenti	egoiste

When used after a noun, **bello** (*beautiful*) and **buono** (*good*) are regular adjectives with four possible endings. When they are used before before a noun, though, they don't take the same endings as all other adjectives ending in **-o**. Instead, they follow these rules:

✔ **bello** follows the rules of the definite article:

- Use **bel** before a singular masculine noun that starts with one or more consonants (exceptions follow): **bel treno** (*beautiful train*); use **bei** with the same kinds of nouns in the plural: **bei treni** (*beautiful trains*).

- Use **bello** before a singular masculine noun starting with **gn-**, **pn-**, **ps-**, **s** + consonant, **z-**, **x-**, or **y-**: **bello spazio** (*beautiful space*); **begli** with the plural: **begli spazi** (*beautiful spaces*).

- Use **bell'** before a singular masculine noun starting with a vowel: **bell'orologio** (*beautiful watch*); use **begli** in the plural: **begli orologi** (*beautiful watches*).

- Before a plural masculine noun that starts with a consonant, use **bei**: **bei gatti** (*beautiful cat*).

- Before a singular or plural feminine noun, use **bella** and **belle**: **bella artista** (*beautiful artist*), **belle artiste** (*beautiful artists*).

✔ **buon** follows the rules of

- The indefinite article when used with singular nouns: For example, before a singular masculine noun that starts with a vowel or consonant, use **buon**: **buon anno** (*good year*).

- The definite article when used with plural nouns: Used with plural nouns it works as a four ending adjective and so you would say: **buoni zii** (*good uncles*), **buone famiglie** (*good families*).

Irregular adjectives

When forming plurals, irregular adjectives modify more letters than just the last one, usually to preserve the soft or hard sound of the singular masculine, as in **bianco, bianca, bianchi, bianche** (*white*). But many times the variations from the norm are accidents of history, for which I can't give you any reason. Table 5-2 breaks down the ending changes for irregular adjectives, with examples.

Table 5-2	Variations of Irregular Adjective Endings	
Type of Adjective to Start	*What the Ending Changes to*	*Examples*
Two-syllable adjective ending in **-co**, **-go**, **-ca**, or **-ga**	**-chi**, **-che**, **-ghi**, **-ghe**	bian**co** (*white*) → bian**chi** bian**ca** → bian**che** lun**go** (*long*) → lun**ghi** lun**ga** → lun**ghe**
Multi-syllable adjective with the accent on the second to last syllable and ending in **-co** or **-ca**	**-ci**, **-che**	simpati**co** (*nice*) → simpati**ci** simpati**ca** → simpati**che**
Multi-syllable adjective ending in **-io** or **-ia**	**-i**, **-ie**	necessar**io** (necessary) → necessar**i** necessar**ia** → necessar**ie**
Two-syllable or multi-syllable adjective preceded by a vowel and ending in **-cio**, **-gio**, **-cia**, or **-gia**	**-ci**, **-gi**, **-cie/-ce**, **-gie/-ge**	sudi**cio** (*dirty*) → sudi**ci** sudi**cia** → sudi**cie** (or sudi**ce**) gri**gio** (*grey*) → gri**gi** gri**gia** → gri**gie** (or gri**ge**)
Two-syllable or multi-syllable adjective preceded by a consonant and ending in **-cio**, **-cia**, **-gio**, or **-gia**	**-i**, **-e**	lis**cio** (*smooth*) → lis**ci** lis**cia** → lis**ce** sa**ggio** (*wise*) → sa**ggi** sa**ggia** → sa**gge**

Invariable adjectives

A few adjectives are *invariable,* meaning that the ending remains the same regardless of how the noun changes gender or number. Key invariable adjectives include the following:

✔ Some adjectives for color: **blu** (*blue*), **beige** (*beige*), **lilla/lillà** (*lilac*), **rosa** (*pink*), **turchese** (*turquoise*), and **viola** (*violet, mauve*)

✔ The word **arrosto** (*roasted*)

✔ The mathematical qualifiers **pari** (*even*) and **dispari** (*odd*)

✔ Adjectives taken from other languages: **snob** (*snobbish*), **chic** (*chic*), **trendy** (*trendy*), and **bordeaux** (*burgundy*)

Write in the masculine singular of the following adjectives.

Q. gialli: _____

A. **giallo** (*yellow*)

1. mosce: _____

4. begli: _____

2. ricchi: _____

5. ipocrite: _____

3. allegre: _____

6. fertili: _____

Choose the adjective in the gender and number appropriate for the word that it describes. Both the ending and the meaning of the sentence should help you choose the right word from the options provided.

Q. Il film era lunga/interessanti/noioso.

A. Il film era **noioso.** (*The movie was boring.*)

7. La canzone è (bello/interessante/lunghe).

8. Paolo compra una macchina (nuova/rosso/grandi).

9. Giuliana è (intelligenti/noioso/brillante).

10. Loro sono (giovani/importante/bella).

11. Le mie sorelle sono (giovane/vecchi/stanche).

12. Le arance non sono (mature/buona/cattivi).

When You Need to Match One Adjective to More than One Noun

An adjective may refer to more than one person or thing, in three ways:

✔ With a plural noun (or name or pronoun), as in **Le suore sono silenziose** (*The nuns are quiet*)

✔ With two separate nouns, as in **Gli uccelli e i gatti sono nemici** (*Birds and cats are enemies*)

✔ With one adjective referring to two different things that are singular and share the same gender, as in **Il professore parla di letteratura e storia tedesca** (*The professor is talking about German literature and history*)

You need to decide the adjective's gender and number so that it matches the noun. Follow these guidelines:

✔ If you have one plural subject, the adjective will be in the plural and match the noun in gender. For example, **I miei fratelli sono piccoli** (*My brothers are short*); **Le mie sorelle sono piccole** (*My sisters are short*).

✔ If you have a masculine noun and a feminine noun, you choose the masculine plural adjective. For example, **Pietro e Luciana sono piccoli** (*Pietro and Luciana are short*).

✔ If you don't know the gender, use the masculine. For example, **Loro sono piccoli** (*They are little*).

✔ If you have one adjective referring to two singular nouns of the same gender, choose the singular form of the adjective in the gender that matches the nouns. For example, in the following sentence, **romana** (*Roman*) matches the gender of the nouns **pittura** (*painting*) and **scultura** (*sculpture*): **Bianca è un'esperta di pittura e scultura romana** (*Bianca is an expert of Roman painting and sculpture*).

Putting Adjectives in Their Place

In English, you place adjectives after verbs that indicate a status or a condition, such as *to be* or *to feel,* as you do in Italian; for example, **Gina è contenta** (*Gina is happy*). When you attach an adjective to a noun, though, in English you place it before the noun to which it refers, as in *a blue sky.* In Italian, you usually do the opposite, as in **Hanno scritto dei libri importanti** (*They've written important books*).

However, you place some commonly used adjectives before the noun. For example, you say **Hanno una bella casa** (*They have a beautiful house*), even though everyone will understand you if you say **Hanno una casa bella.** I give you a list of the most important adjectives that take this placement in the later section, "Recognizing the adjectives that come before nouns."

In a few cases, the adjective changes meaning depending on whether you place it before or after the noun. For example, if you say **È un grand'uomo** (*He's a great man*), you mean something very different from **È un uomo grande** (*He's a big man*). You can find more on these adjectives in the later section, "Using placement to change an adjective's meaning."

Recognizing the adjectives that come before nouns

Italian has some basic adjectives that you place before nouns. For example, you usually say **È una bella casa** (*It's a beautiful house*). But if you say **È una casa bella,** everyone understands you.

Here are the adjectives you usually place before the noun:

✔ **bello** (*beautiful*)

✔ **brutto** (*ugly*)

✔ **buono** (*good*)

✔ **cattivo** (*nasty, evil*)

✔ **breve** (*short*)

✔ **lungo** (*long*)

Using placement to change an adjective's meaning

Some adjectives change meaning depending on whether you place them before or after the nouns they qualify. For example, if you say **Ho rivisto un caro amico** (*I saw a* *dear friend again*), **caro** means *dear to your heart;* but if you say **È un negozio caro** (*It's an expensive store*), **caro** means *expensive.* Here's another example: **Solo** means *lonely* in **Un uomo solo è spesso triste** (*A lonely man is often sad*), and it means *only* in **Sono le sole pesche che abbiamo** (*These are the only peaches we have*). I list the most commonly used adjectives of this sort in Table 5-3.

Table 5-3	Common Adjectives That Change Meaning Depending on Placement	
Adjective	**Translation When Placed before the Noun**	**Translation When Placed after the Noun**
caro	*dear to one's heart*	*expensive*
grande	*great in spirit or deeds*	*big*
piccolo	*not important, minor*	*small*
povero	*pitiable*	*poor*
solo	*the only one*	*lonely*
vecchio	*of many years*	*old*
nuovo	*another*	*new*

Change the order of the words provided so that each set forms a complete sentence. The capitalized word should start the sentence.

Q. contenta, Daria, del, lavoro, sembra

A. **Daria sembra contenta del lavoro.** (*Daria seems to like her job.*)

13. brillante, Bruno, è, ragazzo, un

_____

14. La, le, porta, rosse, scarpe, zia

_____

15. gatto, Hai, il, nero, visto, ?

_____

16. arrosto, carne, Mangiano, solo

_____

17. alla, camicetta, lilla, mamma, Regalo, una

_____

Translate the following sentences. All the verbs are regular and in the present tense of the indicative.

0. Dad will see an old friend.

A. **Papà vede un vecchio amico.**

18. My sister always buys very expensive peaches.

_____

19. Nicola is an old friend.

_____

20. We have a very old car.

_____

21. They're very dear friends, but sometimes they're really boring.

_____

22. She's the only girlfriend who helps her.

_____

23. My wife helps those poor women a lot.

_____

Forming Adverbs the Italian Way

In Italian, adverbs add details and nuances by modifying verbs, adjectives, nouns, entire sentences, and other adverbs. Adverbs can radically change the meaning of what you're saying; for example, **Lia si comporta bene** (*Lia behaves well*) as opposed to **Lia si comporta male** (*Lia behaves badly*). Adverbs are invariable in the sense that they have neither gender nor number, so you don't have to worry about coordinating them to the words they modify.

In Italian, adverbs fall into two categories:

- ✔ **Original:** These adverbs aren't derived from other words, and they vary widely among one another.
- ✔ **Derived:** These adverbs are derived from adjectives.

Original adverbs

Original adverbs don't have a fixed form, so you're forced to simply learn them as you go. Here are some important adverbs to remember:

- ✔ **abbastanza** (*enough*)
- ✔ **adesso/ora** (*now*)
- ✔ **anche** (*also*)
- ✔ **ancora** (*still, yet*)
- ✔ **bene** (*well*)
- ✔ **davvero** (*really*)
- ✔ **domani** (*tomorrow*)
- ✔ **fa** (*ago*)

- ✔ **già** (*already*)
- ✔ **ieri** (*yesterday*)
- ✔ **mai/non . . . mai** (*ever, never*)
- ✔ **male** (*badly*)
- ✔ **no** (*no*)
- ✔ **non** (*not*)
- ✔ **oggi** (*today*)

- ✔ **presto** (*soon, early*)
- ✔ **purtroppo** (*unfortunately*)
- ✔ **sempre** (*always*)
- ✔ **sì** (*yes*)
- ✔ **spesso** (*often*)
- ✔ **subito** (*at once, right away*)
- ✔ **tardi** (*late*)

Some adjectives play the role of adverbs. To use them as adverbs, you always use the masculine singular form. For example, **Sandro e Marco corrono piano** (*Sandro and Marco run slowly*). These adverbs can only qualify verbs, adjectives, and other adverbs (or sentences) because, when you apply them to nouns, names, and pronouns, their "nature" as adjectives takes over and you need to coordinate them with the words they refer to. So you would say **Sandro e Marco sono corridori veloci** (*Marco and Sandro are fast runners*).

Key adjectives that you can use as adverbs include:

- ✔ **comodo** (*comfortable*)
- ✔ **chiaro** (*clear*)
- ✔ **duro** (*hard, tough*)
- ✔ **forte** (*strong*)
- ✔ **giusto** (*right*)
- ✔ **leggero** (*light*)

- ✔ **molto** (*very, much*)
- ✔ **parecchio** (*a lot*)
- ✔ **poco** (*too little*)
- ✔ **quanto** (*how, how much*)
- ✔ **sicuro** (*sure*)

- ✔ **solo** (*alone*)
- ✔ **tanto** (*so, so much*)
- ✔ **troppo** (*too*)
- ✔ **veloce** (*fast*)
- ✔ **vicino** (*near*)

Derived adverbs

You form most derived adverbs by taking the singular form of an adjective and adding **-mente** (the equivalent of *-ly* in English) to it. Here are the basic rules for forming these adverbs, followed by some examples:

- ✔ If the adjective ends in **-o,** you add **-mente** to the feminine singular form of the adjective. For example, **curioso** (*curious*) → **curiosamente** (*curiously*).

- ✔ If the adjective ends in **-e,** you add **-mente** to that adjective. For example, **dolce** (*sweet*) → **dolcemente** (*sweetly*).

- ✔ If the adjective ends in **-e** but the **-e** is preceded by **-l** or **-r,** you drop the **-e** before adding **-mente.** For example, **normale** (*normal*) → **normalmente** (*normally*); **celere** (*rapid*) → **celermente** (*rapidly*).

Form adverbs from the following adjectives, and then translate them into English.

Q. puntuale

A. **puntualmente** (*punctually*)

24. certo: _____

25. difficile: _____

26. generale: _____

27. gentile: _____

28. lento: _____

29. veloce: _____

Complete each sentence by selecting the correct adjective from the options provided and transforming it into an adverb.

esatto   bene   gentile   ~~facile~~   lento   generale

Q. Risolveremo quel problema _____.

A. Risolveremo quel problema **facilmente.** (*We'll solve that problem easily.*)

30. A due anni, suo figlio parla _____.

31. _____, non facciamo sconti.

32. Ha risposto _____ alle domande.

33. La macchina procedeva _____.

34. Roberto la tratta molto _____.

Finding a Place for Adverbs in a Sentence

In general, you place most adverbs close to the words they modify — that is, before the adjective and the noun and after the verb (in both its simple and compound forms). Here are a few examples (note that the adverbs are **spesso** and **molto**):

> **Roberto gioca spesso a golf.** (*Roberto plays golf often.*)
>
> **Mi è piaciuto molto il concerto.** (*I liked the concert a lot.*)

Exceptions to the general rule are the simple adverbs **appena** (*just*), **ancora** (*yet, still*), **già** (*already*), and **mai** (*ever*); and the compound adverbs **non . . . mai** (*ever, never*), **non . . . ancora** (*not yet*), and **non . . . più** (*no more, no longer*). The following guidelines explain where to place them:

> ✔ With a compound verb composed of an auxiliary and a past participle (see Chapter 10), you place the simple adverbs listed previously between the auxiliary and the past participle, as in **Il film è già finito** (*The film has ended already*).
>
> If you have a verbal form consisting of a modal auxiliary and a verb in the infinitive (see Chapter 8), you place the adverb between the two verbs, as in **Volete ancora venire?** (*Do you still want to come?*).
>
> ✔ With compound adverbs, **non** precedes the verb, and **mai/ancora/più** follows it. For example, **Non mangio più il sushi** (*I don't eat sushi anymore*).
>
> If the verb is in a compound form or is accompanied by a modal auxiliary, you place the second word of the adverb between the two verbs, as in **Non ho ancora mangiato il dolce** (*I haven't eaten dessert yet*).

Ancora means *yet* or *still*, but it also means *some more* or *again*. Regardless of meaning, its placement in the sentence remains the same. Here are a few examples:

È ancora presto per telefonargli. (*It's still too early to call him.*)

Vuoi ancora del gelato? (*Do you want some more ice cream?*)

The adverb **sempre,** however, can go either between components of a compound tense or verbal form, or after without any change in meaning. For example, **Ha sempre giocato con lei** and **Ha giocato sempre con lei** both mean *He's always played with her.*

You have more freedom in placing all other adverbs, depending on what you want to emphasize. You can say **Improvvisamente, se ne andarono** (*Suddenly, they left*) or **Se ne andarono improvvisamente** (*They left suddenly*). As usual, when it's a matter of emphasis and style, I can't give you precise rules. Notice where they're placed when reading, and try different options when writing.

Rewrite each sentence, placing the adverb provided in parentheses in its appropriate place. Some exercises may have two correct answers, in which case you should choose whichever one seems most appropriate. Then translate your answer into English.

Q. Non parlano di lui. (bene)

A. **Non parlano bene di lui.** (*They don't speak well of him.*)

35. Vieni. Devo dirti una cosa. (qui)

_____

36. Ho cercato, ma non ho trovato le chiavi. (dappertutto)

_____

37. Non sono arrivati, ma non tarderanno. (ancora)

_____

38. Vuole ballare con lui. (sempre)

_____

39. Hanno camminato, ma hanno perso l'autobus. (velocemente)

_____

40. Ho finito di mangiare. (appena)

_____

41. Non so dov'è andato. (onestamente)

_____

Making Comparisons

In both English and Italian, you can compare things in three ways. You can say something possesses a quality more than, less than, or as much as something else. The two objects you're comparing are called the first and the second term of comparison. You can convey them with names, nouns, pronouns, adjectives, adverbs, and verbs.

Here are the rules for establishing comparisons in Italian:

✔ To say that one object has a quality _more than_ or _less than_ another object, use **più** to convey _more_, **meno** to convey _less_ or _fewer_ (before a countable plural noun), and **di** (or a contracted form of **di**) or **che** to convey _than_. You use **di** only when the second term is a name, a pronoun without a preposition, or an adverb.

> **Bianca è più intelligente di Silvia.** (_Bianca is more intelligent than Silvia._)

> **Sembri meno nervoso di ieri.** (_You seem less nervous than yesterday._)

✔ When the second term is a name or a noun preceded by a preposition; or when you compare two adjectives, two adverbs, or two verbs, you can only use **che** before the second term.

> **Compriamo meno pere che mele.** (_We'll buy fewer pears than apples._)

> **Gli piace sciare più che nuotare.** (_He likes skiing more than swimming._)

With some exceptions that I mention in the later section, "Migliore and peggiore, meglio and peggio: Better and worse," unlike English, Italian doesn't add endings to adjectives or adverbs to convey that one individual possesses a quality to a different degree than someone else. For example, **vecchio** (_old_) remains the same, and you add the words **più** or **meno** before it. In English, you add _-er_ to one- and two-syllable adjectives to assert a difference of degree; for example, _old_ becomes _older_ and _cold_ becomes _colder_.

When you want to say that the degree of a quality (or the amount of an object) keeps on increasing or decreasing, as in _more and more tired, taller and taller,_ and _less and less ready,_ in Italian you use **sempre più** and **sempre meno** (which are invariable) + an adjective, an adverb, or a noun. For example, **Fa sempre più freddo** (_It's colder and colder_); **Abbiamo sempre meno vacanze** (_We have fewer and fewer vacation days_).

To say that one object possesses a quality as much as another object you use the expressions **tanto . . . quanto** or **così . . . come** to convey _as . . . as, as much . . . as,_ or _as many . . . as._ For example, **Bianca è tanto intelligente quanto Silvia** (_Bianca is as intelligent as Silvia_).

When you use an adjective to compare two individuals, you can omit the words **tanto** or **così**, as in **Luciano è alto quanto Carlo** (*Luciano is as tall as Carlo*). You keep **tanto** and **così** when you compare two nouns, as in **Compriamo tante pere quante mele** (*We'll buy as many pears as apples*); two adjectives, as in **Luisa è tanto bella quanto brava** (*Luisa is as beautiful as she's good*); or two verbs, as in **A Gianni piace tanto nuotare quanto sciare** (*Gianni likes swimming as much as skiing*).

You're buying Christmas presents for your children, nieces, and nephews. Using the clues given in parentheses, fill in the missing comparatives in the following dialogue. (***Note:*** Combine the preposition **di** with one of the following articles: **del, dei, delle,** and so on.)

Q. Voglio comprare _____ (*more*) saggi _____ romanzi.

A. Vorrei comprare **più** saggi **che** romanzi. (*I'd like to buy more essays than novels.*)

Cliente: Vorrei fare dei regali educativi **(42)** _____ (*more*) alla moda. A mia figlia piacciono le bambole piccole **(43)** _____ (*less*) bambole grosse, ma le piacciono i videogiochi **(44)** _____ (*more*) bambole.

Commessa: Questo trenino va bene per i bambini che hanno **(45)** _____ (*less*) dieci anni. I bambini **(46)** _____ (*more*) grandi in genere lo trovano noioso.

Cliente: Mio nipote è un bambino **(47)** _____ intelligente **(48)** _____ curioso (*as . . . as*). Ho bisogno di un regalo **(49)** _____ (*more*) interessante **(50)** _____ caro. La mia nipotina è **(51)** _____ (*more*) giovane **(52)** _____ mia figlia. Penso che le piacerebbe un pupazzo di peluche.

Commessa: Questa scimmietta è **(53)** _____ (*less*) bella **(54)** _____ questa tigre, ma ai bambini piace molto.

Designating the best and the worst: The superlatives

Just as in English, in Italian you can rank objects to establish which one is the highest or the lowest in a series or group. And you can declare that one object is excellent at something even if you don't compare it with anything else.

To rank objects as the highest or lowest when the second term is a noun or pronoun, you use **il più/il meno . . . di/in** (*the most/least . . . of/in*). You match the adjective with the noun that it refers to.

> **Luciano è il più alto dei figli.** (*Luciano is the tallest of the children.*)

> **Marta è la meno agile nella squadra.** (*Marta is the least agile on the team.*)

The absolute superlative expresses the greatest degree of an adjective or an adverb, as in **I ragazzi sono lentissimi** (*The boys are so very slow*). In English, you convey it by adding *very, much, by far, incredibly, amazingly,* and so on to an adjective or an adverb.

To express the absolute superlative in Italian, you modify adjectives by dropping the final vowel and adding **-issimo, -issima, -issimi,** or **-issime;** for example, **gentile → gentilissimo** (*very kind*) and **alto → altissimo** (*very tall*). When the adjective or adverb ends in **-i,** it only adds **-ssimo.** For example, **tardi** → **tardissimo** (*very late*). As usual, you coordinate the adjective to the noun in gender and number.

> **Quei vestiti sono carissimi.** (*Those dresses are very expensive.*)

> **Torno a casa prestissimo.** (*I'll be coming home very early.*)

When you want to convey a superlative less emphatically, in Italian you can add **molto** or **assai** (*very*). Despite the fact that **molto** and **assai** mean *very,* the phrase **molto grande** means *large, big,* or *rather big* instead of *very large,* which translates to **grandissimo.**

For some emphasis, you also have the option of repeating a short adjective or adverb, like **grande grande** or **presto presto** (with no comma between them). For example, **Le diede un abbraccio forte forte** (*She gave her a really strong hug*). You typically don't do this with long words because it doesn't sound good.

Migliore and peggiore, meglio and peggio: Better and worse

In Italian you have two ways of saying that someone has *more* or *less* of the qualities expressed by the adjectives **buono** (*good*), **cattivo** (*bad*), **grande** (*great*), and **piccolo** (*small, little*). You can add **più** (*more*) or **meno** (*less*) to the adjective; or use special words as listed in Table 5-4.

With the adverbs **bene** (*well*), **male** (*badly*), **molto** (*much*), and **poco** (*too little*), you only have special forms to express the comparatives and superlatives of these qualities. I list them in Table 5-5.

In all other respects, you use these special forms as you use the other comparatives.

> **Umberto è il più grande dei fratelli.** or **Umberto è il fratello maggiore.** (*Umberto is the oldest of the siblings.*)

> **Penso che il parmigiano sia migliore della fontina.** or **Penso che il parmigiano sia più buono della fontina.** (*I think that parmesan is better than fontina.*)

Table 5-4 Comparatives and Superlatives of Adjectives with Special Forms

Adjective	Comparatives	Relative Superlatives	Absolute Superlative
buono (*good*)	**più buono, migliore** (*better*)	**il più buono, il migliore** (*the best*)	**buonissimo/ottimo** (*very good*)
cattivo (*bad*)	**più cattivo, peggiore** (*worse*)	**il più cattivo, il peggiore** (*the worst*)	**cattivissimo/pessimo** (*very bad*)
grande (*great, big*)	**più grande, maggiore** (*greater, bigger, major*)	**il più grande, il maggiore** (*the greatest, the biggest, the maximum*)	**grandissimo/massimo** (*very big, maximum*)
piccolo (*small*)	**più piccolo, minore** (*smaller, lesser*)	**il più piccolo, il minore** (*the smallest, the least*)	**piccolissimo/minimo** (*very small*)

Table 5-5 Comparatives and Superlatives of Adverbs with Special Forms

Adverb	Comparative	Absolute Superlative
bene (*well*)	**meglio** (*better*)	**benissimo** (*very well*)
male (*badly*)	**peggio** (*worse*)	**malissimo** (*very badly*)
molto (*very, much*)	**più** (*more*)	**moltissimo** (*mostly*)
poco (*too little*)	**meno** (*less*)	**pochissimo** (*very little*)

You're about to audition for your college's winter play (in Italian!). While learning your part, you drop your *caffe latte* on your script, blotting out some words. Now, you need to fill in the holes by choosing the appropriate words to rank qualities and use absolute superlatives. Use the hints in parentheses to fill in the blanks.

Q. Mi piacciono _____ queste bambole! (*very much*)

A. Mi piacciono **moltissimo** queste bambole! (*I like these dolls a lot!*)

Commessa: Che regali deve fare, Signora?

Cliente: Devo fare dei regali a dei bambini. (55) _____
(*young*) ha cinque anni, (56) _____(*old*) ne ha tredici.
Vorrei dei regali (57) _____(*very small*), perché li devo
portare in aereo. Mi piace (58) _____(*very much*) quel
tren, per esempio, ma è troppo grande. Quella tenda, invece, va
(59) _____(*very well*), perché si può piegarlo.

Commessa: Vorrebbe spendere (60) _____(*more*) o
(61) _____(*less*) di cento euro?

Cliente: Cento euro in tutto. Il regalo (62) _____(*least
expensive*) di tutti dovrebbe costare dieci euro, e il regalo
(63) _____(*most expensive*), trenta euro. Vedo una
(64) _____(*very beautiful*) bambola su quello scaffale.

Commessa: È (65) _____(*very beautiful*), ma anche
(66) _____(*very expensive*): costa duecento euro. È
(67) _____(*the most expensive*) di tutte quelle che abbiamo
in negozio.

Cliente: Preferisco non fare regali troppo costosi. Penso che i regali
(68) _____(*the best*) siano quelli che costano
(69) _____(*less*) di tutti.

Answer Key

1 mosce: **moscio** (*floppy*)

2 ricchi: **ricco** (*rich*)

3 allegre: **allegro** (*cheerful*)

4 begli: **bello** (*beautiful*)

5 ipocrite: **ipocrita** (*hypocritical*)

6 fertili: **fertile** (*fertile*)

7 La canzone è **interessante.** (*The song is interesting.*)

8 Paolo compra una macchina **nuova.** (*Paolo is buying a new car.*)

9 Giuliana è **brillante.** (*Giuliana is brilliant.*)

10 Loro sono **giovani.** (*They are young.*)

11 Le mie sorelle sono **stanche.** (*My sisters are tired.*)

12 Le arance non sono **mature.** (*The oranges aren't ripe.*)

13 **Bruno è un ragazzo brillante.** (*Bruno is a bright boy.*)

14 **La zia porta le scarpe rosse.** (*Our aunt wears red shoes.*)

15 **Hai visto il gatto nero?** (*Have you seen the black cat?*)

16 **Mangiano solo carne arrosto.** (*They only eat roasted meat.*)

17 **Regalo alla mamma una camicetta lilla.** (*I'm giving Mom a mauve shirt.*)

18 **Mia sorella compra sempre delle pesche care.**

19 **Nicola è un vecchio amico.**

20 **Abbiamo una macchina molto vecchia.**

21 **Sono dei cari amici, ma a volte sono proprio noiosi.**

22 **È la sola amica che la aiuta.**

23 **Mia moglie aiuta molto quelle donne povere.**

24 certo: **certamente** (*certainly*)

25 difficile: **difficilmente** (*hardly, hard*)

26 generale: **generalmente** (*generally*)

27 gentile: **gentilmente** (*kindly*)

28 lento: **lentamente** (*slowly*)

29 veloce: **velocemente** (*rapidly, fast*)

30 A due anni, suo figlio parla **bene.** (*At 2 years of age, his/her son speaks well.*)

31 **Generalmente**, non facciamo sconti. (*Generally we don't give discounts.*)

32 Ha risposto **esattamente** alle domande. (*He/She answered all the questions correctly.*)

33 La macchina procedeva **lentamente.** (*The car moved ahead slowly.*)

34 Roberto la tratta molto **gentilmente.** (*Roberto treats her very kindly.*)

35 **Vieni qui. Devo dirti una cosa.** (*Come here. I have to tell you something.*)

36 **Ho cercato dappertutto, ma non ho trovato le chiavi.** (*I looked everywhere, but I didn't find my keys.*)

37 **Non sono ancora arrivati, ma non tarderanno.** (*They haven't arrived yet, but they will soon.*)

38 **Vuole ballare sempre con lui.** or **Vuole sempre ballare con lui.** (*She always wants to dance with him.*)

39 **Hanno camminato velocemente, ma hanno perso l'autobus.** (*They walked fast, but they missed the bus.*)

40 **Ho appena finito di mangiare.** (*I've just finished eating.*)

41 **Onestamente, non so dov'è andato.** or **Non so dov'è andato, onestamente.** (*Honestly, I don't know where he went.*)

42–54 Cliente: Vorrei fare dei regali educativi (42) **più che** alla moda. A mia figlia piacciono le bambole piccole (43) **meno delle** bambole grosse, ma le piacciono i videogiochi (44) **più delle** bambole. (*I'd like to give educational gifts, more than fashionable ones. My daughter likes small dolls more than big dolls, but she likes video games more than dolls.*)

Commessa: Questo trenino va bene per i bambini che hanno (45) **meno di** dieci anni. I bambini (46) **più** grandi in genere lo trovano noioso. (*This small train is suitable for children who are younger than 10. Older children usually find it boring.*)

Cliente: Mio nipote è un bambino (47) **tanto** intelligente (48) **quanto** curioso. Ho bisogno di un regalo (49) **più** interessante (50) **che** caro. La mia nipotina è (51) **più** giovane (52) **di** mia figlia. Penso che le piacerebbe un pupazzo di peluche. (*My nephew is a child who's as intelligent as curious. I need a present that's more interesting than expensive. My little niece is younger than my daughter. I think she would like a stuffed puppet.*)

Commessa: Questa scimmietta è (53) **meno** bella (54) **di** questa tigre, ma ai bambini piace molto. (*This little monkey is less nice than this tiger, but children like it a lot.*)

`55` `69`

Commessa: Che regali deve fare, Signora?

Cliente: Devo fare dei regali a dei bambini. (*I have to give presents to some children.*) (55) **Il più giovane** ha cinque anni; (56) **il più vecchio** ne ha tredici. (*The youngest is 5 years old; the oldest is 13.*) Vorrei dei regali (57) **molto piccoli**, perché li devo portare in aereo. (*I like very small gifts, because I have to carry them on the plane.*) Mi piace (58) **moltissimo** quel treno, ma è troppo grande. (*I like that small train very much, but it's too big.*) Quella tenda, invece, va (59) **benissimo**, perché si può piegarlo. (*This tent, instead, works very well, because I can fold it.*)

Commessa: Vorrebbe spendere (60) **più o** (61) **meno** di cento euro? (*Do you want to spend more or less than one hundred euros?*)

Cliente: Cento euro in tutto. (*One hundred euros total.*) Il regalo (62) **meno caro** di tutti dovrebbe costare dieci euro, e il regalo (63) **più caro**, trenta euro. (*The least expensive gift should cost ten euros, and the most expensive, thirty euros.*) Vedo una (64) **bellissimia** bambola su quello scaffale. (*I see a very beautiful doll on that shelf.*)

Commessa: È (65) **bellissima** ma anche (66) **carissima**: costa duecento euro. (*It's very beautiful, but also very expensive: it costs two hundred euros.*) È (67) **la più cara** di tutte quelle che abbiamo in negozio. (*It's the most expensive one among all the ones we have in the store.*)

Cliente: Preferisco non fare regali troppo costosi. (*I prefer not to give gifts that are too expensive.*) Penso che i regali (68) **migliori** siano quelli che costano (69) **meno** di tutti. (*I think that the best presents are those that are also the cheapest.*)

Chapter 6

Prepositions: The Big Challenge

● ●

In This Chapter

▶ Sorting out articles combined with prepositions

▶ Forming complements with prepositions and nouns, names, or pronouns

▶ Locking in set phrases and idiomatic expressions

▶ Pairing verbs and prepositions

● ●

Prepositions are invariable words you need to link other words in a sentence when adding a name, pronoun, or noun by itself isn't enough. For example, *I'm going school* is not a complete sentence. You need to say, *I'm going to school.* Choosing one preposition over another leads you to say different things, such as *I'm speaking to you* or *I'm speaking about you.* One preposition can play different functions. In the sentence *I'm at home,* the word *at* conveys place. In the sentence *He's at ease,* it conveys someone's feelings. On the other hand, different prepositions can convey similar meanings, as with *in the evening* or *at night.*

Prepositions are difficult to learn in any language because their use is idiomatic in many cases. The basic rule, therefore, is practice, practice, and more practice.

In this chapter, I give you some guidelines. I show you the main Italian prepositions (called **preposizioni semplici,** or *simple prepositions*). In Italian, you also encounter other words used as prepositions — adverbs and adjectives in particular. Here, I mention only the few that are indispensable. I also show you how to choose the preposition that corresponds to the one you'd use in English in the same situation, because literal translation won't do. For example, the preposition **di** usually translates to *of,* but in the expression *to think of someone,* you use **a,** which usually means *at* or *to:* **pensare a qualcuno.**

Prepositions can also introduce infinitives. **A** and **di** are the most common in Italian, as *to* is in English. Often, the verb you're using "carries" a specific preposition, which you have no choice but to use. I provide you with a list of commonly used verbs and the prepositions that follow them.

Combining Prepositions with Articles

Italian has eight basic prepositions, corresponding to the basic prepositions used in English. I list them here, starting with the most-frequently used. You find the translation that reflects their meanings in the two languages, but remember that you can't assume that you'll use the same preposition in Italian and English every time.

- ✔ **di** (*of, about*)
- ✔ **a** (*at, to*)
- ✔ **da** (*from, by*)

- ✔ **in** (*in, into*)
- ✔ **con** (*with*)
- ✔ **su** (*on, onto*)

- ✔ **per** (*for, through*)
- ✔ **fra/tra** (*between, among*)

With prepositions, the word order is strict: A preposition precedes and is never separated from the word with which it forms a unit of meaning: **a me** (*to me*); **con coraggio** (*with courage*). *The girl whom I was thinking of* can be translated only as **La ragazza a cui pensavo** (*The girl of whom I was thinking*).

When you have a definite article between a preposition and a noun, you fuse six of the eight prepositions with the articles to form one word. Table 6-1 lists the simple prepositions in their combined forms.

Table 6-1		Prepositions Combined with Articles				
Definite Article	*di*	*a*	*da*	*in*	*con*	*su*
il	del	al	dal	nel	con il	sul
lo, l'	dello, dell'	allo, all'	dallo, dall'	nello, nell'	coll' (or con lo)	sullo, sull'
la, l'	della, dell'	alla, all'	dalla, dall'	nella, nell'	coll' (or con la)	sulla, sull'
i	dei	ai	dai	nei	con i	sui
gli	degli	agli	dagli	negli	con gli	sugli
le	delle	alle	dalle	nelle	con le	sulle

Forming Complements (Preposition + Noun, Name, or Pronoun)

You can form short phrases by putting together a preposition and a noun, a name, or a pronoun. These combinations are called **complementi** (*complements*) because they complete the meaning of a sentence. In Italian, there's a vast array of complements, as you see if you check an Italian grammar book. Here I talk about which prepositions you need in a given context: place, for example. If you want to say, *I'm going from Florence to Palermo,* you need two prepositions that have to do with place. As you gain knowledge of prepositions, you'll realize that you can use the same preposition in different contexts, as happens in English with *in,* for example, which works with both *place* and *time* (as happens in Italian, too). Following are the main contexts and the prepositions you use to talk about each of them.

Possession and specification

If you say that something belongs to someone, or if you convey information about someone or something, you use **di,** as in the following examples: **il succo di mele** (*apple juice*); **le foto del matrimonio** (*the photos of the wedding*); **la paura della fame** (*the fear of hunger*).

In English, you attribute characteristics to people or other things by inverting the word order or placing *of* between an object and another noun representing a feature that object possesses (*the brilliance of diamonds*). You also may add an apostrophe and *s* to a noun or a name or use a possessive adjective, such as *his* or *her.* Here's how Italian works:

✔ Use **di** (*of, about*) to link a feature to a person or thing that has that feature, as in **il piano del tavolo** (*the table top*).

✔ To convey ownership, use possessive adjectives and pronouns, or **di** followed by the thing owned, as in **il gatto di Marta** (*Marta's cat*) or **il suo gatto [di Marta]** (*her cat*).

Qualities and functions

You can talk about features of things by emphasizing a characteristic that makes them what they are, as in **la scollatura a V** (*a V-neck*), or by indicating their function, as in **le carte da gioco** (*playing cards*). In English, you invert the word order or you add an adjective to a noun. So when you have those two constructions in English, you have to decide whether to use **di** (*of*), **a** (*at, in*) or **da** (*by, from*) in Italian.

You can test which preposition works by performing the following experiment. If you say *the table top,* can you change that phrase to *the top of the table?* The answer is yes. In Italian you use **di,** writing **il piano del tavolo.** But if you say *a motor boat,* can you turn it into *the boat of a motor?* Unlikely. You're talking about *a boat with a motor.* In Italian, it's **la barca a motore.** And if you say, *a pleated skirt,* can you turn it into *the skirt's pleated?* Obviously not. It's *a skirt with pleats.* In Italian, it becomes **la gonna a pieghe.** And what about *a golf ball?* Are you talking about *a ball's golf, a golf's ball,* or *a ball you use to play golf?* Clearly the latter. When you describe what something is used for, you choose **da** in Italian: **la pallina da golf.** Here are the general rules:

✔ To indicate a feature of an object, you use noun + **a** + another noun: **la barca che va a vela** is **la barca a vela** (*sailing boat*)

✔ To indicate a feature that explains the function of an object, you use noun + **da** + noun: **la pallina che serve a giocare a da tennis** is **la pallina da tennis** (*tennis ball*)

You also use **da** + number to convey value, as in **Vuoi un anello da 10.000 euro?!** (*You want a ring that costs 10,000 euro?!*), but you use **di** for numbers to count things: **Legge un libro di cinquecento pagine** (*She's reading a 500-page book*).

Insert **di** (*of*), **a** (*characterized by*), **da** (*with the function of*), or no preposition at all between the following sets of nouns.

Q. la camicia _____ notte

A. la camicia **da** notte (*nightgown*)

1. gli occhiali _____ sole

2. i pantaloni _____ righe

3. il giornale _____ ieri

4. la tazzina _____ caffè

5. il discorso _____ Giovanna

6. un saggio _____ trenta pagine

7. il forno _____ microonde

8. l'asilo _____ nido

Place

Place is a label I use to refer to activities ranging from staying still to going through, both physically and metaphorically. English uses only *to* (and *into* or *onto*) to convey motion toward something, whereas Italian uses **in** (*in*), **a** (*at, to*), **da** (*by*, as in *by the window*), and **su** (*on*). Italian chooses the preposition on the basis of various features of place.

In, into, on, over, above, and behind

You use the following prepositions regarding place, depending on what you're discussing:

- ✔ For a point in space, use **a**: **a Genova** (*in/to Genoa*); **all'angolo** (*at/to the corner*); **al Colosseo** (*at/to the Coliseum*); **al primo piano** (*on the first floor*)

- ✔ To indicate geographical position and distance, use **a**: **Siamo a nord-ovest di Trieste** (*We are northwest of Trieste*); **Siamo a 50 chilometri da Siena** (*We're 50 kilometers away from Siena*)

- ✔ For areas with boundaries, use **in** (*in*): **in Italia** (*in/to Italy*); **negli Stati Uniti** (*in/to the United States*)

- ✔ When you say you're *in* or are getting *on* a means of transportation, use **in** (*in, into*) + noun (with or without the article) or **su** (*on, onto*): **in macchina** (*in/inside/into the car*); **nel treno** (*in/into the train*); **sull'aereo** (*on/onto the plane*); **sul treno** (*on/onto the train*)

- ✔ For volumes, use **in** (*in, into*) + noun followed by the article or not: **nel cielo** (*in the sky*); **in aria** (*in the air*)

- ✔ For small islands, use **a/su** (*in, to, on*): **a Capri** (*in/to Capri, on the Isle of Capri*); **a Long Island** (*on/to Long Island*); **sull'Elba** (*on Elba Island*)

- ✔ For large islands, use **in** (*in, to*): **in Sicilia** (*in/to Sicily*); **in Gran Bretagna** (*in/to Great Britain*)

- ✔ For physical place, use **in** + article: **nell'ufficio del dottore** (*in/into the doctor's office*); **nella mia cartella** (*in/into my briefcase*)

- ✔ For expressing *above/over* and *under*, use **sopra** and **sotto** + article: **su/sopra il tavolo** (*on/over the table*); **sotto il tavolo** (*under the table*); **sottoterra** (*underground*)

Whether there's physical contact or not isn't important when choosing between **su** and **sopra**, as in **L'aereo vola sulla/sopra la città** (*The plane is flying over the city*).

✔ For expressing *in front of* and *behind,* use **davanti a** and **dietro a/di: Siamo davanti a San Pietro** (*We're standing in front of St. Peter's*); **La macchina è dietro di te** (*The car is behind you*)

From, through, across, and among

To convey origin, motion through, and separation, you use the following prepositions, depending on what you're discussing:

✔ For conveying someone's origin and being born into a certain family, use **essere + di** (*to be from*): **Sono di Venezia** (*They're from Venice*); **Maria è di buona famiglia** (*Maria comes from a well-to-do family*).

✔ For motion from, origin, distance, and movement out of containers/elements, use **da** (*from, out of*): **La neve cade dal cielo** (*The snow falls from the sky*); **Ha tolto il cellulare dalla borsa** (*She took the mobile phone out of her bag*).

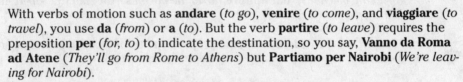

With verbs of motion such as **andare** (*to go*), **venire** (*to come*), and **viaggiare** (*to travel*), you use **da** (*from*) or **a** (*to*). But the verb **partire** (*to leave*) requires the preposition **per** (*for, to*) to indicate the destination, so you say, **Vanno da Roma ad Atene** (*They'll go from Rome to Athens*) but **Partiamo per Nairobi** (*We're leaving for Nairobi*).

✔ For expressing *through,* use **da** and **per: Passate da/per Oslo?** (*Are you going/driving/flying through Oslo?*); **Non passate per il bosco!** (*Don't go through the woods!*).

✔ For expressing *across,* use **dall'altra parte di: Il tabaccaio è dall'altra parte della strada** (*The tobacconist is across the street*).

✔ For expressing *between/among,* use **fra/tra: Tra le case c'è una staccionata** (*There is a fence between the houses*). Italian doesn't distinguish whether you're choosing *between* two things or *among* several things.

Add the appropriate prepositions to the following notes.

0. Parto _____ Amsterdam (destination) _____ Milano (origin).

A. Parto **per** Amsterdam **da** Milano. (*I'll leave for Amsterdam from Milan.*)

9. Roma è a ottocento chilometri _____ Torino.

10. _____ la Francia e l'Olanda c'è il Belgio.

11. Strasburgo è _____ Francia.

12. Per andare _____ Madrid (origin) _____ Berlino (destination) passiamo _____ Monaco.

13. _____ Capri c'è la villa di Tiberio.

14. L'università di Oxford è _____ Inghilterra.

15. Il treno _____ Parigi (origin) _____ Londra passa (destination) _____ la Manica.

Place and function

If you say *I'm going to the doctor's,* you can convey two ideas at once: a physical movement (going to your doctor's office) and the service provided there (you're seeing a doctor because you aren't feeling well). In Italian, you can use the following prepositions to express place and function at the same time:

- ✔ **in** + (no article) noun (neither names nor pronouns): **in chiesa** (*at/to church*); **in ospedale** (*at/to the hospital*); **in casa** (*home, at home*); **in giardino** (*in/to/into the garden*); **in latteria** (*at/to the milk store*); **in ufficio** (*at work*)

- ✔ **a** + noun: **a casa** (*at/to home*), **a teatro** (*at/to the theater*), **a scuola** (*at/to school*)

- ✔ **a** + definite article + noun (neither names nor pronouns): **all'asilo** (*at/to kindergarten*); **al negozio di . . .** (*to the . . . store*); **all'ospedale** (*in/to the hospital*); **al cinema** (*at/to the movie theater*)

- ✔ **da** + noun, name, or pronoun of a person's profession or role: **dal macellaio** (*at/to the butcher's*); **dal dottore** (*at/to the doctor's*); **da zia Lilla** (*at/to Aunt Lilla's*); **da noi** (*at/to our place*)

From the phrases provided, select the proper conclusion to each sentence and write it in the blank.

Devo portarlo in tintoria   al bar   ~~in libreria~~   da lei

in palestra   Siamo alla Polizia   dal gioielliere

0. Vado a comprare dei libri, _____.

A. Vado a comprare dei libri **in libreria**. (*I'm going to the bookstore to buy books.*)

16. Ci hanno rubato la macchina. _____.

17. Dai, passiamo a prendere un caffè _____.

18. Fa i pesi due ore ogni giorno _____.

19. Hai visto quella collana di perle _____?

20. Luigi detesta Marisa. Non verrà a cena _____.

21. Mi sono macchiata il vestito. _____.

Time

With prepositions, time behaves somewhat like space: Things can happen at a specific moment, as in **a Natale** (*at Christmas*), or during a period of time, as in **nel 1975** (*in 1975*). Or they can take a chunk of time, as in **per tre mesi** (*for three months*).

Often you can express time without prepositions, as you can do in English: for example, when something happens on a day of the week, as in **Lo vedo domenica** (*I'll see* *him this Sunday*); when you talk about duration, as in **Stanno in Svezia tre mesi** (*They'll stay/be in Sweden for three months*); and with words that express time, such as **oggi** (*today*), **domani** (*tomorrow*), and **l'anno prossimo** (*next year*). In particular, Italian doesn't use prepositions with dates (see Chapter 3), as in **È nato il 15 agosto 1960** (*He was born [on] August 15, 1960*).

When you need prepositions to talk about a specific point in time, follow these guidelines:

✔ For days of the week, use **di** (*on*), as in **di domenica** (*on Sundays*); for moments of the day, use **di** (*in*), as in **di mattina** (*mornings*); and for seasons, use **in** or **di** (*in*), as in **d'estate** or **in estate** (*in summer*).

✔ If you do something every week on a certain day of the week, in Italian you can use the name of that day with the article, without a preposition, as in **Giochiamo a tennis il sabato** (*We play tennis every Saturday*), or with **di** plus the day of the week, as in **Giochiamo a tennis di sabato** (*We play tennis on Saturdays*). If you're talking about doing something on a certain day in the coming week, you use the name of the day alone, as you do in English: **Giochi a tennis sabato?** (*Will you play tennis Saturday?*).

✔ For holidays or named days and months, use **a** (*at, in*), as in **a Pasqua** (*at Easter*); **a Ferragosto** (*at Ferragosto [on August 15]*); **ad aprile** (*in April*).

✔ For telling the time, use **a** + article, as in **alle 9 di mattina** (*at 9 a.m.*); **alle [ore] 21:40** (*at 9:40 p.m.*); **a mezzogiorno** (*at 12 noon/midday*). (See Chapter 3.)

✔ For expressing that something will happen by a certain time, use **tra/fra** (*in*), as in **tra dieci giorni** (*in ten days*); **tra due settimane** (*in two weeks*). Or use **per** (*by*), as in **per la settimana prossima** (*by next week*).

✔ For expressing origin in time and continuing action, use **da** (*since/from*), as in **da gennaio** (*since/from January*); **dalle sette di mattina** (*since/from 7 in the morning*); **da ieri** (*since/from yesterday*); **dal 15 luglio** (*since/from July 15*).

✔ For expressing the end of a period of time in the future, use **entro** (*by*), as in **entro lunedì** (*by Monday*); **entro la fine dell'anno** (*by the end of the year*).

✔ For expressing the onset of something, use **con/su** (*with/by/at*), as in **con l'arrivo della primavera** (*with the arrival of spring/by spring time*); **sul far del mattino** (*towards/at dawn*).

And when something lasts over a period of time, you use the following prepositions:

✔ For unspecified moments during the day, parts of the day, months, seasons, and years, use **in** or **in** + article (*at, in*) or **durante** (*in, during*): **in mattinata** (*in the morning*); **nel pomeriggio** (*in the afternoon*); **in aprile** (*in April*); **in estate/ nell'estate** (*during the summer/in summer*); **nel 2005** (*in 2005*).

✔ For a specified amount of time and continuing action, use **da** (*for*) when referring to the past: **da tre mesi** (*for three months*) or **dal 20 luglio** (*since July 20*). Use **per** (*for*) when referring to the future and a definite amount of time: **per tre mesi** (*for three months*).

Prima di/del means *before*. It takes **di** before names and pronouns, and it takes **di** + article before nouns. Here are some examples: **Marisa arriva prima di Silvia/lei** (*Marisa arrives before Silvia/her*); **Il treno parte prima dell'autobus** (*The train is leaving before the bus*).

Dopo means *after*. It takes **di** before pronouns and names, but it stands alone when followed by nouns with the article. Here are some examples: **È nato dopo di te** (*He was born after you*); **Mario parte dopo la mamma** (*Mario is leaving after mother*).

Here's an excerpt from my notebook, showing a week's worth of activities and appointments. After familiarizing yourself with it, answer the questions that follow.

Maggio 2007				
giorno	data	ora	attività	note
lunedì	14	9:00	telefonare al medico	prendere un appuntamento ad agosto
martedì	15	18:00	palestra	fissare fli appuntamenti con l'allenatore personal per il 4 giugno
mercoledì	16	20:30	film con Paola	ho visto il film due settimane fa, ma non vedo lei dal 31 dicembre
giovedì	17	17:45	yoga	ogni giovedì dal 17 maggio al 14 giugno
venerdì	18	13:00	pranzo con il redattore	incontro per discutere il lancio del libro a settembre
sabato	19	16:00	telefonare a Michael	Parigi è sei ore avanti rispetto a noi
domenica	20	15:00	partenza per Parigi	prendo la macchina della ditta per andare all'aeroporto

Q. Per quando vuoi prenotare l'appuntamento con il medico?

A. **Per agosto** (or **Per il mese di agosto**) (*For the month of August*)

22. A che ora vai a pranzo con il redattore?

_____

23. Da quando non vedi la tua amica Paola?

_____

24. Hai già visto il film programmato? Che giorno era?

_____

25. Quando parti per Parigi?

_____

26. Quando verrà lanciato il libro?

_____

27. Quante sedute ci sono nel tuo corso di yoga? Quando finisce il corso?

_____

28. Se sono le 4 del pomeriggio da te che ora è a Parigi?

_____

Purpose and agent of action

Are you giving someone a present? Are you doing a favor to or for someone? Are you fighting for freedom? Because Italian looks at these actions as conveying metaphorical movement, you use prepositions indicating motion: **a** (_to_) and **per** (_for_). **A** and **per** are often interchangeable, as they are in English. For example, **Compri i regali per i/ai bambini?** (_Are you buying presents for the kids?_).

TIP

When you write about body parts, in Italian you often use verbs that require the preposition **a** (_to_) afterwards, such as **farsi male a** (_to hurt one's_), **aver male a** (_for something to hurt_), **operare a** (_to perform surgery on/to_). Therefore, you have no choice but to use that preposition, as in **Lo operano al piede sinistro** (_They'll do surgery to his left foot_).

If you use a verb that doesn't require a preposition, such as **rompersi qualcosa** (_to break something_), you add the noun of the organ without any preposition, as in **Maria si è rotta un polso** (_Maria broke a wrist_).

If you consider somebody responsible for something, or the _agent_ of the action, you use **da** (_by_): **La _Nona Sinfonia_ è stata composta da Beethoven.** (_The_ Ninth Symphony _was composed by Beethoven._)

PRACTICE

Choose the appropriate conclusion to each sentence from the options provided and write it in the blank.

~~a Lucia~~	per il gatto	per la produzione del cioccolato
per me	per te	a Lucia

_**Q.**_ Abbiamo detto la verità _____.

_**A.**_ Abbiamo detto la verità **a Lucia.** (_We told Lucia the truth._)

29. Avete comprato il cibo in scatola _____?

30. Dobbiamo sostituire i macchinari _____.

31. Ho dato ventimila euro all'agente di borsa. Li investirà lui _____.

32. Il tuo collega ha lasciato un messaggio sulla scrivania _____.

33. Hai restituito il libro _____?

Tools, reasons, and causes

In everyday life, you do a lot of things with, well, things. These objects can be means of transportation or tools you use to do something; or maybe they're causes of events, or reasons for your actions.

For means of transportation, you use the following prepositions:

- ✔ **in** (*by*) (without the definite article) followed by a noun in the singular (except for objects like **sci** [*skis*], which are used in pairs): **Verranno in macchina** (*They'll come by car*); **Vanno in paese in sci** (*They're going to town by skis*).

- ✔ **con** + article + noun to convey how one has reached one's destination (rather than the means used): The distinction is meaningful in English too, as in the following example: **Arriva con l'aereo delle 20** (*She'll arrive on the 8 p.m. flight*). You also use **con** if you add any qualification to the means used, as in **Va in giro con la moto di suo fratello** (*He drives around with his brother's motorbike*).

- ✔ **per** to convey *by/via*: **L'ho mandato per posta** (*I sent it by mail*).

- ✔ **con** + article + noun to talk about the object used to achieve a result: **Mio padre lucida l'automobile con un prodotto speciale** (*My father polishes the car with a special product*).

- ✔ **da** to express a cause with the verb in the passive form: **La casa è stata distrutta dall'incendio** (*The house was destroyed by the fire*).

The most common prepositions conveying causes and reasons are **da, di,** and **per** (*for, out of, with, because of*). As you can see, you have a lot of options in English as well. This tells you that it's very difficult to give specific rules about how to choose among the various options. It's easier to learn some expressions by heart when you encounter them. Here are a few:

- ✔ **gridare per la rabbia** (*to shout in anger*)

- ✔ **morire di fame/sete** (*to die from hunger/thirst*)

- ✔ **piangere di gioia/di dolore; piangere per la gioia/per il dolore** (*to cry for joy/ in pain*)

- ✔ **ridere dalla/per la gioia** (*to laugh for joy*)

- ✔ **soffrire per la/di nostalgia** (*to suffer from nostalgia*)

- ✔ **tremare per il/di freddo** (*to shiver with cold*)

You've added some comments after performing the activities listed in your notebook. Fill in the blanks with the appropriate prepositions and articles, when needed.

Q. Sono andata al cinema _____ Paola, _____ sua macchina.

A. Sono andata al cinema **con** Paola, **con** la sua macchina. (*I went to the movies with Paola in her car.*)

34. Ho scritto la data dell'appuntamento _____ medico _____ matita.

35. Sono andata in palestra _____ bicicletta. L'allenatore mi ha fatto lavorare _____ pesi.

36. Ho dimenticato l'attrezzatura. Ho dovuto fare yoga _____ tappetino del centro.

37. Il pranzo _____ redattore è stato pagato _____ casa editrice.

38. Ho stampato la carta d'imbarco _____ stampante.

Answer Key

1 gli occhiali **da** sole (*sunglasses*)

2 i pantaloni **a** righe (*striped pants*)

3 il giornale **di** ieri (*yesterday's newspaper*)

4 la tazzina **da** caffè (*demitasse [cup]*)

5 il discorso **di** Giovanna (*Giovanna's speech*)

6 un saggio **di** trenta pagine (*a 30-page essay*)

7 il forno **a** microonde (*the microwave oven*)

8 l'asilo nido (*nursery school*)

9 Roma è **a** ottocento chilometri **da** Torino. (*Rome is 800 kilometers from Turin.*)

10 **Tra** la Francia e l'Olanda c'è il Belgio. (*Belgium is between France and Holland.*)

11 Strasburgo è **in** Francia. (*Strasburg is in France.*)

12 Per andare **da** Madrid **a** Berlino passiamo **da/per** Monaco. (*To go from Madrid to Berlin we'll go through Munich.*)

13 **A** Capri c'è la villa di Tiberio. (*Tiberius's villa is on Capri.*)

14 L'università di Oxford è **in** Inghilterra. (*Oxford University is in England.*)

15 Il treno **da** Parigi **per** Londra passa **sotto** la Manica. (*The train from Paris to London goes under the Channel.*)

16 Ci hanno rubato la macchina. **Siamo alla Polizia.** (*They stole our car. We are at the police station.*)

17 Dài, passiamo a prendere un caffè **al bar.** (*Come, let's go to the bar for a coffee.*)

18 Fa i pesi due ore ogni giorno **in palestra.** (*He/She lifts weights two hours every day at the gym.*)

19 Hai visto quella collana di perle **dal gioielliere?** (*Did you see that pearl necklace at the jewelry store?*)

20 Luigi detesta Marisa. Non andrà a cena **da lei.** (*Luigi can't stand Marisa. He won't go to her place for dinner.*)

21 Mi sono macchiata il vestito. **Devo portarlo in tintoria.** (*I got a spot on my dress. I have to take it to the cleaner's.*)

22 **Alle 13.** (*At 1 p.m.*)

23 **Dal 31 dicembre.** (*Since December 31.*)

24 **Si. Mercoledì il 2 maggio.** (*Yes. Wednesday, May 2.*)

25 **Domenica 20 maggio**. (*Sunday, May 20.*)

26 **A/In settembre.** (*In September.*)

27 **Quattro sedute. / Il 14 giugno**. (*Four sessions. / June 14.*)

28 **Le 10 di sera/le 22.** (*10 p.m.*)

29 Avete comprato il cibo in scatola **per il gatto?** (*Did you buy canned food for the cat?*)

30 Dobbiamo sostituire i macchinari **per la produzione del cioccolato.** (*We have to replace the machine that makes chocolate.*)

31 Ho dato ventimila euro all'agente di borsa. Li investirà lui **per me.** (*I gave 20,000 euros to the investment agent. He'll/She'll invest it for me.*)

32 Il tuo collega ha lasciato un messaggio sulla scrivania **per te.** (*Your colleague left a message for you on your desk.*)

33 Hai restituito il libro **a Lucia?** (*Did you give the book back to Lucia?*)

34 Ho scritto la data dell'appuntamento **con il** medico **con la** matita. (*I wrote the date of the appointment with my physician with a pencil.*)

35 Sono andata in palestra **in** bicicletta. L'allenatore mi ha fatto lavorare **con i** pesi. (*I went to the gym by bike. My trainer made me work with weights.*)

36 Ho dimenticato l'attrezzatura. Ho dovuto fare yoga **con il** tappetino del centro. (*I forgot my gear. I had to do yoga with the center's mat.*)

37 Il pranzo **con il** redattore è stato pagato **dalla** casa editrice. (*The lunch with the editor was paid by the publishing house.*)

38 Ho stampato la carta d'imbarco **con la** stampante. (*I printed the boarding pass with the printer.*)

Chapter 7

Demonstrative, Indefinite, and Possessive Qualifiers

In This Chapter

▶ Pointing to people and things with "this" and "that"

▶ Conveying indefinite persons, qualities, and quantities

▶ Assigning ownership

* *

When you want to point to someone or something because you want to make sure that you and your listener or reader are on the same wavelength you can use a special set of words that help you be specific: words such as *this, my,* and *some.* You add them to names, nouns, and pronouns, as in **Quel corso di filosofia è difficile** (*That philosophy course is difficult*). Or you can use them by themselves as pronouns, as in **"Il nostro viaggio è stato magnifico. E il vostro?"** (*"Our trip was great. And yours?"*).

You have at your disposal different kinds of "pointers" which are the topic of this chapter:

✔ Demonstrative qualifiers, such as **questo** and **quello**, as in **Questa è una bella bambola.** (*This is a beautiful doll.*)

✔ Indefinite words, such as **alcuni** or **nessuno**, as in **Non ho parlato con nessuno.** (*I didn't talk to anyone.*)

✔ Possessive adjectives and pronouns, as in **Hai visto la mia gatta?** (*Did you see my cat?*)

This chapter points out similarities and differences between Italian and English in the use of those qualifiers, tells you how to match them to the words they refer to and how to express that you're talking about part of a larger set, as in **Molti dei miei studenti sono ammalati** (*Many of my students are sick*).

Pointing to Something with Questo (This) and Quello (That)

The demonstrative qualifiers **questo** (*this*) or **quello** (*that*) are words you use to point to people, things, and situations. You can use them as adjectives or pronouns. They function as adjectives when you add a noun afterwards. They function as pronouns when they refer to a noun, name, or pronoun you've already mentioned.

When you use either **questo** or **quello,** you coordinate it in gender and number with the person or thing to which it refers. **Questo** follows the role of the "four ending adjectives" while **quello** follows the definite article. When you use either as an adjective followed by a noun, besides gender and number you need to choose the spelling of its ending depending on the vowel or consonant of the word that follows, as you do with the definite article (see Chapter 2). So, for example, you say **quell'alta torre** (*that high tower*), but **quella torre alta** (*that high tower*).

Demonstrative qualifiers mean exactly the same in Italian and English, with the following exceptions when it comes to using **questo** and **quello** as pronouns:

- ✔ You use the form **quelli** (*those ones*) *only* as a pronoun: **Quelli non vogliono pagare il conto** (*Those [people] don't want to pay the bill*). When you refer to a group of females only you use **quelle** (*those ones*), which is the regular plural of **quella.**

- ✔ You can use **questo** or **quello** reinforced with the adverbs of place **qui/qua** (*here*) for **questo** or **lì/là** (*there*) for **quello.** You can point to a thing: **Questo qui è il mio quaderno** (*This [one] is my notebook*). When you employ them to point to a person, you often do it to convey a negative nuance: **Non ti fidare di questa qui** (*Don't trust this one*); **Non parlare a quello là** (*Don't talk to that one*).

- ✔ You can add an adjective to **questo** or **quello** instead of repeating a noun and an adjective: **"Vuoi la giacca blu o quella verde?" "Quella verde."** (*"Do you want the blue or the green jacket?" "The green one."*)

Translate the following sentences into Italian.

0. I'll buy the long dress; she'll buy the short one.

A. **Compro il vestito lungo; lei compra quello corto.**

1. This is my wife.

_____

2. My children? These are not my children.

_____

3. Those trees are tall.

_____

4. Do you want that jacket? This one is new.

_____

5. Which scarf do you want? The yellow one or the red one?

_____

6. They hired that one (feminine), but they made a big mistake.

_____

7. Listen (singular) to this one. He thinks he knows everything.

_____

Conveying Something Indefinite

In this section I talk about indefinite words that you can use as adjectives or as pronouns and about indefinite words that you can use only as pronouns. Mind that in Italian indefinite adjectives and pronouns are often singular even though they may convey either a singular or a plural meaning. An example is the adjective **qualche** (*some*) (which never changes its ending), as in the phrase: **Abbiamo ancora qualche dubbio** (*We still have some doubts*); or the pronoun **chiunque** (*anyone*): **Sono disposto a discutere della questione con chiunque!** (*I'm willing to discuss that issue with anyone!*)

I also show you how indefinite words can help you select a section out of a larger whole, as in the following example: **Molti di noi non gli hanno creduto** (*Many of us didn't believe him*). **Molti** (*many*) is the section and the larger whole is **noi** (*us*).

Indefinite words used as adjectives or pronouns

In Table 7-1 I list indefinite words that can be used as adjectives or pronouns. I indicate which ones

✔ You can employ only in the singular, the plural, or both.

✔ Are invariable, which means that they only come in one form no matter the gender and number of the person or thing to which they refer. If they are singular (which is almost always the case) you conjugate the verb in the third-person singular. If the verb is in a compound form which includes the past participle (check Chapter 9), you use the past participle in the masculine singular, unless you're sure that the indefinite adjective or pronoun refers to a group of females.

✔ Vary in gender and number, ending in **-o, -a, -i** or **-e**; or only in number, ending in **-e** or **-i**; you match variable indefinites with the nouns to which they refer, as you do with describing adjectives (see Chapter 5).

Table 7-1 **Indefinite Adjectives/Pronouns**

Masculine Singular (Default)	Meaning as an Adjective	Meaning as a Pronoun	Use	Feminine Singular	Plural (M/F)	Examples	Notes
del, dello, dell'	some, any, a few	N/A	It's an indefinite article made of the preposition di (of) + the definite article; in the singular it accompanies uncountable nouns	della, dell'	dei, degli/delle	Singular: **Vorrei del pane.** (*I'd like some bread.*) Plural: **Vorrei delle pesche.** (*I'd like some peaches.*)	Not to be confused with the same word meaning of the: **Mi piace molto la crosta del pane.** (*I like the crust of the bread a lot.*)
alcuno	not any	some, any, a few	In the plural it means some, a few, as in **Sono venuti alcuni amici** (*Some friends came*); in negative sentences if you say: **Alcuni amici non sono venuti** (*Some friends didn't come*), you mean that some came and others didn't; you use **nessuno** (*no one*), to say that no one came	alcuna	alcuni/ alcune	**Alcuni arrivano sempre tardi.** (*Some are always late.*)	In the singular it's used in writing in negative sentences, instead of **nessuno, nessuna** (*no, no one*): **Non ho alcun bisogno di aiuto.** (*I don't need any help.*)
qualche	a, some kind of, a few, any	N/A	It's invariable and used with countable nouns; when referring to "something" singular it means **uno, una** (*one, a, some kind of*); when referring to "something" plural it means some	qualche	N/A	**Troverò qualche soluzione.** (*I'll find a solution/some kind of solution.*); **Qualche ragazzo si è offeso.** (*Some/ A few boys were offended.*)	
ciascuno	each	each	It's used with countable nouns, or referring to them as a pronoun; only singular	ciascuna	N/A	**Ciascuna proposta verrà esaminata.** (*Each proposal will be examined.*); **Ciascuno può esprimere la propria opinione.** (*Everyone can express their opinion.*)	

Masculine Singular (Default)	Meaning as an Adjective	Meaning as a Pronoun	Use	Feminine Singular	Plural (M/F)	Examples	Notes
ogni	every, each	N/A	It's used with countable nouns; only singular	ogni	N/A	**Ogni medaglia ha il suo rovescio.** (*Every coin has a flip side.*)	
qualunque	any	N/A	It's used with countable nouns; only singular. It means *any one you want/you prefer*	qualunque	N/A	**Telefona a qualunque ora.** (*You can call any time.*)	
un certo	a, a certain	N/A	It's used with countable nouns; in the singular you add the article **un** (MS) or **una** (FS); as a pronoun in the plural, it means *those unspecified items or people*	una certa	certi/certe	**Devo finire certi lavori.** (*I need to finish certain jobs.*); **Ha telefonato una certa Signora Rossi.** (*A Mrs. Rossi called.*); **Certi sostengono che non c'è il surriscaldamento globale.** (*Some people maintain that there is no global warming.*)	Used without the article when followed by collective singular words, such as **gente** (*people*)
[l', un] altro	[the, an] other	[the] other[s]	It's used also with the definite or indefinite article	[l', un'] altra	[gli] altri [le] altre	**L'altro giorno pioveva.** (*It was raining the other day.*); **È passato un altro ragazzo a cercarti.** (*Another boy came looking for you.*)	Used in various combinations: **l'un l'altro** (*each other, one another*), **l'uno ... l'altro** (*one ... the other*), **gli uni ... gli altri** (*some ... others; the ones ... the others*)
nessuno	no	no one, nobody	It's only used in the singular	nessuna	N/A	**Non vidi nessuna bambina.** (*I saw no little girl./I didn't see any little girl.*)	If used at the beginning of a negative sentence, **non** (not) is omitted: **Nessuno ha telefonato.** (*No one called.*) (Check Chapter 16 about negative questions and answers.)

(continued)

Table 7-1 (continued)

Masculine Singular (Default)	Meaning as an Adjective	Meaning as a Pronoun	Use	Feminine Singular	Plural (M/F)	Examples	Notes
molto	much, a lot	much, a lot	It's used with uncountable nouns in the singular, and countable nouns in the plural	molta	molti/ molte	**Hai bisogno di molto zucchero?** (*Do you need a lot of sugar?*); **Hanno perso molte partite.** (*They lost a lot of games.*)	
tanto	so much, so many	so much, so many	It's used with uncountable nouns in the singular, and countable nouns in the plural	tanta	tanti/tante	**Ha fatto tanta fatica!** (*She made such a big effort!*); **Abbiamo visto tante farfalle!** (*We saw [so] many butterflies!*)	
troppo	too much, too many	too much, too many	It's used with uncountable nouns in the singular, and countable nouns in the plural	troppa	troppi/ troppe	**C'è troppo zucchero.** (*There's too much sugar.*); **Abbiamo troppe barche.** (*We have too many boats.*)	
poco	too little, few	few	When it means *too little* it's used with singular uncountable nouns; in the plural it means *few* with plural countable nouns	poca	pochi/ poche	**Ho poco vino.** (*I have too little wine.*); **Poche persone gli credono.** (*Only a few people believe him.*)	
parecchio	a lot of, several	several	It's used with uncountable nouns in the singular, and countable nouns in the plural	parecchia	parecchi/ parecchie	**Ho ancora parecchio tempo.** (*I still have a lot of time.*); **Hai ancora parecchi compiti da fare?** (*Do you still have several assignments to do?*)	
tutto il	entire, whole, all	N/A	It's used with countable and uncountable nouns; in the singular it means *the entire, the whole; in the plural it means all*	tutta la	tutti i/ tutte le	**Hanno consumato tutta la benzina!** (*They used the entire tank of gas!*); **Hai visto tutti i suoi film?** (*Have you seen all his/her movies?*)	

In Italian as in English, the indefinite adjectives/pronouns *both* and *either* are used only with plural, countable nouns. The most common phrase is **tutti e due** (M)/**tutte e due** (F), but especially in writing, you'll also see **ambedue** (M and F) and **entrambi** (M)/**entrambe** (F).

Indefinite words used solely as pronouns

In Table 7-2 I list separately some indefinite words that you can only use as pronouns. Most of these indefinite pronouns are singular and invariable, but they do convey a generic, singular or plural meaning. Look at the following example: **"Hai contattato qualcuno?" "Sì, ho contattato tre avvocati"** (*"Did you contact someone?" "Yes, I contacted three lawyers"*).

In English nowadays you use *everyone* meaning "all people." You add third-person plural possessive adjectives and personal pronouns, as in *Everyone thinks that their team is better.* In Italian you can't use **ognuno** that way. You use **tutti** (masculine plural), as in **Tutti pensano che la loro squadra** or **tutte** (feminine plural) if you know the group includes only women.

To convey *whoever, whatever,* and *whichever,* you can use

- **chiunque** + verb in the subjunctive, as in **Chiunque sia stato, lo scopriranno.** (*Whoever did it, they'll find them.*)

- **chiunque** + **di** + noun/pronoun to refer to people, as in **Chiunque sia stato di loro, lo scopriranno.** (*Whoever did it, they'll find them.*)

- **qualunque** or **qualsiasi** + noun, as in **Qualunque regalo tu le faccia, non sarà contenta.** (*Whatever present you give her, she won't be happy.*)

Chiunque, qualunque, and **qualsiasi** require the verb in the subjunctive (see Chapters 14 and 15 for coverage of the subjunctive) as shown in the examples above.

Table 7-2 Indefinite Pronoun

Masculine Singular (Default)	Feminine	Translation	Example	Notes
uno	una	one, someone	Ha telefonato una. (Someone/A woman called.)	
ognuno	ognuna	everyone, each, each one	Ognuno è contento. (Everyone is happy.)	It takes the verbs in the singular but refers to a generic singular or plural subject. Use the feminine when you refer to women only.
qualcuno	qualcuna	someone, somebody	"Hai contattato qualcuno?" "Sì, ho contattato tre avvocati." ("Did you contact someone?" "Yes, I contacted three lawyers.")	It takes the verbs in the singular but refers to a generic singular or plural subject. Use the feminine when you refer to women only.
chiunque		anyone, anybody	Chiunque avrebbe fatto ciò che hai fatto tu. (Anyone would've done what you have.)	It takes the verb in the singular but refers to a generic singular or plural subject.
qualcosa		something, anything	Posso fare qualcosa per te? (Can I do something for you?)	Add altro (else) to qualcuno or qualcosa to translate someone else, something else: Chiediamo a qualcun altro (Let's ask someone else).
tutto		everything	Ada ha capito tutto. (Ada understood everything.); Hanno parlato di tutto. (They spoke about everything)	It's used as the direct object of a sentence. When you use it as subject you need to add ciò: Tutto ciò è falso (All this is false).
niente, nulla		nothing	Niente serve quanto essere pazienti. (Nothing helps so much as being patient.)	Skip the adverb non (not) when you begin a sentence with niente/nulla. (See Chapter 16 for negative questions and answers.)

Complete the following sentences by choosing among the indefinite adjectives or pronouns in parentheses.

Q. Mia zia ha comprato (alcuni; alcune; degli) vestiti.

A. Mia zia ha comprato **alcuni** vestiti. (*My aunt bought some clothes.*)

8. Siamo andate (tutte; molte; tutte e due) a teatro.

9. Non sono venuti (l'uno e l'altro; né l'uno né l'altro; nessuno) al matrimonio.

10. (Ogni; Qualcuno; Ognuno) è libero di fare quello che vuole.

11. "C'è ancora (della; molto; parecchio) Coca-Cola in frigo?" "No, ma c'è (del; poco; una certa) succo d'arancia."

12. C'è (uno; qualcuno; ciascuno) in casa?

13. Hai mangiato (molta; tutti; tutto)?!

Indefinite words that express a part of a set: Partitive articles, indefinites, and the pronoun ne

When you employ an indefinite pronoun, you often express the set of which the pronoun refers to as a part. For example, in this sentence, **Alcuni di loro non verranno alla festa** (*Some of them won't come to the party*). **Alcuni** (*some*) is the indefinite pronoun and **loro** (*of them*) is the set. You can employ the following formulas using pronouns and other words to convey a part of a larger whole:

✔ **ognuno/ciascuno** (*each*), **chiunque** (*any*), **nessuno** (*none*), **qualcuno** (*any, some*), **uno** (*one*) + the preposition **di** (*of*) or **tra** (*among*) + the verb in the third-person singular

  If there's a past participle, you leave it in the masculine, as in **Qualcuno di voi ha scritto al giornale** (*Some of you wrote to the paper*), unless you know that the group consists of only females. For example, **Una delle ragazze si è fatta male** (*One of the girls got hurt*).

✔ **alcuni** (*some, a few*), **molti** (*many, a lot of*), **parecchi** (*several*), **pochi** (*few*), **tanti** (*so many*), **troppi** (*too many*) + **di** or **tra** + the verb in the third-person plural

  Alcuni di voi hanno chiesto un rinvio. (*Some of you have asked for a postponement.*)

✔ The indefinite article **del, dello, dell', della, dell'** (*some*) in the singular + nouns that are uncountable or indicate things in bulk, such as **acqua** (*water*), **vino** (*wine*), or **pioggia** (*rain*)

  Vuoi del vino? (*Do you want some wine?*)

✔ The adverbial phrase **un po' di** (*a little of*) + uncountable concrete nouns or abstractions

Sì, vorrei un po' di vino grazie. (*Yes, I'd like some wine thank you.*)

Ci vuole un po' di costanza. (*You need a little perseverance.*)

You use **di** after an indefinite pronoun when an adjective follows. For example, **Hai visto qualcosa di interessante alla mostra?** (*Did you see something/anything interesting at the exhibit?*).

When you don't want to repeat the noun or pronoun representing a set already mentioned in a sentence with an indefinite pronoun, you can replace the set with the pronoun **ne** (*of those, them*), either placed before the verb or attached to the infinitive or the gerund. (For the other meanings of **ne** and a discussion of pronoun placement, turn to Chapter 4.) If you use a past participle or another adjective, you coordinate it with the word **ne** refers to:

"Hai comprato delle/alcune/molte/troppo banane?" "Ne ho comprate troppe!" (*"Did you buy some/many/too many bananas?" "I bought too many [of those]!"*)

If you use **uno/nessuno** (*one/none*), the past participle takes the singular, coordinated in gender with the item you're talking about:

"Hai visto i tuoi amici?" "No, non ne ho visto nessuno." (*"Did you see your friends?" "No, I didn't see any [of them]."*)

You can employ any quantifier, not just indefinites, to express a part of a set. For example, **"Hai comprato dieci borse?!" No, ne comprate 2!"** (*"Did you buy ten handbags?" "No! We bought two!"*).

From the options provided, select the proper conclusion to each sentence and write it in the blank.

~~Ne ho venduta poca.~~   Non abbiamo incontrato nessuno.   Ma no, ce ne hanno messe cinque!

Erano in cinquantamila!   Qualcuno di voi è disponibile?   Grazie, ne vorrei mezzo litro.

Q. Hai venduto tanta limonata?

A. **Ne ho venduta poca.** (*No, I sold very little.*)

14. Abbiamo bisogno di tre volontari.

_____

15. Avete incontrato qualcuno al centro commerciale?

_____

16. Ci hanno messo tre ore da Bologna a Firenze?

_____

17. Quanti erano alla manifestazione?

_____

18. Vuole dell'acqua minerale?

_____

Assigning Ownership with Possessive Qualifiers

In English you assign ownership by adding a possessive adjective (*my* or *our*) to the object owned, by referring to that object through a possessive pronoun (*mine* or *ours*), or by adding *'s* (or just the apostrophe) to the noun or name that conveys the owner. In Italian you have three options: add a possessive adjective to the owner, introduce the owner with the preposition **di** (*of*), or employ the idiomatic expression **essere di [insert owner's name]**, which means something like *to belong to*.

Unlike in English, in the third-person singular Italian, the possessive adjective or pronoun doesn't convey whether the owner is male or female. That information is clarified only by the context of the sentence; for example, **la sua gatta** can mean *his/her cat*.

Table 7-3 lists possessive adjectives and pronouns, which are identical in Italian, along with the corresponding definite articles.

Table 7-3	Possessive Qualifiers and Pronouns			
Translation	*Masculine Singular*	*Masculine Plural*	*Feminine Singular*	*Feminine Plural*
my, mine	mio, il mio	miei, i miei	mia, la mia	mie, le mie
your, yours	tuo, il tuo	tuoi, i tuoi	tua, la tua	tue, le tue
his, hers, its	Suo, il suo	Suoi, i suoi	Sua, la sua	Sue, le sue
our, ours	nostro, il nostro	nostri, i nostri	nostra, la nostra	nostre, le nostre
your, yours	vostro, il vostro	vostri, i vostri	vostra, la vostra	vostre, le vostre
their, theirs	Loro, il loro	Loro, i loro	Loro, la loro	Loro, le loro

In Italian you use the definite article with possessive adjectives and pronouns, except in two cases:

✔ You don't use the article with the names of close relatives except for the use with **loro.**

✔ When you use a possessive word after the verb **essere** (*to be*) at this stage you can use the article or skip it, whichever comes easier, as when you say **Quell'automobile è la mia** (*That car is mine*) or **Quell'automobile è mia** (*That car is mine*).

Note, however, that the presence or absence of the article conveys a slightly different meaning: **Quell'automobile è la mia** (pronoun) means *That car is mine* (as opposed to being yours or hers, and so forth). **Quell'automobile è mia** (adjective), on the other hand, means simply *That car belongs to me* (as in, *I bought it, I didn't rent it*).

If you select one or more items out of a group of things owned, in Italian you can use

✔ Any quantifier (a number or an indefinite pronoun) followed by **dei, degli, delle** + possessive qualifier + noun in the plural: **Sono tre dei miei amici** (*They're three of my friends*).

✔ **uno** or **dei** + possessive adjective + noun: **È un mio amico** (*He's a friend of mine*); **Sono dei miei amici** (*They're friends of mine*). But, **È un amico dei miei** means *He's a friend of my parents*.

Revise the following sentences by replacing the **di** plus noun/name or the **essere di** constructions with the appropriate possessive.

Q. Quel gatto appartiene a Paolo?

A. **Quel gatto è suo?** (*Is that cat his cat?*)

19. I genitori di Marisa celebrano le nozze d'oro.

_____

20. La figlia di Federico e Piera ha quindici anni.

_____

21. È il collega dell'avvocato.

_____

22. Sono arrivate tre amiche degli zii.

_____

23. Quella macchina appartiene a voi?

_____

24. Non toccare quella bambola! Appartiene a noi!

_____

Answer Key

1. Questa è mia moglie.

2. I miei bambini? Questi non sono i miei bambini.

3. Quegli alberi sono alti.

4. Vuoi quella giacca? Questa è nuova.

5. Quale sciarpa vuoi? Quella gialla o quella rossa?

6. Hanno assunto quella lì/là, ma hanno fatto un grosso errore.

7. Ascolta questo qui. Crede di sapere tutto lui.

8. Siamo andate **tutte e due/tutte** a teatro. (*We both/all went to the theater.*)

9. Non sono venuti **né l'uno né l'altro** al matrimonio. (*Neither one nor the other came.*)

10. **Ognuno** è libero di fare quello che vuole. (*Everyone/Each is free to do as they please.*)

11. "C'è ancora **della** Coca-Cola in frigo?" "No, ma c'è **del** succo d'arancia." (*Do we have any Coke in the refrigerator?*)

12. C'è **qualcuno** in casa? (*Is there anyone at home?*)

13. Hai mangiato **tutto**?! (*Did you eat everything?!*)

14. **Qualcuno di voi è disponibile?** (*Is anyone available?*)

15. **Non abbiamo incontrato nessuno.** (*We didn't meet anyone.*)

16. **Ma no, ce ne hanno messe cinque!** (*Oh no, it took them five!*)

17. **Erano in cinquantamila!** (*There were 50,000 people!*)

18. **Grazie, ne vorrei mezzo litro.** (*Yes, thank you, I'd like half a liter.*)

19. **I suoi genitori celebrano le nozze d'oro.** (*Her parents celebrate their gold wedding anniversary.*)

20. **La loro figlia ha quindici anni.** (*Their daughter is 15 years old.*)

21. **È il suo collega.** (*He's one of his colleagues.*)

22. **Sono arrivate tre delle lore amiche.** (*Three of their friends have arrived.*)

23. **Quella macchina è vostra?** (*Is that car yours?*)

24. **Non toccare quella bambola! È nostra!** (*Don't touch that doll! It's ours!*)

Chapter 8

Linking Sentences with Conjunctions and Relative Pronouns

• •

In This Chapter

▶ Joining thoughts thanks to conjunctions

▶ Linking clauses with relative pronouns

• •

*I*n Chapters 1 through 7 I talk about handling various words — articles, nouns, verbs, indefinite words, among others — to form one meaningful sentence. But in speech and writing, you use many sentences, not just one. You can string them out one after another, separating them with a period. But you often need to link together thoughts expressed in different sentences. I devote this chapter to showing you how to do that with coordinating or subordinating conjunctions or with relative pronouns.

When you rely on conjunctions, you employ invariable words whose only purpose in life is to join clauses. I only give you a few suggestions about coordination and subordination here because this is a broad and complex topic that you're sure to work on in depth in advanced Italian courses (or books). In both Italian and English, you encounter coordinating and subordinating conjunctions. Here's a rundown of both:

▶ You use coordinating conjunctions — such as **e** (*and*), **o/oppure** (*or*), or **ma** (*but*) — when you link together clauses that are (grammatically) of equal standing.

> **Vai in crociera o stai sul lago?** (*Are you going on a cruise or are you staying at the lake?*)

▶ You use subordinating conjunctions — such as **perché** (*because*), **quando** (*when*), or **finché** (*in so far as*) — when you link together dependent and independent clauses.

> **Quando torni dobbiamo parlare.** (*When you come back we need to talk.*)

You can point to a person, thing, or situation already mentioned by linking two clauses with a relative pronoun, thus building a dependent clause called a *relative clause*. For example, **L'attrice che ha vinto l'Oscar è francese** (*The actress who won the Oscar is French*). In the example, **che** (*who*) is a relative pronoun that introduces the relative clause **ha vinto l'Oscar è francese** (*won the Oscar is French*).

In the section reserved for relative pronouns, I introduce you to a special set of combined demonstrative + relative pronouns that do double duty: The (implied) demonstrative pronoun belongs to the independent clause while the relative component introduces the dependent clause, as in **Ha visto chi ha mandato questo pacco?** (*Did you see who sent this package?*). In this example, **chi** combines **la persona che** (*the person who*) and **quello che** (*the one who*). (You can also use the non-combined form if you wish, but the combined form is handy.) (For more on demonstrative qualifiers, turn to Chapter 6.)

Linking Words and Clauses with Conjunctions and Prepositions

As you know, a clause is a grouping of words that includes a verb, which sometimes is all you need: **Entrate!** (*Come in!*). But in most situations, you need a subject, an object, adjectives and other qualifiers, other nouns introduced by a preposition, and so forth to express your meaning. When you're on a roll with sentence construction and want to keep going, you can link full sentences together using conjunctions and prepositions. Here's the breakdown of these linking words:

✔ Coordinating conjunctions: These conjunctions link together two (or more) sentences that remain meaningful even if you take the conjunction away; for example, **Va negli USA, [ma] non va a New York** (*He's going to the US, [but] he's not going to New York*). This process is called *coordination,* and you have an array of coordinating conjunctions to choose from.

✔ Subordinating conjunctions: These conjunctions tie one or more dependent clauses to an independent one, as in **Gioco con te se mi impresti la tua bici** (*I'll play with you if you lend me your bike*). This process is called *subordination.* I also tell you about how to use prepositions to construct a subordinate clause with the verb in the infinitive.

Connecting words or sentences with coordinating conjunctions

You can use coordinating conjunctions in various ways:

✔ To link names, nouns, pronouns, adjectives, and adverbs in the same sentence, as in **Mi piacciono i romanzi e i resoconti di viaggio** (*I like novels and travel books*), or **Vorrei un vestito elegante, ma comodo** (*I'd like an elegant but comfortable dress*).

✔ To coordinate verbs in the infinitive, such as when they follow a modal auxiliary (see Chapter 10). For example, **No so né sciare né arrampicare** (*I can neither ski nor climb*).

✔ To coordinate complete sentences, as in **Lia scrive poesie e Ugo suona il piano** (*Lia writes poems and Ugo plays the piano*).

Table 8-1 lists coordinating conjunctions you can use to link words or sentences.

Table 8-1	Coordinating Conjunctions		
Coordinating Conjunction	*Translation*	*Coordinating Conjunction*	*Translation*
allora, poi	*then*	**ma, però, tuttavia**	*but, however*
anzi, piuttosto (**di** + infinitive)	*rather*	**né . . . né**	*neither . . . nor*
cioè	*that is*	**non solo . . . ma anche**	*not only . . . but also*
comunque	*however*	**o, oppure**	*or*
e	*and*	**o . . . o**	*either . . . or*
e . . . e, sia . . . sia	*both . . . and*	**perciò, dunque**	*therefore*
infatti	*in fact, indeed*	**quindi**	*so, therefore, thus*

When you use the conjunction **e**, you can invert the order of the sentences. Think of them in mathematical terms: In multiplication or addition, the product or sum doesn't change if you move numbers around. This is also the case with **o** (*or*), **o . . . o** (*either . . . or*), **né . . . né** (*neither . . . nor*), and **sia . . . sia** (*either . . . or*). But with other conjunctions (as with division and subtraction), order matters. If you establish a contrast with **ma** (*but*) or **tuttavia** (*however*); point to a conclusion or a consequence with **quindi** (*thus*) or **perciò** (*therefore*); or convey a temporal sequence with **allora, poi** (*then*), you can't swap the sentence order. For example, **Mia le fa un regalo, ma non dirglielo** (*Mia will give her a present, but don't tell her*).

Rewrite the sentences with the conjunctions in the proper places. When it comes to coordinating conjunctions, you may have more than one correct option.

Q. Luca non vuole parlarti, allora ha bisogno dei tuoi consigli.

A. **Luca non vuole parlarti, tuttavia, ma, però ha bisogno dei tuoi consigli.** (*Luca doesn't want to talk to you, but he needs your advice.*)

1. Avete studiato poco. Vi hanno bocciato all'esame.

_____

2. Hanno comprato l'automobile di una loro amica. Ne compreranno una nuova.

_____

3. Studia in Australia. Pensa di trasferirsi là.

_____

4. Vai al cinema con Giulia. Vai al ristorante con Maria.

_____

5. Vado a Parigi. Non posso restare più di tre giorni.

_____

Joining a dependent clause with an independent one

If you subordinate one sentence to another, you establish a relationship of dependence between a main or independent clause and a subordinate or dependent one. With subordination, the meaning of the combined sentences is very different from their meanings if left independent of one another. Consider this example: **Mangio la verdura perché fa bene** (*I eat vegetables because they're good for me*) means that you eat vegetables because they're healthy food. **Mangio la verdura. La verdura fa bene.** (*I eat vegetables. Vegetables are good for one's health.*) means that you may eat them because you like them, because you have nothing else in the refrigerator, or for any other reason. The fact that you eat veggies isn't necessarily tied to their health benefits.

You can subordinate a dependent clause to a dependent one in two ways:

- ✔ With a subordinating conjunction
- ✔ With a preposition or prepositional phrase that does the work of a conjunction

I expand on these methods in the following sections.

With a subordinating conjunction
Table 8-2 lists the most common subordinating conjunctions.

Table 8-2	Subordinating Conjunctions		
Subordinating Conjunction	*Translation*	**Subordinating Conjunction**	*Translation*
affinché	*in order to*	**nonostante**	*although*
[non] appena	*as soon as*	**perché**	*because, why, so that, in order that*
che	*that*	**più ... di quanto, più ... che, più ... di quello che**	*more ... than, more ... than what*
come	*as, how*	**poiché, dal momento che, dato che**	*as, for, since, given that*
così ... come, tanto ... quanto, tale ... quale	*as ... as, as much ... as, such ... as*	**prima che**	*before*
da quando	*ever since*	**purché**	*as long as, provided that*
dopo che	*after*	**quando**	*when, as*
dove	*where*	**quanto, quanti, quanta, quante**	*how much, how many*

Subordinating Conjunction	Translation	Subordinating Conjunction	Translation
finché	until	se	if, whether
finché non	until	sebbene, benché	although, even though
meno . . . di quanto, meno . . . che, meno . . . di quello che	less . . . than, less . . . than what	senza che	without + subjunctive
mentre	whereas, while	tanto, tanta, tanti, tante che	so [much so] that, to the point that

Conjunctions are invariable, with the exception of words you use to convey comparisons, such as **tante . . . quante** (*as many . . . as*).

When you link sentences through subordination, the main clause and the conjunction you've chosen determine the mood and tense of the verb in the dependent clause. In Chapter 15, I detail how to link sentences with the declarative and the *if . . . then* constructions, which often use the subjunctive. Other constructions require the conjunction in the dependent clause, including **affinché, perché** when it means *in order to*, **a meno che** (*unless, except if*), **nonostante/nonostante che** (*although*), **prima che** (*before*), **purché** (*as long as, provided that*), **sebbene, benché** (*although, even though*), and **senza che** (*without*). For example, **Mi spiegate cosa sta succedendo sui mercati affinché non perda tutti i miei soldi?** (*Can you explain to me what's happening in the markets so I won't lose all my money?*).

As I say in the introduction to this chapter, the syntax of subordination is complex, so in the following exercise all you have to do is to choose the correct conclusion to the first part of the combined sentence. I've chosen the conjunctions on your behalf!

From the options provided, select the proper conclusion to each sentence and write it in the blank.

devo darti altre informazioni	perché sei una persona fidata	~~lui russava~~	non li vediamo più
perché non avete telefonato	sebbene avessi molti dubbi	senza che suo padre lo sapesse	più di quanto non pensassi

Q. Mentre lei faceva il discorso _____.

A. Mentre lei faceva il discorso **lui russava.** (*While she was giving her speech he was snoring.*)

6. Da quando si sono trasferiti in campagna _____.

7. Tina ha venduto la casa _____.

8. Ho aderito alla proposta dell'avvocato _____.

9. Prima che tu parta per Nuova Delhi _____.

10. Quel vestito costa _____.

11. Te lo dico _____.

12. Volevamo sapere _____.

With a preposition or prepositional phrase

As long as the subject of both clauses is the same, you can introduce a dependent clause with a preposition, or with phrases that include a preposition, followed by an infinitive. In the sentence **Ho deciso di andare a pescare** (*I've decided to go fishing*), the preposition **di** (*to*) introduces a dependent clause. In fact, you can replace the preposition with the declarative conjunction **che** (*that*): **Ho deciso che vado a pescare** (*I've decided that I'll go fishing*). Table 8-3 lists prepositions and phrases with prepositions that can introduce verbs in the infinitive.

When you use the preposition **da,** the infinitive can refer to the object of the sentence, as in **Dammi un libro da leggere** (*Give me a book to read/that I can read/for me to read*). And you can have two different subjects when you use **su** + article, as in **Partimmo sul sorgere del sole** (*We left while the sun was rising*).

Table 8-3	Prepositions Working as Conjunctions		
Preposition	*Translation*	*Preposition*	*Translation*
a	*to* + infinitive (or gerund)	**in modo da**	*in such a way to* + infinitive, *so as to* + infinitive
a tal punto da	*to the point of* + gerund	**invece di**	*instead of* + gerund
da	*to* + infinitive	**oltre a**	*besides* + gerund
di	*of* + gerund	**per**	*to* + infinitive, *for* + gerund
dopo + past infinitive	*after* + gerund	**prima di**	*before* + gerund
fino a	*to the point of* + gerund	**senza**	*without* + gerund
in + article + infinitive	*in* + gerund	**su** + article + infinitive	*on* + gerund, *while* + finite verb

Each of the following exercises features separate sentences or combined sentences linked by a subordinating conjunction. You can add a preposition to link the sentences that are independent, and you can replace the subordinating conjunction with a preposition. In both cases you should end up with a combined sentence in which the two clauses are linked by a preposition and the verb in the infinitive. Remember that if the verb is in the present perfect in the original sentence, you need a past infinitive.

Q. È andato via. Ha fatto male.

A. Ha fatto male ad andare via. (*You [formal]/he/she did the wrong thing by leaving.*)

13. Dopo che ho parlato con Laura, ho deciso di accettare quel lavoro.

_____

14. Ha preso la macchina. Non ha preso l'autobus.

_____

15. È stato arrestato perché non ha pagato le tasse.

_____

16. Vi prego. Fate silenzio.

_____

17. Devo dire la verità. Le cose non stanno come dici tu.

_____

18. Prima che lei si sposasse, Laura aveva una carriera brillante.

_____

Joining Clauses That Belong Together

You may need a full sentence to point to a person or a thing already mentioned. For example, if you say **L'attrice ha vinto l'Oscar. L'attrice è francese,** you can link the two sentences by using a relative pronoun, which introduces a relative clause. The two sentences become **L'attrice che ha vinto l'Oscar è francese** (*The actress who won the Oscar is French*). In this sentence, **che ha vinto l'Oscar** (*who won the Oscar*) is the relative clause, and *who* is the relative pronoun.

In English you often can skip the relative pronoun unless it's the subject of the relative clause. In Italian you may not. For example, in English you may say *Did you like the wine that we drank last night?* or *Did you like the wine we drank last night?* Either is correct. In Italian, though, you must include **che** (*that*): **Ti è piaciuto il vino che abbiamo bevuto ieri sera?**

Italian has a set of relative pronouns that have counterparts in English, such as **che** (*who, whom*) or **le quali** (*who,* feminine plural). But Italian also has a set of combined relative pronouns. They convey (but don't spell out) a demonstrative pronoun, such as **quello** (*that*) or **colui** (*the one*), and a relative pronoun, such as **che** (*who*), to form the combined pronoun **chi** (*who*), which means **colui che** (*the one who*). In English the only exact equivalent is *what,* which means *the things that/which;* in Italian, it's **quanto.** Because these pronouns have no exact counterparts in English, turn to the later section, "Economy of speech: Combined pronouns" to see what they mean and how they work.

Dealing just with your average relative pronouns

Italian has two sets of (non-combined) relative pronouns: invariable and variable.

✔ Invariable relative pronouns don't change their endings to match the words they replace in gender and number (for once!). An example is **che** (*who, whom*), which can refer to a singular, plural, masculine, or feminine person or thing, as in **Le bambine che hai visto al parco sono le mie sorelle** (*The little girls you saw in the park are my sisters*).

✔ Variable relative pronouns are formed of two words: the relative word **quale** and the definite article. **Quale** changes in number, but not in gender: **quale, quali.** It always takes the definite article, which conveys both gender and number — **il, la, i, le** (*the*) — to form the pronoun **il quale** (and its variations) meaning *who, whom, which*. For example, **La bambine le quali hai visto al parco sono le mie sorelle** (*The little girls you saw in the park are my sisters*).

When you use the variable set, you coordinate the pronoun with the word in the preceding clause that the pronoun replaces. You change the ending of the pronoun in number and the article in both gender and number (for more on rules of coordination, refer to Chapter 2). For example, in the sentence **La gatta della quale ti avevo parlato è morta** (*The female cat about whom I talked to you died*), **la gatta** is feminine singular, as is the relative pronoun **della quale.**

You also have to contend with the pronoun **cui**, which never changes and can't be used as subject or direct object. You can only use it in two ways:

✔ Accompanied by the definite **il, la, i, le** (*the*), which conveys both gender and number to form the pronoun **il cui** (and its variations). In this form, **il cui** means *whose.*

> **Hai visto quel film il cui titolo ora non ricordo?** (*Did you see that movie whose title I can't remember right now?*)

✔ Accompanied by a preposition but without an article, as in **da cui** (*by/from whom*).

Table 8-4 illustrates the functions of the variable and invariable relative pronouns.

Table 8-4			Relative Pronouns			
Translation	*Invariable*	*Masculine Singular*	*Feminine Singular*	*Masculine Plural*	*Feminine Plural*	*Use*
who, whom, that, which	**che**	**il quale**	**la quale**	**i quali**	**le quali**	Subject or direct object
of, about which/whom		**del quale**	**della quale**	**dei quali**	**delle quali**	Indicates specification or possession

Translation	Invariable	Masculine Singular	Feminine Singular	Masculine Plural	Feminine Plural	Use
of, about which/whom	di cui					Indicates specification
whose		il cui	la cui	i cui	le cui	Indicates specification or possession
whose		del quale	della quale	dei quali	delle quali	Indicates specification or possession
to/for whom	[a] cui	al quale	alla quale	ai quali	alle quali	Indicates aim or purpose
from whom/which, by whom/ which, to whom/which, or any other preposition (see Chapter 6)	da cui, a cui, or any other preposition (see Chapter 6)	dal quale, al quale	dalla quale, alla quale	dai quali, ai quali	dalle quali, alle quali	Other complements (check Chapter 6)

When it comes to deciding which pronoun to use, if you use a relative pronoun as subject or direct object, you can choose between the invariable form **che** or the variable form **il quale.**

- ✔ Choose the word **che** when it's very clear to whom you're referring, as in **Ho visto Giovanna che andava in palestra** (*I saw Giovanna, who was going to the gym*).

- ✔ Choose the variable form **il quale** (or one of its forms) when you want to avoid ambiguity. If you say **Ho incontrato il figlio della signora Maria, che ti manda tanti saluti** (*I met Maria's son, who sends you his greetings*), in Italian nothing makes you really certain who sent you greetings, whether **Maria** or **il figlio.** But if you say **Ho incontrato il figlio della signora Maria, il quale ti manda saluti,** you know for sure that you're talking about **il figlio,** which is masculine singular, because **il quale** is masculine singular as well.

When you use a preposition with the relative pronoun because you want to convey an indirect object, you can choose between **cui** (plus article *or* plus preposition) or **quale** (plus preposition *and* article). When in English

- ✔ You use *of* or *about* before a relative pronoun, use **di + cui** in Italian, as in **Non possiamo fare la vacanza di cui ti ho parlato** (*We can't take the vacation which I spoke to you about*). (But remember that the formula **Non possiamo fare la vacanza della quale ti ho parlato** is perfectly correct and used all the time.)

✔ You use the pronoun *whose,* meaning that someone already mentioned possesses a certain trait, or that something already mentioned has a certain characteristic, in Italian use **il cui (la cui, i cui, le cui).** For example, **Ho visto una ragazza la cui bellezza mi ha colpito** (*I saw a girl whose beauty struck me*); **Abbiamo fatto una riunione il cui scopo non mi era chiaro** (*We had a meeting whose purpose wasn't clear to me*).

✔ You need any other preposition before the relative pronoun, you can use indifferently **cui** or **il quale.** You add only the preposition to **cui: con cui** (*with whom/which*), **da cui** (*by whom/which*), **su cui** (*on whom/which*); and you add a combined article to **quale: con il quale** (*with whom/which*), **dal quale** (*by whom/which*), **sul quale** (*on whom/which*). (For combined articles and the use of prepositions, consult Chapter 6.) For example, you can say **La persona sulla quale avevamo contato non ci può aiutare** or **La persona su cui avevamo contato non ci può aiutare** (*The person on whom we had counted can't help us*).

If you need a preposition with the relative pronoun (either **il quale** or **cui**) you may not skip it. However, with **cui** only, you may (but don't have to) skip the preposition **a** (*to*) or **per** (*for*) to indicate aim or purpose (not motion), and leave **cui** all by itself, as in **La faccenda cui ti riferisci è stata sistemata** (*The problem you're referring to has been solved*).

Join the following sentences using the appropriate relative pronouns. Use both the invariable or variable forms; at times, both will be correct. (***Tip:*** You need to place the relative pronoun after the word to which it refers, which means that you may have to change the word order of the new sentence, as I show in the example.)

Q. Ti ho parlato di quella persona. È arrivata.

A. **La persona di cui/della quale ti ho parlato è arrivata.** (*The person I was telling you about has arrived.*)

19. Ho fatto un sogno. Volavo sopra il Polo Nord.

_____

20. Il professore è famoso. Darà la conferenza.

_____

21. Ci siamo dimenticati di quei libri. Puoi portarli tu?

_____

22. Volevo regalare un CD di Pavarotti a quella amica. Ce l'ha già.

_____

23. Siamo passati dall'aeroporto di Oslo. È molto bello.

_____

24. Siamo passati da quell'aeroporto. Ci ha fatto perdere la coincidenza.

_____

Economy of speech: Combined pronouns

In addition to relative pronouns, Italian has combined relative pronouns. A combined pronoun is a single word that conveys two meanings: a demonstrative word (see Chapter 7) and a relative pronoun. For example, the pronoun **quanto** (*what, all that which*) contains both the demonstrative **quello** (*that*) **tutto quello** (*all that*) and the relative pronoun **che** (*which*). For example, **Farò quanto mi è possibile/Farò tutto quello che mi è possibile** (*I'll do what I can*).

You can use the combined or non-combined form of the relative pronouns — it's your choice. The combined forms are very convenient, just as the pronoun *what* is in English.

If you use a non-combined form, you can see that each of the two components of the pronoun plays a different function. Consider this example: **Non faccio favori a coloro che non lo meritano** (*I don't do favors to those who don't deserve them*). With the demonstrative component **a coloro** (*to those*), you convey aim or purpose; in fact, you need the preposition **a** (*to*). The relative component **che** (*who*) is the subject of the relative clause. And because in this case the demonstrative **coloro** is plural, the verb of the relative clause is plural, too.

If you collapse the two components in a combined form, you're also collapsing the two grammatical functions. So, in keeping with the preceding example, **a coloro che** becomes **a chi** (*those who*): The pronoun takes the preposition **a** to convey aim or purpose, but it's a singular pronoun, so you need the verb in the singular in the relative clause, as in **Non faccio favori a chi non lo merita** (*I don't do favors to those who don't deserve them*).

Remember that the combined pronouns can convey

✔ A direct object and a subject, as in **Lisa ringrazia chi le ha mandato i fiori/Lisa ringrazia coloro che le hanno mandato i fiori** (*Lisa thanks those who sent her flowers*) or **Lisa ringrazia colei/colui che le ha mandato i fiori** (*Lisa thanks the person who sent her flowers*). (Given the context at your disposal, the pronoun **chi** can refer to all the persons mentioned.)

✔ Two direct objects, as in **Invito quanti voglio** or **Invito tutti coloro che voglio** (*I'm inviting all those I want to invite*).

✔ An indirect object and a subject, as in **Siamo riconoscenti per quanto hanno fatto per noi** or **Siamo riconoscenti per quello che hanno fatto per noi** (*We're thankful for what they did for us*).

Table 8-5 presents the combined pronouns and their non-combined counterparts along with some examples.

Table 8-5	Combined Demonstrative + Relative Pronouns		
Combined Pronoun	**Demonstrative + Relative Pronoun**	*Translation*	*Example*
chi	**colui che** (MS), **colei che** (FS), **coloro che** (M/F)	*the one, those who*	**Chi è uscito per ultimo non ha chiuso la porta.** (*The person who went out last didn't lock the door.*)
quanto	**tutto quello che** (refers to situations only)	*what, all that which*	**Farò quanto mi è possibile.** (*I'll do what I can.*)
quanti, quante, quelli che, quelle che	**tutti coloro che** (MP), **tutte coloro che** (FP)	*all those who, people who*	**La festa è riservata a quanti hanno ricevuto l'invito.** (*The party is reserved for those who have received the invitation.*)

Rewrite the following sentences, replacing the demonstrative and relative pronouns with the appropriate double pronouns.

Q. Parleremo con coloro che verranno alla riunione.

A. **Parleremo con chi verrà alla riunione.** (*We'll speak with those who will come to the meeting.*)

25. Coloro che studiano sodo sono promossi.

_____

26. Ci sono quelli che credono ancora a Babbo Natale.

_____

27. Pagheremo quello che dobbiamo pagare.

_____

28. C'è molto di vero in quello che dici.

_____

29. Dalle a quelle che ne hanno più bisogno.

_____

Answer Key

1. **Avete studiato poco, infatti/perciò/dunque/quindi vi hanno bocciato all'esame.** (*You studied too little, so you flunked the exam.*)

2. **Hanno comprato l'automobile di una loro amica, quindi/perciò/allora non ne compreranno una nuova.** (*They bought the car of a friend of theirs, therefore they won't buy a new one.*)

3. **Non solo studia in Australia, ma/anzi/infatti pensa anche di trasferirsi là.** (*Not only does he/she study in Australia, but he's/she's thinking of moving there.*)

4. **O vai al cinema con Giulia o vai al ristorante con Maria.** (*Either you go to the movies with Giulia or you go to dinner with Maria.*)

5. **Vado a Parigi, tuttavia/però, non posso restare più di tre giorni.** (*I'm going to Paris, but I can't stay more than three days.*)

6. Da quando si sono trasferiti in campagna **non li vediamo più.** (*Since they moved to the country we no longer see them.*)

7. Tina ha venduto la casa **senza che suo padre lo sapesse.** (*Tina sold the house without her father knowing it.*)

8. Ho aderito alla proposta dell'avvocato **sebbene avessi molti dubbi.** (*I accepted the lawyer's proposal even though I had many doubts.*)

9. Prima che tu parta per Nuova Delhi **devo darti altre informazioni.** (*Before you leave for New Delhi, I should give you more information.*)

10. Quel vestito costa **più di quanto non pensassi.** (*That dress costs more than I thought.*)

11. Te lo dico **perché sei una persona fidata.** (*I'm telling you because you're a trustworthy person.*)

12. Volevamo sapere **perché non avete telefonato.** (*We wanted to know why you didn't call.*)

13. **Dopo aver parlato con Laura ho deciso di accettare quel lavoro.** (*After talking to Laura I decided to accept that job.*)

14. **Invece di prendere l'autobus ha preso la macchina.** (*Instead of taking the bus he/she took the car.*)

15. **È stato arrestato per non aver pagato le tasse.** (*He was arrested for not paying his taxes.*)

16. **Vi prego di fare silenzio.** (*Please, keep silent.*)

17. **A dire la verità, le cose non stanno come dici tu.** (*To tell the truth, things aren't as you say.*)

18. **Prima di sposarsi, Laura aveva una carriera brillante.** (*Before she got married, Laura had a brilliant career.*)

19. **Ho fatto un sogno in cui/nel quale volavo sopra il Polo Nord.** (*I had a dream in which I was flying over the North Pole.*)

20 **Il professore che darà la conferenza è famoso.** (*The professor who will give the lecture is famous.*)

21 **Puoi portare tu quei libri di cui ci siamo dimenticati?** (*Can you bring those books which we forgot?*)

22 **L'amica [a] cui/alla quake volevo regalare un CD di Pavarotti, ce l'ha già.** (*The friend to whom I wanted to give a Pavarotti CD already has it.*)

23 **Siamo passati dall'aeroporto di Oslo, che è molto bello.** (*We flew through the Oslo airport, which is beautiful.*)

24 **L'aeroporto da cui/dal quale siamo passati ci ha fatto perdere la coincidenza.** (*The airport we went through made us miss our connection.*)

25 **Chi studia sodo è promosso.** (*Those who study hard get promoted.*)

26 **C'è chi crede ancora a Babbo Natale.** (*There are still those who believe in Santa Claus.*)

27 **Pagheremo quanto dobbiamo pagare.** (*We'll pay what we must pay.*)

28 **C'è molto di vero in quanto dici.** (*There's a lot of truth in what you say.*)

29 **Dalle a chi ne ha più bisogno.** (*Give them to those who need them most.*)

Part III
What Would You Do without Verbs and Tenses?

"Passato remoto? Sounds like a Japanese channel changer."

In this part . . .

Here come the verbs! Verbs are the core of both English and Italian because they convey so much meaning. If you say *Go!,* that's all you need to express what you have in mind. Italian loves verbs, and to prove it, it has many more verb forms than English (check out the table of moods and tenses on the Cheat Sheet at the front of this book), and every verb varies greatly from person to person and tense to tense.

In this part, I explain how to distinguish the core of a verb (the stem) from the endings you add for each person in the various moods and tenses. I introduce conjugations, regular verbs, and a lot of irregular verbs (which you patiently have to learn by heart). I talk about the present and various ways to convey the past. I show you how to coordinate the past participle with the subject of the sentence or its object, when to use **essere** (*to be*) and **avere** (*to have*), where to place pronouns, and how to add verbs such as **potere** (*can*), **dovere** (*must*), and **volere** (*will*), which are called modal auxiliaries. Finally, I introduce the future tense, which is used in Italian more or less like in English.

Chapter 9

Writing in the Present

● ●

In This Chapter

▶ Conjugating regular and irregular verbs

▶ Managing the present progressive

▶ Dealing with the gerund, the infinitive, and personal pronouns

● ●

The present tense of the *indicative mood,* which allows you to convey statements of fact or describe feelings and emotions, allows you to talk about the present (obviously!) and the future (not so obviously). (I cover the future more in Chapter 12.) The present tense takes two forms in both Italian and English:

✔ The present (also called the *present simple*), which you use to describe situations, recurring actions, and habits:

> **Noi viviamo in Italia.** (*We live in Italy.*)
>
> **Io leggo il giornale ogni mattina.** (*I read the paper every morning.*)

✔ The present progressive, with which you talk about what's happening or what you're doing at a specific moment:

> **Lia sta parlando al telefono.** (*Lia is talking on the phone.*)

In this chapter, I show you how to form the present simple by adding endings to the verb (as you do in English when you add *-s* to the third-person singular). I also show how to form the present progressive, which you create by using the verb **stare** (*to stay, to be*) in the present and adding the main verb in the gerund. Finally, I talk about when to use the present or the present progressive and how to add verbs in the infinitive to modal auxiliaries such as **potere** (*can, may*) or **dovere** (*must, shall*). I also talk about verbs that have no subject and how to add pronouns to verbs in the infinitive and the gerund.

The Reliable Guys: Regular Verbs

Conjugated verbs are formed with a stem and an ending. The default form of the verb, which you find in dictionaries, is the *infinitive,* as in *to work.* In Italian, most infinitives end in **-are, -ere,** or **-ire.** When you take these endings out you are left with the stem of the verb. Here are the three options, illustrated by three regular verbs:

✔ **-are: guardare** (*to look at, to watch*)

✔ **-ere: temere** (*to fear*)

✔ **-ire: sentire** (*to hear*)

Regular verbs form the present by adding endings to the stem according to a fixed pattern, which changes depending on whether the verb ends in **-are, -ere,** or **-ire.** All you have to do is to figure out the conjugation pattern and apply it to each verb of that type. Table 9-1 shows you the regular verb endings. I follow that with a chart that shows sample conjugations of a regular verb.

Table 9-1	Endings for the Present Tense of the Indicative		
Person	*-are Verb Endings*	*-ere Verb Endings*	*-ire Verb Endings*
io	**-o**	**-o**	**-o**
tu	**-i**	**-i**	**-i**
lui/lei/Lei/esso	**-a**	**-e**	**-e**
noi	**-iamo**	**-iamo**	**-iamo**
voi	**-ate**	**-ite**	**-ite**
loro/Loro/essi/esse	**-ano**	**-ono**	**-ono**

The following table conjugates the present indicative of **guardare** (*to look at, to watch*).

guardare (*to look at, to watch*)	
io guard**o**	noi guard**iamo**
tu guard**i**	voi guard**ate**
lui/lei/Lei/esso guard**a**	loro/Loro/essi/esse guard**ano**
Guardiamo sempre la TV. (*We always watch TV.*)	

In order to preserve the hard sound of the infinitive, verbs ending in **-care** and **-gare,** such as **giocare** (*to play*) and **pagare** (*to pay*), add an **h** before the suffixes beginning with **-e** or **-i.** Verbs ending in **-iare,** such as **studiare** (*to study*) and **consigliare** (*to advise*), keep only one **i** when the ending begins with **i.** But those accented on the **i,** such as **sciare** (*to ski*), **inviare** (*to send*), and **spiare** (*to spy*), keep the **i** of the stem, which means that in some persons they have two.

Conjugate the verbs listed in parentheses to match the subject.

Q. io _____ (*giocare*)

A. io **gioco** (*I play*)

1. noi _____ (*arrivare*)

2. tu _____ (*leggere*)

3. tu _____ (*sciare*)

4. noi _____ (*dormire*)

5. tu _____ (*cadere*)

6. loro _____ (*insegnare*)

7. lei _____ (*consigliare*)

8. lui _____ (*partire*)

9. io _____ (*mangiare*)

10. noi _____ (*conoscere*)

Finding Surprises at Every Turn: Irregular Verbs

Verbs are classified regular or irregular depending on how they behave throughout their entire conjugation, in all moods and tenses. So the remarks that follow explain why a verb that may be regular in the present indicative — such as **vedere** (_to see_) — is considered irregular: It changes the stem in the simple past, from **ved-** to **vid-.** Verbs can be irregular in that they

- Change the stem in some persons within one tense: For example, **essere** (_to be_), becomes **io sono** (_I am_), **noi siamo** (_we are_).

- Use one stem in one tense and a different stem in another one: For example, the present indicative of **vivere** is regular, but its simple past (see Chapter 10) is irregular, changing the stem from **viv-** to **vis-** in some persons.

- Take endings different from the regular ones: For example, the simple past of **cadere** (_to fall_) is **io caddi** (_I fell_) rather than **cadei,** which is the form regular verbs take in the first-person singular.

Auxiliary verbs and modal auxiliaries

Auxiliary verbs do what the adjective says: They help the main verb. The key auxiliary verbs in Italian and English are **essere** (_to be_) and **avere** (_to have_), which people use to construct compound tenses, as in **Noi eravamo andati** (_We had gone_).

Modal verbs, which provide different nuances to what you're saying, also act as auxiliaries; they're followed by the infinitive of the main verb. The modals include **dovere** (_must, shall_), **potere** (_can, may_), and **volere** (_will, to want to_). Italian also uses **sapere** as a modal auxiliary, meaning _to know how to._

Using essere (to be) and avere (to have)

The following tables show the conjugation of the verbs **essere** and **avere**.

essere (_to be_)	
io **sono**	noi **siamo**
tu **sei**	voi **siete**
lui/lei/Lei/esso/essa **è**	loro/Loro/essi/esse **sono**
Sono stanca. (_I'm tired._)	

avere (_to have_)	
io **ho**	noi **abbiamo**
tu **hai**	voi **avete**
lui/lei/Lei/esso/essa **ha**	loro/Loro/essi/esse **hanno**
Abbiamo tre bambole. (_We have three dolls._)	

Expressing mood with modal auxiliaries

Like their English counterparts, **dovere** (*must, shall*), **potere** (*can, may*), and **volere** (*will, to want to*) are *modal auxiliaries,* which are usually followed by another verb in the infinitive. **Sapere** (*to know how to*) can be used in the same way as the other modals.

The meanings of **dovere** and **potere** are close to those of their English counterparts, with the following exceptions:

- ✔ **Dovere** also translates *to have to,* as in **Devo parlargli** (*I have to talk to him*). And you can use **dovere** by itself, meaning *I owe:* **Le devo la mia gratitudine** (*I owe her my gratitude*).

- ✔ **Potere** means both *can* and *may.* For example: **Posso entrare?** (*May I come in?*) or **Puoi fare tu la spesa?** (*Can you do the shopping?*). When you use *can* in English to convey that you need to overcome an obstacle to do something, Italian uses **potere** (*can*) or **riuscire a** (*to succeed*), as in these examples: **Riesci a passare/Puoi passare dal salumiere?** (*Can you stop by the deli?*) and **Ugo riesce a riparare la TV?** (*Will Ugo be able to repair the TV set?*).

- ✔ **Volere** can be translated literally as *will,* as in *he does as he wills.* But in English, *will* is used to convey the future, which you convey in Italian by adding specific endings to the main verb (see Chapter 12). Italian **volere** corresponds to *to want to* followed by an infinitive, as in **Voglio parlare con lei** (*I do want to talk to her*).

The following tables show conjugations of each of the modal auxiliary verbs.

dovere (*must, shall*)	
io **devo**	noi **dobbiamo**
tu **devi**	voi **dovete**
lui/lei/Lei/esso/essa **deve**	loro/Loro/essi/esse **devono**
Devono andare a casa. (*They must go home.*)	

potere (*can, may*)	
io **posso**	noi **possiamo**
tu **puoi**	voi **potete**
lui/lei/Lei/esso/essa **può**	loro/Loro/essi/esse **possono**
Può giocare con noi. (*He/she can play with us.*)	

volere (*will, want, wish*)	
io **voglio**	noi **vogliamo**
tu **vuoi**	voi **volete**
lui/lei/Lei/esso/essa **vuole**	loro/Loro/essi/esse **vogliono**
Vogliono vederti. (*They want to see you.*)	

sapere (*to know how to*)	
io **so**	noi **sappiamo**
tu **sai**	voi **sapete**
lui/lei/Lei/esso/essa **sa**	loro/Loro/essi/esse **sanno**
Sai giocare a scacchi? (*Do you know how to play chess?*)	

Replace the words underlined in each sentence with the appropriate form. Choose from these auxiliary and modal auxiliary verbs: **avere, essere, dovere, potere, sapere, volere.**

Q. Luciano <u>rimane</u> _____ l'unico che va a trovare la nonna.

A. Luciano **è** l'unico che va a trovare la nonna. (*Luciano is the only one who visits Grandma.*)

11. Federico <u>possiede</u> _____ più case di Angelo.

12. Lei <u>ha tutte le conoscenze necessarie per</u> _____ riparare la televisione.

13. Bianca <u>ha il permesso di</u> _____ andare in India.

14. <u>Sono obbligati a</u> _____ denunciare quel funzionario corrotto.

15. <u>Ti fa piacere</u> _____ andare a cena con me?

Irregular verbs of the first conjugation: -are

Andare (*to go*), **dare** (*to give*), **fare** (*to do, to make*), and **stare** (*to stay, to be*) are the only irregular verbs of this first conjugation, but they're quite important. The following tables show you the conjugations of all four verbs.

andare (*to go*)	
io **vado**	noi **andiamo**
tu **vai**	voi **andate**
lui/lei/Lei/esso/essa **va**	loro/Loro/essi/esse **vanno**
Andiamo sempre nello stesso ristorante. (*We always go to the same restaurant.*)	

dare (*to give*)	
io **do**	noi **diamo**
tu **dai**	voi **date**
lui/lei/Lei/esso/essa **dà** (always accented)	loro/Loro/essi/esse **danno**
Gli **dà** un libro. (*He/she gives him a book.*)	

fare *(to do, to make)*	
io **faccio**	noi **facciamo**
tu **fai**	voi **fate**
lui/lei/Lei/esso/essa **fa**	loro/Loro/essi/esse **fanno**
Faccio una torta. (*I'm making a cake.*)	

stare *(to stay, to be)*	
io **sto**	noi **stiamo**
tu **stai**	voi **state**
lui/lei/Lei/esso/essa **sta**	loro/Loro/essi/esse **stanno**
Stiamo bene. (*We're well.*)	

Add the appropriate verbal form, choosing among **andare, dare, fare,** and **stare.**

Q. Tu _____ male?

A. Tu **stai** male? (*Are you not feeling well?*)

16. _____ noi qualcosa da mangiare al gatto.

17. _____ tu all'ufficio postale?

18. I miei genitori _____ bene.

19. Aldo _____ in panetteria.

20. I miei amici _____ una partita a carte.

Irregular verbs of the second conjugation: -ere

Most irregular verbs belong to the second conjugation, so it's impossible to list them all here. What I give you is patterns of change so that if you know that **cogliere** changes the stem to **colgo-** in the first-person singular of the present indicative, you can try your best guess with **togliere** and see whether it does the same (it does).

Among verbs ending in **-cere,** some you use all the time are irregular. They include **piacere** (*to please,* but it corresponds in meaning to *to like*), **dispiacere** (*to be sorry*), **tacere** (*to be silent*), and **giacere** (*to lie down*). For these verbs, you double the **c** in the first-person singular and the first- and third-person plural. ***Note:* Piacere** is used primarily in third-person singular and plural forms.

piacere (*to be pleasing*)	
io pia**ccio**	noi pia**cciamo**
tu pia**ci**	voi pia**cete**
lui/lei/Lei/esso/essa pia**ce**	loro/Loro/essi/esse pia**cciono**
Mi **piacciono** le pesche. (*I like peaches.*)	

Bere (*to drink*) and **sedere/sedersi** (*to sit*) are even more irregular. **Bere** changes the stem to **bev-** in all persons.

bere (*to drink*)	
io **bevo**	noi **beviamo**
tu **bevi**	voi **bevete**
lui/lei/Lei/esso/essa **beve**	loro/Loro/essi/esse **bevono**
Bevono solo acqua. (*They drink only water.*)	

Sedere/sedersi uses the stem **sied-** in all persons except the first- and second-person plural. **Sedersi** is a reflexive verb, so I've included the reflexive pronouns in parentheses. (I illustrate how to form and use reflexive verbs in Chapter 17.)

sedere/sedersi (*to sit down*)	
io (mi) **siedo**	noi (ci) **sediamo**
tu (ti) **siedi**	voi (vi) **sedete**
lui/lei/Lei/esso/essa (si) **siede**	loro/Loro/essi/esse (si) **siedono**
Anna **siede** a capotavola. (*Anna sits at the head of the table.*)	

Rimanere (*to remain*) changes the stem in the first-person singular and the third-person plural, which drops the **-ere** and becomes **rimang-**. Verbs that behave like **rimanere** include **dolere** (*to hurt, to feel sorry*) and **valere** (*to be worth*).

rimanere (*to remain*)	
io **rimango**	noi **rimaniamo**
tu **rimani**	voi **rimanete**
lui/lei/Lei/esso/essa **rimane**	loro/Loro/essi/esse **rimangono**
Rimanete a Pairigi? (*Will you remain in Paris?*)	

The verb **tenere** (*to keep*) changes the stem to **teng-** in the first-person singular and third-person plural and to **tien-** in the second- and third-person singular. All verbs formed by adding prefixes to **tenere** do the same, including **appartenere** (*to belong*), **mantenere** (*to maintain*), **ottenere** (*to obtain*), and **ritenere** (*to think*).

tenere (*to keep*)	
io **tengo**	noi **teniamo**
tu **tieni**	voi **tenete**
lui/lei/Lei/esso/essa **tiene**	loro/Loro/essi/esse **tengono**
Tengono i nostri documenti. (*They keep our documents.*)	

Spegnere (*to turn off*) also takes the form **spengere**, transposing the **g** and **n**. The first-person singular and plural come from **spengere,** and the other persons come from **spegnere.**

spengere/spegnere (*to turn off*)	
io **spengo**	noi **spegniamo**
tu **spegni**	voi **spegnete**
lui **spegne**	loro **spengono**
Spegniamo la luce. (*We turn the light off.*)	

Some verbs change **gl** to **lg** for the stem of the first-person singular and the third-person plural. For example, the stem of **scegliere** (*to choose*) becomes **scelg-** for those persons, but it otherwise uses the standard **scegl-** stem you get from cutting the ending off the infinitive. The verbs **cogliere** (*to pick*) and **togliere** (*to take out*) behave the same way.

scegliere (*to choose*)	
io **scelgo**	noi **scegliamo**
tu **scegli**	voi **scegliete**
lui/lei/Lei/esso/essa **sceglie**	loro/Loro/essi/esse **scelgono**
Scegliamo la tua proposta. (*We choose your proposal.*)	

Irregular verbs of the third conjugation: -ire

The third conjugation in **-ire** has fewer irregular verbs. I illustrate some basic patterns in this section.

Salire (*to get on, to go up*) changes the stem to **salg-** in the first-person singular and the third-person plural.

salire (*to get on, to go up*)	
io **salgo**	noi **saliamo**
tu **sali**	voi **salite**
lui/lei/Lei/esso/essa **sale**	loro/Loro/essi/esse **salgono**
Salgono sull'autobus. (*They're getting on the bus.*)	

A lot of verbs in ending **-ire** add **-isc-** to the stem in the first- and third-person singular and the third-person plural before adding the regular endings. The following table shows the conjugation of **agire** (*to act, to behave*) as an example.

agire (*to act, to behave*)	
io **agisco**	noi **agiamo**
tu **agisci**	voi **agite**
lui/lei/Lei/esso/essa **agisce**	loro/Loro/essi/esse **agiscono**
Anna **agisce** onestamente. (*Anna behaves honestly.*)	

Here are some other common verbs included in this group. Consult a dictionary if you find a verb you don't know and you think it may behave like these.

- **capire** (*to understand*)
- **colpire** (*to hit, to strike*)
- **costruire** (*to build*)
- **finire** (*to end, to finish*)

- **guarire** (*to recover, to heal*)
- **gestire** (*to manage*)
- **preferire** (*to prefer*)
- **restituire** (*to return*)

- **spedire** (*to send, to mail*)
- **tossire** (*to cough*)
- **tradire** (*to betray*)
- **unire** (*to unite*)

Apparire (*to appear*) doesn't add **-isc-,** but it does drop the **r** and adds an **-i-** in the first-person singular and the third-person plural: io **appaio**, tu **appari**, lui/lei/Lei/esso/essa **appare**, noi **appariamo**, voi **apparite**, loro/Loro/essi/esse **appaiono. Riapparire** (*to reappear*) and **scomparire** (*to disappear*) follow the same pattern.

Even more irregular are the verbs **dire** (*to say, to tell*), **morire** (*to die*), **uscire** (*to go out*), and **venire.** Consult a dictionary or *Italian Verbs For Dummies,* by Teresa L. Picarazzi (Wiley), for the conjugations.

Modify the verbs listed in parentheses to match the subjects.

Q. lei _____ (chiarire)

A. lei **chiarisce** (*she clarifies*)

21. lui _____ (colpire)

22. noi _____ (agire)

23. io _____ (preferire)

24. voi _____ (conoscere)

25. loro _____ (proibire)

26. tu _____ (gestire)

27. noi _____ (dormire)

More irregular verbs: Those that end in -arre, -urre, and -orre

Some Italian verbs don't exhibit regular endings in the infinitive. These verbs end in **-arre**, **-urre**, or **-orre**.

Verbs ending in **-arre**, such as **trarre** (*to draw*), change those ending letters to **-agg-** in the first-person singular and the third-person plural. They behave as if they were regular verbs in **-are** in the second-person singular and first- and second-person plural. Other verbs that follow this pattern include **attrarre** (*to attract*), **contrarre** (*to contract, to narrow*), and **distrarre** (*to distract*).

trarre (*to draw*)	
io **traggo**	noi **traiamo**
tu **trai**	voi **traete**
lui/lei/Lei/esso/essa **trae**	loro/Loro/essi/esse **traggono**
Traggono le loro conclusioni. (*They're drawing their own conclusions.*)	

Verbs ending in **-orre**, such as **porre** (*to put*), add **-ong-** to the stem in the first-person singular and third-person plural. They take **pon-** in the second-person singular and the first- and second-person plural.

porre (*to put, to suppose*)	
io **pongo**	noi **poniamo**
tu **poni**	voi **ponete**
lui/lei/Lei/esso/essa **pone**	loro/Loro/essi/esse **pongono**
Pongono la prima pietra. (*They're laying the foundation stone.*)	

The following verbs end in **-orre** and behave like **porre**:

- **deporre** (*to depose*)
- **imporre** (*to impose*)
- **opporre** (*to oppose*)
- **proporre** (*to propose*)
- **supporre** (*to suppose*)

And verbs ending in **-urre**, such as **produrre** (*to produce*), add **-uc-** to the stem before adding the standard endings.

produrre (*to produce*)	
io **produco**	noi **produciamo**
tu **produci**	voi **producete**
lui/lei/Lei/esso/essa **produce**	loro/Loro/essi/esse **producono**
L'Italia **produce** molto vino. (*Italy produces a lot of wine.*)	

The following verbs behave like **produrre:**

- **condurre** (*to conduct*)
- **introdurre** (*to introduce*)
- **ridurre** (*to reduce*)
- **sedurre** (*to seduce*)

Having to Do without a Subject: Impersonal Verbs

You can have people doing things, or you can have things happening without anyone in particular doing them. Italian has several verbs called *impersonal verbs* that need no subject. In English, if you use a verb in the third-person singular, it takes *it* as its subject.

You use these impersonal verbs only in the third-person singular in finite forms such as the present indicative or the past simple, and you use them in the infinitive, the past participle, and the gerund. Several verbs regarding the weather are impersonal, including the following common ones:

- **lampeggiare** (*to flash [lightning]*) → **lampeggia** (*there's lightning*)
- **nevicare** (*to snow*) → **nevica** (*it snows*)
- **piovere** (*to rain*) → **piove** (*it rains*)
- **tirare vento** (*to be windy*) → **tira vento** (*it's windy*)
- **tuonare** (*to thunder*) → **tuona** (*it thunders*)

Other weather-related verbs are formed with **fare** (*to do*) + an adjective or noun, such as:

- **fare freddo** (*to be cold*) → **fa freddo** (*it's cold*)
- **fare caldo** (*to be hot*) → **fa caldo** (*it's hot*)

Here are some other impersonal verbs that have nothing to do with the weather but are used often:

- **bisognare** (*need, to have to*) → **bisogna,** as in **Bisogna partire.** (*It's necessary to leave.*)
- **bastare** (*to be sufficient*) → **basta,** as in **Basta parlarle.** (*It's sufficient to talk to her.*)
- **cominciare** (*to begin*), → **comincia,** as in **Comincia a piovere.** (*It's beginning to rain.*)
- **importare** (*to matter*) → **importa,** as in **Importa che cosa pensano loro.** (*It matters what they think.*)

  Don't confuse the two meanings of **importare,** *to matter* and *to import,* as in **Importano mele dal Giappone** (*They import apples from Japan*).

- **sembrare** (*to seem*) conjugates to **sembra,** as in **Mi sembra giusto.** (*It seems right to me.*)

You can use **essere** followed by an adjective, an adverb, or a noun, as an impersonal verb, as in **È ora di andare** (*It's time to go*). In English, it's similar to saying *It's beautiful/important/a shame*.

Out of the list of impersonal verbs, **bastare, cominciare, importare** (*to matter*), and **sembrare** can be used either impersonally or personally, as in the following examples:

> **Le mele bastano.** (*The apples we have are sufficient.*)
>
> **Cominciamo il lavoro domani.** (*We'll start our job tomorrow.*)
>
> **Le loro opinioni importano molto.** (*Their opinions matter a lot.*)
>
> **Sembrano contenti.** (*They seem happy.*)

What's Happening Right Now: The Present Progressive Tense

In Italian, you can convey that you're in the midst of doing something with the present simple *or* with the present progressive. For instance, if someone asks you **Che cosa stai facendo?** (*What are you doing?*), you can answer **Sto lavando la macchina** (*I'm washing the car*) or **Lavo la macchina** (*I wash the car*). Both are equally correct and idiomatic. But you should use the present progressive when you want to emphasize what's happening in that specific moment: **Abbassa la TV. Non vedi che sto parlando al telefono?** (*Turn down the TV. Don't you see I'm speaking on the phone?*); **Sta cominciando a piovere** (*It's beginning to rain*).

In Italian, you use only the present simple, not the present progressive, with **essere** (*to be*) or **stare** (*to stay, to be*) to talk about conditions in general, as in **Pietro è gentile con te** (*Pietro is being nice to you*); **Indossa un vestito blu** (*She's wearing a blue dress*).

You form the present progressive by adding the gerund to the verb **stare,** as in **Stiamo mangiando** (*We're eating*). The gerund is invariable in gender and number, so you don't have to match it to any other word. To form it, you add **-ando** to the stem of an **-are** verb, or add **-endo** to the stem of an **-ere** or **-ire** verb. Table 9-2 illustrates the patterns for sample verbs of the three conjugations.

Table 9-2		Creating Gerunds	
Verb Type	**Infinitive**	**Gerund Ending**	**Gerund**
-are	**guardare** (*to look at, to watch*)	-ando	**guardando** (*looking*)
	andare (*to go*)		**andando** (*going*)
-ere	**temere** (*to fear*)	-endo	**temendo** (*fearing*)
	vedere (*to see*)		**vedendo** (*seeing*)
-ire	**sentire** (*to hear*)	-endo	**sentendo** (*hearing*)
	finire (*to finish*)		**finendo** (*finishing*)

Most verbs form the gerund regularly. Even those ending in **-ire,** which add **-isc-** to some persons, follow a regular pattern. For instance, you form the gerund as **finendo** (*finishing*), from the infinitive **finire** (*to finish*).

Most of the verbs that form the gerund irregularly are verbs that add some letters to the stem, such as **bere** (*to drink*), which becomes **bev-** and has the gerund **bevendo** (*drinking*). The main irregular verbs follow; I give the infinitive first followed by the gerund:

- ✔ **condurre** (*to lead*) → **conducendo** (*leading*)
- ✔ **bere** (*to drink*) → **bevendo** (*drinking*)
- ✔ **dire** (*to say*) → **dicendo** (*saying*)
- ✔ **fare** (*to do*) → **facendo** (*doing*)
- ✔ **porre** (*to lay*) → **ponendo** (*laying*)
- ✔ **produrre** (*to produce*) → **producendo** (*producing*)
- ✔ **trarre** (*to draw*) → **traendo** (*drawing*)

Fill in the gaps in the following sentences with the appropriate form of the verb suggested in parentheses.

0. A noi _____ spesso di incontrarci in centro. (capitare)

A. A noi **capita** spessso di incontrarci in centro. (*It often occurs to us to meet downtown.*)

28. _____ chiamare un tecnico per fare aggiustare la lavapiatti. (bisognare)

29. _____ a grandinare. (comininciare)

30. Guarda! _____. (nevicare)

31. In negozio _____ ad arrivare gli abiti della stagione autunnale. (incominciare)

32. Non _____ di andare al supermercato. (esserci bisogno)

33. Per arrivare all'aeroporto in tempo, _____ partire alle quattro del pomeriggio. (bastare)

34. _____ da ieri sera. (piovere)

Using Pronouns with Verbs in the Infinitive or the Gerund

With a verbal form composed of a modal auxiliary and a verb in the infinitive or a present progressive (with the gerund), *and* with an unstressed pronoun that conveys either a direct object (such as **mi** [*me*] or **la** [*her*]) or an indirect object meaning *to* or *for* (such as **gli** [*to him*]; check Chapter 4 on pronouns for more information), you can place these pronouns in two different places without any change in meaning. It's only a matter of taste and style. Here are your options:

REMEMBER

- Place the pronoun before the modal auxiliary and before the present progressive form: **Lo posso fare** (*I can do it*); **Vi sto parlando** (*I'm talking to you*).

- Attach the pronoun to the verb in the infinitive or the verb in the gerund: **Posso farlo** (*I can do it*); **Sto parlandovi** (*I'm talking to you*).

  The infinitive drops the final **-e** to ease pronunciation, as in **Dobbiamo venderglielo** (*We must sell it to him/her*).

In Table 9-3, I list the personal pronouns you can place in those positions (but refer to Chapter 4 for a full list and for a review of their functions). For each pronoun type, the table shows both pronoun placements for an example sentence with a modal auxiliary and an example sentence in the present progressive. (The pronouns are underlined in the examples.) As you can see, when you have a modal auxiliary followed by an infinitive, you can place any unstressed pronoun before the verbal form, as in **Lo posso aiutare;** or attached to the infinitive, as in **Posso aiutarlo** (*I can help him*). When you have the present progressive, you can add any unstressed pronoun before the verbal form, as in **Lo sto aiutando;** or attached to the gerund, as in **Sto aiutandolo** (*I'm helping him*).

Table 9-3	Pronoun Placement with Modal Auxiliaries and the Present Progressive			
Type of Pronoun	*Pronouns*	*Pronoun Before Verb*	*Pronoun Attached to Verb*	*Translation*
Direct object pronouns	**mi, ti, lo/la, ci, vi, li/le** (*me, you, him/her, it, us, you, them*)	**Lo posso aiutare. La sto aiutando.**	**Posso aiutarlo. Sto aiutandola.**	*I can help him. I'm helping her.*
Indirect object pronouns	**mi, ti, gli, le, ci, vi, gli** (*to me, to you, to him, to her, to us, to you, to them*)	**Le voglio dire una cosa. Le sto raccontando una storia.**	**Voglio dirle una cosa. Sto raccontandole una storia.**	*I want to tell her something. I'm telling her a story.*
The pronouns ci and ne	**ci** (*here, there, about this, about that*); **ne** (*from here, from there, about this, about that, about him/her/them*)	**Ci stanno pensando. Ne posso parlare.**	**Stanno pensandoci. Posso parlarne.**	*They're thinking about it. I can talk about it.*
Double pronouns	**ve ne, me lo, te lo, ce le, gliene** (*about it to you, them to us, about it to him/her*)	**Non ve ne posso parlare. Me lo stanno portando.**	**Non posso parlarvene. Stanno portandomelo.**	*I can't talk to you about it. They're bringing it to me.*

In the following sentences, attach the appropriate pronoun or the adverbial particle **ci** to the infinitive or the gerund, and rewrite the sentence.

Q. Umberto le vuole regalare *un paio di* orecchini.

A. Umberto vuole **regalarle** un paio di orecchini. (*Umberto wants to give her a pair of earrings.*)

35. Ci possono imprestare la loro macchina.

_____

36. Gli dobbiamo restituire i soldi.

_____

37. "Insomma, chi viene alla festa? Me lo volete dire?!"

_____

38. Li dovete pagare?

_____

39. "Puoi comprare tre CD?" "Ne posso comprare due."

_____

40. "State andando dal macellaio?" "Ci stiamo andando."

_____

Answer Key

1 noi **arriviamo** (*we arrive*)

2 tu **leggi** (*you read*)

3 tu **scii** (*you ski*)

4 noi **dormiano** (*we sleep*)

5 io **cado** (*you fall*)

6 loro **insegnano** (*they teach*)

7 lei **consiglia** (*she advises*)

8 lui **parte** (*he leaves*)

9 io **mangio** (*I eat*)

10 noi **conosciamo** (*we know*)

11 Federico **ha** più case di Angelo. (*Federico has more houses than Angelo.*)

12 Lei **sa** riparare la televisione. (*She knows how to repair the TV set.*)

13 Bianca **può** andare in India. (*Bianca can go to India.*)

14 **Devono** denunciare quel funzionario corrotto. (*They must turn in that corrupt officer.*)

15 **Vuoi** andare a cena con me? (*Do you want to go to dinner with me?*)

16 **Diamo** noi qualcosa da mangiare al gatto. (*We'll feed the cat.*)

17 **Vai** tu all'ufficio postale? (*Are you going to the post office?*)

18 I miei genitori **stanno** bene. (*My parents aren't well.*)

19 Aldo **va** in panetteria. (*Aldo is going to the bakery.*)

20 I miei amici **fanno** una partita a carte. (*My friends are playing a card game.*)

21 lui **colpisce** (*he hits*)

22 noi **agiamo** (*we act*)

23 io **preferisco** (*I prefer*)

24 voi **conoscete** (*you know*)

25 loro **proibiscono** (*they prohibit*)

26   tu **gestisci** (*you manage*)

27   noi **dormiamo** (*we sleep*)

28   **Bisogna** chiamare un tecnico per fare aggiustare la lavapiatti. (*We need to call a technician to have the dishwasher fixed.*)

29   **Comincia/Sta cominciando** a grandinare. (*It's starting to hail.*)

30   Guarda! **Nevica./Sta nevicando.** (*Look! It's snowing.*)

31   In negozio **incominciano** ad arrivare gli abiti della stagione autunnale. (*The fall season clothes are starting to arrive in the store.*)

32   Non **c'è bisogno** di andare al supermercato. (*There's no need to go to the supermarket.*)

33   Per arrivare all'aeroporto in tempo, **basta** partire alle quattro del pomeriggio. (*To get to the airport in time, it's sufficient to leave at 4 p.m.*)

34   **Piove** da ieri sera. (*It has been raining since last night.*)

35   Possono **imprestarci** la loro macchina. (*They can lend us their car.*)

36   Dobbiamo **restituirgli** i soldi. (*We must give him back the money.*)

37   "Isomma, chi viene alla festa? Volete **dirmelo**?!" (*"So, who's coming to the party? Would you tell me?"*)

38   Dovete **pagarli?** (*Do you have to talk to him?*)

39   "Puoi comprare tre dischi?" "Posso **comprarne** due." (*"Can you buy two CDs? "I can buy two [of them]."*)

40   "State andando dal macellaio?" "Stiamo **andandoci**." (*"Are you going to the butcher?" "We're going there."*)

Chapter 10

Glancing Back at the Past: The Present Perfect and Preterit

. . . .

In This Chapter

▶ Forming past participles

▶ Choosing the right auxiliary

▶ Making sure the past participle coordinates with the subject or object

▶ Using the present perfect with modal auxiliaries

▶ Recognizing the preterit

. . . .

*W*hen you talk or write about the past in English you mostly use the simple past. You say *I went home* no matter whether you went home two minutes ago or two months ago. In Italian, you mostly use the *present perfect,* or **passato prossimo** (literally, *near past*). For example, **Sono andata a casa** (*I went home*). Italian has two other forms that you translate in English with the simple past: the **imperfetto** (*imperfect*) and the **preterit** (known by Italians as the **passato remoto**). In this chapter I focus on the present perfect, which is the most common form of the past tense and at the end of the chapter I talk about the preterit, which is used primarily in historical narratives and fairy tales. In Chapter 11 I cover the imperfect tense.

The present perfect tense is a *compound tense* because it comprises an auxiliary and the verb that conveys the action you're talking about. In Italian the present perfect is made of the present indicative of either **avere** (*to have*) or **essere** (*to be*) and the past participle of the main verb, as in **Ho mangiato il gelato** (*I ate the ice cream*).

In order to form the present perfect of a particular verb, you need to follow these steps:

1. Choose between **essere** (*to be*) and **avere** (*to have*) as the auxiliary verb.

2. Modify the verb's infinitive in order to turn it into a past participle.

3. Choose the ending of the past participle, which may take the default form in **-o** or may need to be coordinated with the subject or the object of the sentence.

Later in this chapter, I explain how you can add a modal auxiliary (*can, may, shall, must, will*) to a verbal form in the present perfect, as in **Ho potuto vederlo** (*I was able to see him/I could see him*).

Step 1: Turning a Verb into a Past Participle

Words such as **amato** (*loved*), **andato** (*gone*), **tenuto** (*kept*), **visto** (*seen*), and **studiato** (*studied*) are past participles. They're forms of the verbs used in several compound tenses (for a complete list, see the table about moods and tenses on the Cheat Sheet). In Italian, past participles behave like adjectives (see Chapter 5), varying in gender and number, because in most cases they must be coordinated with the words they refer to.

I deal with coordination between past participle and subject or object of the sentence in the section, "Step 3: Coordinating the Past Participle with the Subject or Object," later in this chapter. I start with telling you how to form past participles.

Forming the past participle of regular verbs

In Chapter 9 I talk about regular and irregular verbs, and I warn you that a verb may be regular in the present tense and irregular in another tense, such as the preterit. When it comes to the past participle, most verbs, even those that are irregular in other tenses, form the past participle according to the rules I spell out in this section. Table 10-1 starts you off with regular verbs.

Table 10-1	Forming the Past Participles of Regular Verbs		
Infinitive	*Singular Past Participle (M, F)*	*Plural Past Participle (M, F)*	*Translation*
guardare (*to look at, to watch*)	guard**ato**, guard**ata**	guard**ati**, guard**ate**	*looked at, watched*
temere (*to fear*)	tem**uto**, tem**uta**	tem**uti**, tem**ute**	*feared*
sentire (*to hear*)	sent**ito**, sent**ita**	sent**iti**, sent**ite**	*heard*

The verb **fare** only keeps the **f-** of the infinitive and doubles the **-t-** to become **fatto, fatta, fatti, fatte**; **dare** keeps the **d-** and becomes **dato, data, dati, date**.

Verbs of the second conjugation in **-cere** and **-scere** add an **-i** before the suffixes of the past participle in order to preserve the soft sound of the infinitive. For example, **conoscere** (*to know*) → **conosciuto, conosciuta, conosciuti, conosciute** (*known*).

Forming the past participle of irregular verbs

Even with irregular verbs, the endings of the past participles never change. What changes is the stem of the verb, which in most cases loses some letters — really, it contracts. Remember that verbs formed by adding prefixes to the main verb take the same ending as the basic verb when it comes to the past participle. So **rompere** (*to break*) → **rotto** (*broken*), and **corrompere** (*to corrupt*) → **corrotto** (*corrupted*).

Irregular verbs of the second conjugation

You find many irregular verbs in the second conjugation in **-ere**. Most of them form the past participle by contracting the infinitive before adding the endings. For example, **rimanere** (*to remain*) drops **-nere** and becomes **rimasto, rimasta, rimasti, rimaste; dipingere** (*to paint*) drops the **-gere** and becomes **dipinto.** Because patterns are erratic to say the least, my suggestion is this: Learn them by heart as you encounter them, and check a dictionary when you want to use a new verb. After all, that's what learners of English have to do with verbs such as *to go,* which becomes *gone* in the past participle.

Table 10-2 lists the most common irregular verbs ending in **-ere.**

Table 10-2	The Past Participle of Verbs Ending in -ere		
Infinitive	*Past Participle*	*Infinitive*	*Past Participle*
accendere (*to light, to turn on*)	**acceso** (*lighted, turned on*)	**nascere** (*to be born, to rise*)	**nato** (*born*)
appendere (*to hang*)	**appeso** (*hung*)	**nascondere** (*to hide*)	**nascosto** (*hid*)
bere (*to drink*)	**bevuto** (*drunk*)	**perdere** (*to lose*)	**perso** (*lost*)
chiedere (*to ask*)	**chiesto** (*asked*)	**piangere** (*to cry*)	**pianto** (*cried*)
chiudere (*to close*)	**chiuso** (*closed*)	**prendere** (*to take*)	**preso** (*taken*)
cogliere (*to pick*)	**colto** (*picked*)	**rispondere** (*to answer*)	**risposto** (*answered*)
correre (*to run*)	**corso** (*ran*)	**scegliere** (*to choose*)	**scelto** (*chose*)
cuocere (*to cook*)	**cotto** (*cooked*)	**scendere** (*to go down*)	**sceso** (*went down*)
discutere (*to discuss*)	**discusso** (*discussed*)	**scrivere** (*to write*)	**scritto** (*written*)
dissuadere (*to deter*)	**dissuaso** (*deterred*)	**sorgere** (*to rise*)	**sorto** (*rose*)
dividere (*to divide*)	**diviso** (*divided*)	**spegnere** (*to extinguish*)	**spento** (*extinguished*)
fingere (*to pretend*)	**finto** (*pretended*)	**spingere** (*to push*)	**spinto** (*pushed*)
giungere (*to arrive*)	**giunto** (*arrived*)	**togliere** (*to take out*)	**tolto** (*took out*)
leggere (*to read*)	**letto** (*read*)	**vedere** (*to see*)	**veduto, visto** (*seen*)
mettere (*to put*)	**messo** (*put*)	**vincere** (*to win*)	**vinto** (*won*)
muovere (*to move*)	**mosso** (*moved*)	**vivere** (*to live*)	**vissuto** (*lived*)

Irregular verbs of the third conjugation

A few verbs of the third conjugation in **-ire** are irregular. They behave similarly to the verbs of the second conjugation that drop pieces of the infinitive before adding the endings of the past participle. Table 10-3 lists the most important irregular **-ire** verbs.

Some verbs begin their lives with a contracted infinitive. Their past participles are erratic, so here comes one more short list for you to learn. The basic ones are **trarre** (*to draw*) → **tratto** (*drawn*); **porre** (*to put, to lay*) → **posto** (*put, laid*); and **produrre** (*to produce*) → **prodotto** (*produced*).

Table 10-3	Irregular Verbs Ending in -ire
Infinitive	*Past Participle*
apparire (*to appear*)	**apparso** (*appeared*)
aprire (*to open*)	**aperto** (*opened*)
dire (*to say*)	**detto** (*said*)
morire (*to die*)	**morto** (*died*)
offrire (*to offer*)	**offerto** (*offered*)
venire (*to come*)	**venuto** (*came*)

Form the past participle of the following verbs in the default masculine singular form.

Q. risorgere

A. **risorto** (*resurrected*)

1. apparire: _____

2. comporre: _____

3. congiungere: _____

4. convincere: _____

5. percorrere: _____

6. promuovere: _____

7. riprendere: _____

8. riprodurre: _____

9. ritrarre: _____

10. rivedere: _____

11. rinvenire: _____

Reconstruct the infinitive of the following past participles.

Q. distratti

A. **distrarre** (*to distract*)

12. aggiunte: _____

13. ammessa: _____

14. assolti: _____

15. bevuto: _____

16. concesse: _____

17. piaciuta: _____

18. cresciuti: _____

19. discusse: _____

20. disposto: _____

21. morse: _____

22. sorretta: _____

Step 2: Figuring Out Which Auxiliary to Use

When you want to form any compound tense that requires the past participle, you need to choose between the auxiliaries **avere** and **essere**. In order to make that choice, you have to know

- Whether the verb is active (**Io vado** [*I'm going*]), passive (**Il film è girato** [*The film is shot*]), or reflexive (**Io mi guardo** [*I'm looking at myself*]). Consult Chapter 17 for coverage of the passive and reflexive uses of verbs.

- Whether the verb is transitive (**Luigi ama Susanna** [*Luigi loves Susanna*]) or intransitive (**Bruno corre** [*Bruno runs/is running*]).

In this chapter, I only talk about the active form of transitive and intransitive verbs.

The distinction between transitive and intransitive verbs is clear-cut in Italian. When a verb can be followed directly by an object (called, in fact, the *direct object*), it's transitive, as in **Suono il pianoforte** (*I play the piano*). So *transitive* means that the verb's action is transferred to an object directly, without adding any other part of speech (in particular a preposition). When you have a preposition plus a person, the noun is an indirect object, which takes a transitive verb — for example, **Ho scritto a Mirko** (*I wrote to Mirko*). Intransitive verbs take a preposition, but the preposition is usually coupled with a place, as in **Vado in ufficio** (*I'm going to the office*).

I'm not saying that in real life you always find verbs followed by objects, direct or indirect. I'm saying that a transitive verb *can* be followed by a direct object, whereas an intransitive verb *cannot*. But you can use a transitive verb by itself, without expressing the object, as in **Le scrivo** (*I'm writing to her*). And you can use an intransitive verb by itself, for example when you say **Vengo** (*I'm coming*). But **scrivere** is transitive because you *can* add a direct object to it: **Le scrivo una cartolina** (*I'm writing her a postcard*); and **venire** isn't transitive because if you add an object, you do need a preposition: **Lui arriva da Mosca** (*He's coming from Moscow*). Any Italian dictionary will tell you whether the verb is transitive (**v. tr.**) or intransitive (**v. intr.**).

In English, the presence of a preposition isn't decisive when it comes to determining whether a verb is transitive or intransitive. If you say, *I've looked for you all day,* the verb *to look for* is transitive because the verb isn't *to look* but *to look for*. If you change the preposition from *for* to *at,* the meaning changes completely. And *to look* used by itself has a third meaning (and is an intransitive verb). Verb + preposition packages are called *phrasal verbs,* of which English has a lot and Italian only a few. So when you encounter a verb with a preposition, the presence of the preposition and a place is a good indicator that the verb is intransitive.

You need the auxiliary **avere** (*to have*) with the following verbs:

- **Avere,** which is transitive and regular in its past participle, **avuto** (*had*)

    Donatella ha avuto fortuna. (*Donatella has had good luck.*)

- Transitive verbs in the active form, such as **amare** (*to love*), **leggere** (*to read*), and **mandare** (*to send*)

    Ho cercato tuo fratello. (*I looked for your brother.*)

✔ A few intransitive verbs that convey an action performed by the subject (except verbs of motion), such as **dormire** (*to sleep*), **pranzare/cenare** (*to dine*), **parlare** (*to speak*), and **gridare** (*to shout*)

> **Ho dormito poco.** (*I slept very little.*)

You need the auxiliary **essere** (*to be*) with the following intransitive verbs:

✔ **Essere,** which becomes **stato, stata, stati, state** (*been*)

> **Sei stato in Cina?** (*Have you been to China?*)

✔ **Stare** (*to stay* and *to be* in set phrases such as **stare bene/male** [*to be well/ unwell*]), which takes the same past participle as **essere: stato, stata, stati, state** (*stayed, felt*)

> **Lucio è stato male.** (*Lucio was ill.*)

✔ Most verbs of motion, used literally or metaphorically

> **Siamo arrivati a Hong Kong.** (*We arrived at Hong Kong.*)

> **Il dollaro è sceso rispetto all'euro.** (*The dollar has fallen against the euro.*)

✔ Most intransitive verbs conveying a change of status in the subject, such as **invecchiare** (*to age*), **nascere** (*to be born*), **crescere** (*to grow up*), and **morire** (*to die*)

> **Mio padre è invecchiato molto.** (*My father has aged a lot.*)

✔ Reflexive verbs, such as **lavarsi** (*to wash oneself*) and **addormentarsi** (*to fall asleep*)

> **Mi sono svegliato.** (*I woke up.*)

> **Mi sono tagliato un dito.** (*I cut my finger.*)

✔ The passive voice, as in **essere amato** (*to be loved*) and **essere mangiato** (*to be eaten*)

> **La casa è stata venduta.** (*The house has been sold.*)

See Chapter 17 for more on the reflexive and passive constructions.

You can use either **avere** or **essere** with the following verbs:

✔ Those conveying weather conditions, such as **piovere** (*to rain*), **nevicare** (*to snow*), and **grandinare** (*to hail*). For example, **È/Ha piovuto** (*It rained*). You use them only in the third-person singular without any subject. (Check Chapter 9 for details.)

✔ Some verbs of motion, such as **correre** (*to run*), **passare** (*to spend [time], to go by*), **finire** (*to end, to finish*), and **volare** (*to fly*). These verbs take **essere** when you use them without a direct object and **avere** with a direct object. For example, **Sono corsi a casa** (*They ran home*); but **Hanno corso la Maratona di New York** (*They ran the New York Marathon*). Also included in this category is **cominciare** (*to begin*), which takes **essere** when you use it without any subject, as in **È cominciato a piovere** (*It started to rain*), and takes **avere** when it's used with a subject, as in **Abbiamo cominciato le vacanze** (*We began our vacation*).

The intransitive verb **vivere** (*to live, to reside*) can take both **avere** and **essere** without any change in meaning, as in **Hanno vissuto dieci anni a Barcellona/Sono vissuti dieci anni a Barcellona** (*They lived ten years in Barcelona*).

Using the words in parentheses, add the appropriate auxiliaries to the following sentences.

Q. Sono _____ dieci anni in Argentina. (vivere)

A. Sono **vissuti** dieci anni in Argentina. (*They lived ten years in Argentina.*)

23. Con chi _____ tu? (parlare)

24. Dopo quella gita, loro _____ dieci ore filate! (dormire)

25. I miei colleghi _____ in Marocco. (essere)

26. Mio figlio _____ di dieci centimetri in un anno! (crescere)

27. I miei figli _____ *Il signore degli anelli.* (vedere)

28. Voi _____ allo stadio? (andare)

Step 3: Coordinating the Past Participle with the Subject or Object

Since past participles have four endings, you have to decide what words to match them to, just like you do with adjectives. Here are three possibilities you may have:

✔ You choose the **-o** ending of the past participle when the auxiliary is **avere** followed by

- A transitive verb used by itself or followed by an expressed direct object; for example, **Mia sorella ha già mangiato** (*My sister has eaten*); **Mia sorella ha mangiato la carne** (*My sister has eaten the meat*).

- An intransitive verb that takes **avere,** including **correre** (*to run*), **vivere** (*to live*), and **agire** (*to behave*). For example, **Ida e Gianna non hanno dormito** (*Ida and Gianna didn't sleep*).

✔ You have to coordinate the past participle with the subject (see Chapter 2 on coordination), when the auxiliary is **essere** and

- The verb is intransitive (the action is performed by the subject and the verb stands alone or takes no direct object). For example, **Pietro e Gianni sono andati via** (*Pietro and Gianni left*).

- The verb is reflexive (the subject is also the recipient of the action). For example, **I due ragazzi si sono lavati** (*The two boys washed themselves*). (I cover the reflexive in depth in Chapter 17.)

- The verb is in the passive voice (the action is performed upon the subject by someone else). For example, **L'attrice è stata premiata con l'Oscar dalla giuria** (*The actress was awarded an Oscar by the jury*). (I cover the passive voice in Chapter 17.)

✔ You have to coordinate the past participle with the direct object of a sentence when the auxiliary is **avere** and the object precedes the verb, which happens when

- You use the direct object pronouns **mi, ti, lo, la, ci, vi, li, le** (*me, you, him, her, it, us, you, them*), which are placed before the verb. For example, **"Hai visto i miei fratelli?" "Sì, li ho visti andare via"** (*"Did you see my brothers?" "I saw them leave"*).

- You use the pronoun **ne** (*of this/that/these/those*), which refers to something already mentioned (see Chapter 4 for more information on pronouns and **ne** in particular). Because **ne** is invariable, you have to look for the word that it replaces in order to ascertain its gender and number. For example, **"Quanti libri hai letto?" "Ne ho letti sei"** (*"Did you read all those books?" "I read six of them"*).

Use the words in parentheses to add the appropriate past participles to the following sentences, matching them to the appropriate words if necessary.

Q. Abbiamo _____ bene in quel ristorante. (cenare)

A. Abbiamo **cenato** bene in quel ristorante. (*We dined well in that restaurant.*)

29. "Avete pagato le mele?" "Le abbiamo _____." (pagare)

30. "Avete trovato delle albicocche?" Non ne abbiamo _____." (trovare)

31. "Hai visto Elena?" "Non l'ho _____." (vedere)

32. I miei genitori sono _____ a Parigi per Pasqua. (essere)

33. Mirella è _____ molti anni in Australia. (vivere)

34. Mirella ha _____ a lungo da sola. (vivere)

35. Nell'incidente aereo sono _____ centocinquante persone. (morire)

Adding a Modal Auxiliary to a Verbal Form in the Present Perfect

In English, you can't form the present perfect of the modal auxiliaries *can, may, shall, must,* or *will.* In fact, you use substitutes (for other tenses as well): *to be able to* or *to have the possibility of* for *can* or *may; to have to* for *must* or *shall;* and *to want to* for *will.* You can form the present perfect and then add the verb that conveys the main action. That's what you do in Italian with the modal auxiliaries themselves: **dovere** (*must, shall*), **potere** (*can, may*), or **volere** (*will, to want, to wish*). You form the present perfect and add an infinitive. For example, **Ho potuto aiutare mio fratello** (*I was able to help my brother*). Of course, you still have to choose an auxiliary: Usually you adopt the one of the infinitive that follows. Therefore, you have three cases:

✔ If you use a modal auxiliary, for example **potere** (*can, to be able to*), and you want to form the present perfect followed by the verb **leggere,** which is transitive and takes **avere,** you say **Ho potuto leggere la tua lettera** (*I was able to/could read your letter*).

✔ If you use a modal auxiliary, for example **dovere** (*must, shall, to have to*), and you use it with the verb **camminare**, which is intransitive but takes **avere**, you say **Hanno dovuto camminare per tre ore** (*They had to walk for three hours*).

✔ If you use a modal auxiliary, for example **volere** (*to want to*), and you use it with the verb **tornare**, which is intransitive and takes **essere**, you say **Sono voluti tornare** (*They wanted to come back*).

You use the auxiliary **avere** when the modal auxiliary introduces the verb **essere** (*to be*). For example, **Ho potuto essere generoso** (*I've been able to/I could be generous*).

Based on the appointments listed on the following agenda, write sentences describing what you did between May 13 and May 20, 2007. Add the modal auxiliaries listed in parentheses to each of your sentences, and write all sentences in the present perfect tense. Because the sentences are in the first-person singular, you have to decide whether you're writing them as a man or a woman. I give you both options in the answer key.

0. Lunedì 4, 14:00 (dovere)

A. **Lunedì 14, alle 14, ho dovuto prenotare un appuntamento con il medico.** (*Monday 14, at 2 p.m., I had to make an appointment with the physician.*)

MAGGIO 2007			
giorno	data	ora	attività
lunedì	14	9:00	prenotare un appuntamento dal medico
martedì	15	18:00	andare in palestra
mercoledì	16	20:30	andare al cinema con Paola
giovedì	17	17:45	andare a yoga
venerdì	18	14:00	parlare del libro con il curatore
sabato	19	09:00	stampare la carta d'imbarco
domenica	20	07:00 10:00	svegliarsi alle 7 partire per Parigi con Michael

36. Martedì 15, 18:00 (potere)

_____

37. Mercoledì 16, 20:30 (volere)

_____

38. Giovedì 17, 17:45 (potere)

_____

39. Venerdì 18, 14:00 (dovere)

_____

40. Sabato 19, 9:00 (dovere)

_____

41. Domenica 20, 7:00 (dovere)

_____

42. Domenica 20, 10:00 (dovere)

_____

Writing and Reading about the Distant Past: The Preterit

The preterit tense (or, in Italian, the **passato remoto**), is used to express events that took place in the distant past and have no relationship with the present. It is used frequently in writing, especially in narratives. Nowadays, in spoken Italian, the tense used mostly to talk about the past is the present perfect, but in some central and southern regions of Italy people use the preterit. Here are two examples of the preterit in action:

> **Dante nacque nel 1265.** (_Dante was born in 1265._)
>
> **Manzoni scrisse I Promessi Sposi.** (_Manzoni wrote the Promessi Sposi._)

Even though the majority of Italians use the present perfect for talking and writing, the preterit is used in fairy tales, short stories, and novels as well as when describing historical events in nonfiction biographies, histories, and encyclopedia articles, so you do need to recognize it. Unfortunately, it's the most irregular of all verb forms in Italian.

The preterit of regular verbs

As with all regular verbs, the regulars of the preterit vary their endings depending on the verb's conjugation. I list them in Table 10-4, followed by an example for the three conjugations.

Table 10-4	Suffixes for Regular Verbs in the Preterit		
Person	*Suffix for -are Verbs*	*Suffix for -ere Verbs*	*Suffix for -ire Verbs*
io	**-ai**	**-ei** (or **-etti**)	**-ii**
tu	**-asti**	**-esti**	**-isti**
lui/lei/Lei/esso/essa	**-ò**	**-é** (or **-ette**)	**-ì**
noi	**-ammo**	**-emmo**	**-immo**
voi	**-aste**	**-este**	**-iste**
loro/Loro/essi/esse	**-arono**	**-erono** (or **-ettero**)	**-irono**

Note that several **-ere** verbs have two alternative forms in the first- and third-person singular and third person plural.

The following tables show you how to conjugate the preterit of the regular verbs **guardare** (*to look at, to watch*), **temere** (*to fear*), and **sentire** (*to hear*).

guardare (*to look at, to watch*)	
io guard**ai**	noi guard**ammo**
tu guard**asti**	voi guard**aste**
lui/lei/Lei/esso/essa guard**ò**	loro/Loro/essi/esse guard**arono**
Guardarono il Titanic che affondava. (*They wached the Titanic sink.*)	

temere (*to fear*)	
io tem**ei** (or tem**etti**)	noi tem**emmo**
tu tem**esti**	voi tem**este**
lui/lei/Lei/esso/essa tem**é** (or tem**ette**)	loro/Loro/essi/esse tem**erono** (tem**ettero**)
Tememmo il peggio. (*We feared the worst.*)	

sentire (*to hear*)	
io sent**ii**	noi sent**immo**
tu sent**isti**	voi sent**iste**
lui/lei/Lei/esso/essa sent**ì**	loro/Loro/essi/esse sent**irono**
La giovane donna **sentì** il gallo cantare. (*The young woman heard the rooster sing.*)	

Complete each sentence with the verb in the preterit; use the verb provided in parentheses, which conjugates regularly in the preterit. For verbs in which the person has more than one possible conjugation, use the more common version.

Q. Noi _____ a lungo. (dormire)

A. Noi **dormimmo** a lungo. (*We slept a lot.*)

43. Tu _____ a scuola. (andare)

44. Voi _____ per la Polonia. (partire)

45. Mia sorella _____ di perdere il bambino. (temere)

46. Suo marito _____ il garage. (pulire)

47. Tu ed io _____ la sua posizione. (capire)

The preterit of irregular verbs

Many irregular verbs have only the first-person singular and the third-person singular and plural irregular (1, 3, 3, pattern). The **tu, noi,** and **voi** form are regular; for example, the verbs **scrivere** (*to write*), **piacere** (*to like*), **mettere** (*to put*), **conoscere** (*to know*). Take a look at the sample conjugation for **scrivere;** when you know the infinitive and the first-person singular (**scrissi**) you can easily form the other two persons (**scrisse** and **scrissero**). The **tu** form is the regular **-esti** ending; the **noi** form takes **-emmo,** and the **voi** form uses **-este** (the regular second conjugation endings). You can find the various conjugations for other verbs in Appendix A.

scrivere (*to write*)	
io **scrissi**	noi scrivemmo
tu scrivesti	voi scriveste
lui/lei/Lei/esso/essa **scrisse**	loro/Loro/essi/esse **scrissero**
Scrissero molto durante le vacanze. (*They wrote a lot during the holidays.*)	

Find the conjugation of the following verbs from their infinitive and first-person singular forms:

Q. Chiedere (*to ask*), chiesi

A. **Chiedesti, chiese, chiedemmo, chiedeste, chiesero**

48. decidere (*to decide*), decisi, _____, _____, _____, _____, _____

49. leggere (*to read*), lessi, _____, _____, _____, _____, _____

50. prendere (*to get*), presi, _____, _____, _____, _____, _____

51. venire (*to come*), venni, _____, _____, _____, _____, _____

52. vivere (*to live*), vissi, _____, _____, _____, _____, _____

Some verbs, though, do not derive directly from the infinitive and don't follow the 1, 3, 3 pattern. For example, **dare** (*to give*), **dire** (*to say*), **bere** (*to drink*), **stare** (*to stay*), and **fare** (*to do, to make*) are entirely irregular in the preterit. Because the preterit has so many variations, and because you won't use it enough to justify memorizing all the conjugations in this erratic tense, your best bet is to simply look up the conjugations for verbs in this tense when you need them. I provide the conjugations of the most commonly used verbs in Appendix A, but any English-Italian dictionary will provide them as well.

Fill in the blanks with the preterit of the verbs provided in parentheses. Use Appendix A or a dictionary to find the conjugations.

Q. Tu _____ molto amareggiato. (rimanere)

A. Tu **rimanesti** molto amareggiato. (*You were really disappointed.*)

53. A Bianca _____ lo spettacolo. (piacere)

54. Carlo _____ un passaggio a Elisa. (dare)

55. I ragazzi _____ una corsa. (fare)

56. Lui _____ un quesito. (porre)

57. Loro _____ le trattative. (aprire)

Even though the preterit is the tense of historical and fictional writing, writers can write in any tense — it all depends on what they want to convey. As a writer, you may practice whichever tense is better suited to the situation. The passage you find in this exercise is in the present tense, which conveys closeness. It's as if you were right there where the action is taking place. The preterit, on the other hand, creates more distance between yourself and what you're narrating. It's definitive; things happened in a certain way and can't be changed. Do you want closeness or distance? Perhaps in the preterit the following story is more poignant and sad. Transpose all the verbs that are in the present tense into the preterit, except for the ones I underline and for which I give you the correct tense in parentheses. I supply the correct revisions for those verbs because the first one, **riporta,** should be changed to the imperfect (Chapter 11), and the second one, **poteva essere,** should be changed to the past conditional (Chapters 14 and 15).

Q. Quell'inverno la temperatura **raggiunge** i venti gradi sotto zero.

A. Quell'inverno la temperatura **raggiunse** i venti gradi sotto zero.

• • • • • • •

(58) Guarda la ragazza senza nascondere la sua ammirazione. Lei (59) restituisce il suo sguardo, ma non (60) dimostra nessun interesse per lui. Seduti sulla panchina nel parco, ognuno dei due (61) continua a fare quello che stava facendo prima di notare la presenza dell'altro: lei (62) continua a leggere il suo libro, lui a far giocare il cane con un bastone, che il cane <u>riporta</u> (riportava) dieci, venti volte. Dopo cinque minuti, lui si (63) alza e si (64) mette a passeggiare avanti e indietro. Lei gli (65) lancia un'occhiata distratta, poi si (66) rimette a leggere. (67) Vanno avanti per un mese senza dire una parola. Poi, un giorno, lei al parco non (68) viene più. Lui si (69) domanda per mesi e mesi, dopo, se lei <u>poteva essere</u> (avrebbe potuto essere) il grande amore della sua vita.

• • • • • • •

Answer Key

1 apparire: **apparso** (*appeared*)

2 comporre: **composto** (*composed*)

3 congiungere: **congiunto** (*joined*)

4 convincere: **convinto** (*convinced*)

5 percorrere: **percorso** (*covered [of distance]*)

6 promuovere: **promosso** (*promoted*)

7 riprendere: **ripreso** (*taken up again*)

8 riprodurre: **riprodotto** (*reproduced*)

9 ritrarre: **ritratto** (*portrayed*)

10 rivedere: **rivisto/riveduto** (*seen again*)

11 rinvenire: **rinvenuto** (*recovered [one's senses]*)

12 aggiunte: **aggiungere** (*to add*)

13 ammessa: **ammettere** (*to admit*)

14 assolti: **assolvere** (*to acquit*)

15 bevuto: **bere** (*to drink*)

16 concesse: **concedere** (*to concede*)

17 piaciuta: **piacere** (*to like*)

18 cresciuti: **crescere** (*to grow*)

19 discusse: **discutere** (*to discuss*)

20 disposto: **disporre** (*to dispose, to lay*)

21 morse: **mordere** (*to bite*)

22 sorretta: **sorreggere** (*to support*)

23 Con chi **hai parlato** tu? (*Who did you talk to?*)

24 Dopo quella gita, loro **hanno dormito** dieci ore filate! (*After that excursion, they slept ten hours straight!*)

25 I miei colleghi **sono stati** in Marocco. (*My colleagues were in Morocco.*)

26 Mio figlio **è cresciuto** di dieci centimetri in un anno! (*My son has grown ten centimeters in a year!*)

27   I miei figli **hanno visto/veduto** *Il signore degli anelli*. (*My children saw* The Lord of the Rings.)

28   Voi **siete andati** allo stadio? (*Did you go to the stadium?*)

29   "Avete pagato le mele?" "Le abbiamo **pagate**." (*"Did you pay for the apples?" "We paid for them."*)

30   "Avete trovato delle albicocche?" "Non ne abbiamo **trovate**." (*"Did you find apricots?" "We didn't find any."*)

31   "Hai visto Elena?" "Non l'ho **vista**." (*"Have you seen Elena?" "I haven't seen her."*)

32   I miei genitori sono **stati** a Parigi per Pasqua. (*My parents were in Paris at Easter.*)

33   Mirella è **vissuta** molti anni in Australia. (*Mirella lived many years in Australia.*)

34   Mirella ha **vissuto** a lungo da sola. (*Mirella lived alone for a long time.*)

35   Nell'incidente aereo sono **morte** centocinquanta persone. (*One hundred and fifty people died in the plane accident.*)

36   **Martedì 15, alle 18:00, sono potuta/potuto andare in palestra.** (*Tuesday the 15th at 6 p.m., I was able to go to the gym.*)

37   **Mercoledì 16, alle 20:30 sono voluta/voluto andare al cinema con Paola.** (*Wednesday the 16th at 8:30 p.m., I wanted to go to the movies with Paola.*)

38   **Giovedì 17, alle 17:45 sono potuta/potuto andare a yoga.** (*Thursday the 17th at 5:45 p.m., I was able to go to yoga.*)

39   **Venerdì 18, alle 14:00, ho dovuto parlare del libro con il curatore.** (*Friday the 18th at 2 p.m., I had to talk about the book with my editor.*)

40   **Sabato 19, alle 9:00, ho dovuto stampare la carta d'imbarco.** (*Saturday the 19th at 9 a.m., I had to print the boarding pass.*)

41   **Domenica 20, mi sono dovuta svegliare alle 7.** (*Sunday the 20th, I had to wake up at 7 a.m.*)

42   **Alle 10 Michael ed io siamo dovuti partire per Parigi.** (*At 10 a.m, Michael and I had to leave for Paris.*)

43   Tu **andasti** a scuola. (*You went to school.*)

44   Voi **partiste** per la Polonia. (*You left for Poland.*)

45   Mia sorella **temé/temette** di perdere il bambino. (*My sister feared she might lose the baby.*)

46   Suo marito **pulì** il garage. (*Her husband cleaned the garage.*)

47   Tu ed io **capimmo** la sua posizione. (*You and I understood his position.*)

48   **decidesti, decise, decidemmo, decideste, decisero**

49   **leggesti, lesse, leggemmo, leggeste, lessero**

50   **prendesti, prese, prendemmo, prendeste, presero**

51 venisti, venne, venimmo, veniste, vennero

52 vivesti, visse, vivemmo, viveste, vissero

53 A Bianca **piacque** lo spettacolo. (*Bianca liked the show.*)

54 Carlo **diede** un passaggio a Elisa. (*Carlo gave Elisa a ride.*)

55 I ragazzi **fecero** una corsa. (*The boys ran in a race.*)

56 Lui **pose** un quesito. (*He asked a question.*)

57 **Aprirono** le trattative. (*They opened the negotiations.*)

58 – 69

• • • • • • •

(58) **Guardò** la ragazza senza nascondere la sua ammirazione. (*He looked at the girl without hiding his admiration.*) Lei (59) **restituì** il suo sguardo, ma non (60) **dimostrò** nessun interesse per lui. (*She returned his stare, but didn't show any interest in him.*) Seduti sulla panchina nel parco, ognuno dei due (61) **continuò** a fare quello che stava facendo prima di notare la presenza dell'altro: lei (62) **continuò** a leggere il suo libro, lui a far giocare il cane con un bastone, che il cane riportava dieci, venti volte. (*Seated on the park bench, each of them kept on doing what they were doing before noticing the other's presence; she continued to read her book, he to play with his dog, throwing a stick which the dog brought back ten, twenty times.*) Dopo cinque minuti, lui si (63) **alzò** e si (64) **mise** a passeggiare avanti e indietro. (*After five minutes, he got up and began walking back and forth.*) Lei gli (65) **lanciò** un'occhiata distratta, poi si (66) **rimise** a leggere. (*She glanced at him absentmindedly, then she returned to her reading.*) (67) **Andarono** avanti per un mese senza dire una parola. (*They went on like this for a month without ever saying one word.*) Poi, un giorno, lei al parco non (68) **venne** più. (*Then, one day, she stopped coming to the park.*) Lui si (69) **domandò** per mesi e mesi, dopo, se lei poteva essere il grande amore della sua vita. (*He wondered for months and months, afterwards, if she could have been the great love of his life.*)

• • • • • • •

Chapter 11

When Things Lasted (In the Past): The Imperfect

*T*he imperfect is true to its name because when you use it, you don't focus on whether or not the action you're talking about was concluded sometime in the past but rather on the fact that it lasted for a while. For example, **Quando era giovane, andava ogni weekend a ballare** (*When she was young, she went dancing every weekend*). In this statement, you don't know if she's still dancing or how well; all you're interested in is that she used to do it in the past. In English you can convey an imperfect action in the past with the formula *used to* + infinitive.

Because the imperfect allows you to talk about things that lasted in the past, it's also very useful when you want to talk about feelings, emotions, states of affairs, and habits. Here are some situations you can use as guidelines for choosing the imperfect over another past tense. You employ it to talk about

✔ Conditions and states of affairs: **Quando ero bambino andavo a scuola vicino a casa.** (*When I was a child, I went to a school close to home.*)

✔ Actions that may have or may not have been completed in the past but that were happening at the time: **Quando suo fratello ha telefonato, Ada scriveva una lettera.** (*When her brother called, Ada was writing a letter.*)

✔ Habitual activities: **Quando ero bambino, passavo sempre l'estate in montagna.** (*When I was a child, I used to spend/I would always spend the summer in the mountains.*)

Note: You'll find the imperfect commonly used in journalism because it's ideal for narratives, even if the action is over and done with. For example, **Ieri tre operai morivano in una fonderia, uccisi da un tubo di metallo che cadeva dal soffitto.** (*Yesterday, three workers died in a foundry, killed by a metal tube that fell from the ceiling*).

The imperfect is a simple tense. As usual, you'll encounter regular and irregular verbs, but fortunately the imperfect doesn't have many irregularities; I outline the major ones in this chapter. Besides telling you how to form the imperfect of regular and irregular verbs, in this chapter I give you some guidelines on how to choose between the present perfect and the imperfect and when to use the imperfect progressive (yes, Italian has that one too) rather than the imperfect. I also mention the **trapassato prossimo** (*past perfect*), which you use when two things occurred in the past but one is closer to you in time than the other.

Forming the Imperfect

Luckily for you, the imperfect is a very regular tense, even for verbs that are irregular in other tenses. And even with the few verbs that are irregular in the imperfect, what changes is the stem of the verb; the endings are always the same. In this section, I start by telling you what the endings are, and then I move on to the few irregularities you'll encounter.

Adding endings to regular verbs

Italian has three conjugations, for which the endings are **-are, -ere,** and **-ire.** To form the imperfect, you add endings to the stem of the verb, which you get by dropping the infinitive ending. So the stem of **guardare** (*to look at, to watch*) is **guard-,** of **temere** (*to fear*) is **tem-,** and of **sentire** (*to hear*) is **sent-.** The endings that you apply for the imperfect vary depending on the verb's conjugation. I list the endings in Table 11-1 and then provide a sample conjugation.

Table 11-1	Endings of the Imperfect		
Person	*Suffixes for -are Verbs*	*Suffixes for -ere Verbs*	*Suffixes for -ire Verbs*
io	**-avo**	**-evo**	**-ivo**
tu	**-avi**	**-evi**	**-ivi**
lui/lei/Lei/esso/essa	**-ava**	**-eva**	**-iva**
noi	**-avamo**	**-evamo**	**-ivamo**
voi	**-avate**	**-evate**	**-ivate**
loro/Loro/essi/esse	**-avano**	**-evano**	**-ivano**

guardare (*to look at*)	
io guard**avo**	noi guard**avamo**
tu guard**avi**	voi guard**avate**
lui/lei/Lei/esso/essa guard**ava**	loro/Loro/essi/esse guard**avano**
Loro **guardavano** un film. (*They were watching a movie.*)	

The auxiliary verb **avere** — as well as the modal auxiliaries **dovere** (*must, shall*), **potere** (*can, may*), **volere** (*will, want*), and **sapere** (*to know how to*), which usually are followed by a verb in the infinitive — form the imperfect regularly, but in other tenses they're irregular. The following list shows the meanings of the modal auxiliaries in the imperfect tense. I provide them in the first-person singular, but you have to choose the appropriate person (first-, second-, or third-person singular or plural) when you use them.

- ✔ **Potevo** (*could, was able to, was capable of*): Conveys capacity, power, or permission. For example, **Poteva lavorare solo due ore al giorno** (*She could only work two hours a day*).

- ✔ **Dovevo** (*had to*): Conveys necessity, need, or obligation. For example, **Dovevano parlargli prima di partire** (*They had to talk to him before leaving*).

- ✔ **Volevo** (*wanted to*): Conveys intention or desire. For example, **I bambini volevano giocare a calcio** (*The children wanted to play soccer*).

- ✔ **Sapevo** (*could*): Conveys skill and ability. For example, **Sapeva giocare a golf** (*She could play golf/She knew how to play golf*).

A few scoundrels: Irregular verbs

As I say throughout this book, in most cases it's hard to give criteria for recognizing irregular verbs. All I can do is to list them, and all you can do is to learn them by heart (or consult a dictionary). This section covers irregular verbs in the imperfect.

Essere (to be): Always irregular

The verb **essere** (*to be*) is irregular in all moods and tenses. In the imperfect, it takes a special stem, **er-**, and adds the endings of the first conjugation in **-are** (even if in the infinitive it's a verb of the second conjugation in **-ere**), but after dropping the letters **-av-**, except in the first- and second-persons plural. Here's the conjugation (quite honestly, it's easier to show you than to explain!):

essere (*to be*)	
io **ero**	noi **eravamo**
tu **eri**	voi **eravate**
lui/lei/Lei/esso/essa **era**	loro/Loro/essi/esse **erano**
Io **ero** stanca. (*I was tired.*)	

Regular verbs that take an expanded stem

Because of space limitations, I can't list all the regular verbs that take an expanded stem in the imperfect, so I give you the most common ones in Table 11-2, along with their modified stems. These few verbs drop the **-re** of the infinitive, add **-eve-,** and then add the regular endings of the imperfect of the second conjugation in **-ere.**

Verbs formed by adding a prefix to a basic verb, as in adding **ri-** to **fare** (*to do, to make*) to get **rifare** (*to redo, to remake*), follow the pattern of the basic verb. For example, add **dis-** to **porre** (*to lay*) to get **disporre** (*to dispose*). In the case of **condurre,** which is a verb with a prefix to begin with, you can change that prefix, using **tra-,** for example, to get **tradurre** (*to translate*).

Table 11-2	Verbs with an Expanded Stem
Infinitive	*Expanded Stem for the Imperfect*
bere (*to drink*)	**bevev-**
condurre (*to lead*)	**conducev-**
dire (*to say, to tell*)	**dicev-**
fare (*to do, to make*)	**facev-**
porre (*to lay*)	**ponev-**
trarre (*to draw*)	**traev-**

condurre (*to lead*)	
io conduc**evo**	noi conduc**evamo**
tu conduc**evi**	voi conduc**evate**
lui/lei/Lei/esso/essa conduc**eva**	loro/Loro/essi/esse conduc**evano**
Lei **conduceva** una vita semplice. (*She led a simple life.*)	

fare (*to do, to make*)	
io fac**evo**	noi fac**evamo**
tu fac**evi**	voi fac**evate**
lui/lei/Lei/esso/essa fac**eva**	loro/Loro/essi/esse fac**evano**
Noi **facevamo** alpinismo da giovani. (*We used to go climbing when we were young.*)	

Conjugate the following verbs in the imperfect in the person suggested for each entry.

Q. noi _____ (agire)

A. noi **agivamo** (*we acted*)

1. tu _____ (andare)   5. loro _____ (essere)

2. lei _____ (bere)   6. noi _____ (fare)

3. lui _____ (supporre)   7. io _____ (produrre)

4. lei _____ (dire)   8. voi _____ (trarre)

Crafting the Imperfect Progressive

Like English, Italian has an imperfect progressive tense. You form the imperfect progressive by conjugating the regular verb **stare** (*to stay*) in the imperfect and then adding the gerund of the main verb. For example, **Io stavo leggendo** (*I was reading*). The gerund is invariable (it has only one form), so you don't have to worry about matching it to another word in the sentence. You form the gerund by adding **-ando** to the stems of verbs ending in **-are,** and you add **-endo** to the stems of verbs ending in **-ere** or **-ire.** I talk about it more at length in Chapter 9, where you can also check the gerunds of irregular verbs. Here's an example of a verb in the imperfect progressive:

guardare (*to look at, to watch*)	
io **stavo guardando**	noi **stavamo guardando**
tu **stavi guardando**	voi **stavate guardando**
lui/lei/Lei/esso/essa **stava guardando**	loro/Loro/essi/esse **stavano guardando**
Voi **stavate guardando** la partita di calcio. (*You were watching the soccer game.*)	

In Italian you use the imperfect progressive in the same way you use it in English: to emphasize what you were doing (or what was happening) at a given moment. If you ask the question **Che cosa stavano facendo?** (*What were they doing?*), what you leave unsaid is *at that moment* or *at the time we're talking about.* And you can answer **Stavano guardando la TV** (*They were watching TV*).

However, Italian is more flexible than English when it comes to the distinction between a simple tense and its progressive form. So you can also say **Che cosa facevano?** (*What were they doing?*), and answer **Guardavano la TV** (*They were watching TV*). You choose between the two versions not because you need to follow a rule but because the progressive form may seem more appropriate in a specific instance.

In Italian, you use the progressive form to talk about emotional and mental states. For example, **Stavo pensando di licenziarmi** (*I was thinking of quitting that job*). But you don't use it to talk about conditions, as in **Indossava un vestito blu** (*She was wearing a blue dress*), or with the verb **essere** (*to be*), as in **Era carino con te** (*He was being nice to you*).

In the following sentences, fill in the blanks with the appropriate form of the verb suggested in parentheses. Use the imperfect or the imperfect progressive.

Q. Quando ho visto quell'incidente, _____ dal negozio. (uscire)

A. Quando ho visto quell'incidente, **stavo uscendo** dal negozio. (*When I saw that accident, I was walking out of the store.*)

9. Durante la stagione delle piogge, non _____ mai di piovere. (smettere)

10. Quando l'ho incontrato, Sandro _____ in palestra. (andare)

11. Sandro _____ in palestra tutti i giorni. (andare)

12. Quando mi hai chiamato io_____ la pasta. (cucinare)

13. Da bambino al mare lui _____ sempre i castelli di sabbia. (fare)

14. Anni fa noi _____ sempre a scacchi. (giocare)

15. La moto è arrivata a velocità fortissima proprio mentre Ida _____ la strada. (attraversare)

When the Going Gets Tricky: Comparing the Imperfect and Present Perfect

In this section I give you guidelines about

✔ How to choose between the imperfect (or the imperfect progressive) and the present perfect

- Imperfect/imperfect progressive: **Guardavo/Stavo guardando la TV con i miei amici.** (*I watched/I was watching TV with my friends*.)

- Present perfect: **Ho guardato la TV fino a mezzanotte.** (*I watched TV until midnight.*)

✔ What happens when you link sentences together using the present perfect in one and the imperfect in the other, as in **Guardavo** [imperfect] **la TV quando è mancata** [present perfect] **la luce** (*I was watching TV when the electricity went out*); or you want to emphasize that specific moment, as in **Stavo guardando** [imperfect progressive] **la TV quando è mancata** [present perfect] **la luce** (*I was watching TV when the electricity went out*).

Choosing one over the other: Imperfect or present perfect?

In English and Italian you employ the present perfect to talk about situations that began in the past and are still affecting the present, as in **Il grande direttore d'orchestra è morto nella sua casa di famiglia** (*The great conductor died at his family's home*).

But in other situations, Italian uses the imperfect or the present perfect, and the English translation for both of the Italian tenses is the same. Compare the following examples:

Mia figlia era una bambina vivace. (*My daughter was a lively kid.*)

Mia figlia è stata in Spagna l'estate scorsa. (*My daughter was in Spain last summer.*)

In the first sentence, the verb *was* needs to be in the imperfect in Italian because the sentence conveys a condition lasting over time. In the second sentence, the trip to Spain is an event that was concluded in the past. You have to get used to asking the following questions to decide whether to use the imperfect or the present perfect:

- ✔ Am I talking about an event? If yes, use the present perfect.
- ✔ Am I talking about a situation, a condition, or something lasting? If yes, use the imperfect.

Using different tenses in different sentences

Sometimes, you'll find yourself in a situation where, when looking at a sentence in isolation, you find it's difficult to decide whether you're talking about a condition that lasted in the past or an event that happened and is over. If in English you have a sentence such as *My son was a quiet kid,* what tense do you use in Italian? The present perfect? **Mio figlio è stato un bambino tranquillo?** Or the imperfect? **Mio figlio era un bambino tranquillo?** Neither of them is right or wrong. What tense you use depends on the context, and the simplest context you can think of may be another sentence.

Suppose that you're talking about your son, who's now 20 years old, and you're looking back to the time to when he was a kid. You have three possible situations; you can think of

- ✔ Two situations that both lasted in the past and for which you use the imperfect: **Quando mio figlio era bambino, era molto tranquillo.** (*When my son was a kid, he was very quiet.*)

- ✔ A condition that lasted in the past as compared to an event (in this case, the onset of adolescence) that changed that situation and for which you use the present perfect: **Mio figlio era un bambino tranquillo, ma con l'adolescenza è diventato molto vivace.** (*My son was a quiet child, but with adolescence he became very lively.*)

- ✔ Two situations that have a beginning and an end, no matter the length of time they cover, and for which you use the present perfect: **Mio figlio è stato un bambino tranquillo fino ai quattordici anni, ma poi è diventato molto vivace.** (*My son was a quiet kid until the age of 14; afterwards he became very lively.*)

As the examples show, you need to appreciate the nuances in order to make the best decision. People will understand you if you use the wrong tense in situations such as the one illustrated in this example, but if you want to write well, you need to develop sensitivity to those nuances.

For each of the following sentences, choose the correct verb from among the options in parentheses.

Q. (Hai giocato/Giocavi/Stavi giocando) a carte tutta la sera?

A. **Hai giocato** a carte tutta la sera? (*Did you play cards all evening?*)

16. Alla festa (ha indossato/indossava/stava indossando) un vestito rosso.

17. Da bambino (ha giocato/giocava) sempre con il lego, e infatti da grande (ha fatto/faceva) l'architetto.

18. Da giovane, mia nonna (ha messo/metteva) sempre il cappello quando (usciva/è uscita).

19. (Sono andata/Stavo andando/Andavo) al mare quando (ha cominciato/cominciava/stava cominciando) a piovere.

20. (Ha viaggiato/Viaggiava) sull'autobus, (ha letto/leggeva) il giornale e (ha fatto/faceva) la maglia, tutto allo stesso tempo!

Conveying Two Past Actions in Sequence: The Past Perfect

In Italian, the past perfect is called **trapassato prossimo**. You need this tense when two actions occurred in the past and one occurred before the other. In Italian, you also use this tense in situations where English uses the simple past, even though it's correct to use the past perfect in English too, as in **Le ho chiesto cos'aveva fatto** (*I asked her what she had done/I asked her what she did*).

You use the past perfect

✔ When you're talking about an event that happened in the past before the situation you're describing. You convey the situation with the imperfect and the event with the past perfect.

> **Non sapevo** [situation lasting over time] **che tu gli avevi telefonato** [event]. (*I didn't know you had already called him.*)

✔ When you're describing a situation that lasted over time before an event you're talking about. You convey the event with the present perfect and the situation with the past perfect.

> **Quando siamo usciti** [event], **aveva smesso di piovere** [situation lasting over time]. (*By the time we went out, it had stopped raining.*)

You form the past perfect by conjugating the auxiliary verb **essere** or **avere** in the imperfect. Then you add the past participle of the main verb, such as **detto** (*said*) or

andato (*gone*), to get **avevo detto** (*I had said*) or **ero andato** (*I had gone*). Head to Chapter 10 for information about the following:

- ✔ How to form the past participle (**amato** [*loved*], **fatto** [*done, made*], and so on)
- ✔ How to choose between **essere** and **avere** as the auxiliary
- ✔ Which of the four endings of the past participle you need: **-o, -a, -i,** or **-e**

Complete the following sentences by adding the past perfect in the person suggested in parentheses. Choose the appropriate auxiliary, and pay attention to the ending of the past participle.

Q. Ieri Anna ci ha portato il libro che le _____. (chiedere, noi)

A. Ieri Anna ci ha portato il libro che le **avevamo chiesto.** (*Yesterday Anna brought us the book we asked for/had asked for.*)

21. Non sembrate sorpresi. _____ già _____ la notizia della sua pro-mozione? (sapere, voi)

22. _____ sempre _____ un marito modello, ma un bel giorno è sparito. (essere, lui)

23. Mariella non sapeva che Anna e Luisa _____ in Olanda. (nascere, loro)

24. Me le _____? Ma io non le trovo più. (dare, tu)

25. Gliel' _____, ma non ci hanno creduti. (dire, noi)

Practicing Your Navigation Among the Three Past Tenses

In the following exercises you practice using the three past tenses, two of which I cover in Chapter 10 (the present perfect and preterit) and the imperfect, which I cover in this chapter.

Think of a hypothetical vacation you spent at the beach when you were 7 years old. Some things you did began and ended while you were on vacation — you learned how to swim, for example — others occurred over a stretch of time — the vacation itself, for example, or your being 7 years old, which covered, of course, an entire year of your life. When you translate the sentences listed below, decide when it's appropriate to use the imperfect or the present perfect. You may also need the past perfect when two events happened both at that time, but one preceded the other.

Translate the following sentences from English into Italian using the appropriate past tense.

Q. This photograph represents a place similar to one I used to know.

A. **Questa fotografia rappresenta un posto simile a un posto che io conoscevo.**

26. As a child, I used to go to the seashore every year.

27. I used to go on vacation with my parents and my siblings.

28. I learned to swim when I was 7.

29. My father taught me to swim.

30. I used to build sandcastles.

31. I had a lot of friends at the beach.

32. At the beach, we always played bocce on the sand.

33. My mother had bought me a mask and fins so I could watch the fish under water.

34. I never saw again the friends I had met at the beach.

The following passage is the biography of an Italian writer, Lalla Romano, written mostly in the present tense. Answer the questions that follow in one of the three past tenses. Her birth, dates of publications, and so forth are best conveyed in the preterit. When an activity covers a chunk of time or an emotional or existential state, you should talk about it in the imperfect. And when it comes to assessing her role in Italian literature, you should use the present perfect (Chapter 10).

Lalla (Graziella) Romano nasce l'11 novembre, 1906, a Demonte (Cuneo). Nel 1924 Lalla Romano si iscrive alla Facoltà di Lettere e Filosofia dell'Università di Torino, dove frequenta soprattutto le lezioni di Filosofia, di Letteratura francese e di Storia dell'arte. Mentre frequenta l'università incomincia a dipingere i primi autoritratti. Tra il 1938 e il 1940 scrive dei racconti sulla vita del mondo dell'arte a Torino e continua ad esporre quadri. Tra il 1944 e il 1951 avviene il passaggio definitivo dalla pittura alla letteratura. Tra il 1953 e il 1969 pubblica numerosi romanzi, tra cui *La penombra che abbiamo attraversato*, nel 1964 e *Le parole tra noi leggere*, nel 1969. Nel 1982 incomincia la collaborazione al *Corriere della Sera*. Lalla Romano continua a pubblicare saggi e romanzi fino alla sua morte, avvenuta nel 2001. Le sue opere vengono tradotte in molte lingue, incluso il giapponese. Lalla Romano è uno degli scrittori italiani più importanti del XX secolo.

Q. Quando nasce Lalla Romano?

A. **Lalla Romano nacque l'11 novembre 1906.** (*Lalla Romano was born on November 11, 1906.*)

35. Quando si iscrive all'Università?

_____

36. Che corsi frequenta?

_____

37. Che attività artistica inizia negli anni dell' Università?

_____

38. Che cosa fa tra il 1938 e il 1940?

_____

39. Che cosa pubblica nel 1969?

_____

40. Quando inizia a collaborare al _Corriere della Sera?_

_____

41. A che cosa si dedica negli anni fino alla sua morte?

_____

42. I suoi romanzi vengono tradotti?

_____

43. Lalla Romano è uno scrittore importante?

_____

Answer Key

1 tu **andavi** (*you were going*)

2 lei **beveva** (*she was drinking*)

3 lui **supponeva** (*he supposed*)

4 lei **diceva** (*she said*)

5 loro **erano** (*they were*)

6 noi **facevamo** (*we used to do*)

7 io **producevo** (*I produced*)

8 voi **traevate** (*you drew*)

9 Durante la stagione delle piogge, non **smetteva** mai di piovere. (*During the rain season, it never stopped raining.*)

10 Quando l'ho incontrato, Sandro **stava andando/andava** in palestra. (*When I met him, Sandro was going to the gym.*)

11 Sandro **andava** in palestra tutti i giorni. (*Sandro used to go to the gym every day.*)

12 Quando mi hai chiamato **stavo cucinando** la pasta. (*When you called me, I was cooking pasta.*)

13 Da bambino al mare **lui faceva** sempre i castelli di sabbia. (*As a child he always built sandcastles on the beach.*)

14 Anni fa **noi giocavamo** sempre a scacchi. (*Years ago we used to play chess all the time.*)

15 La moto è arrivata a velocità fortissima proprio mentre Ida **stava attraversando** la strada. (*The motorbike arrived at very high speed right when Ida was crossing the street.*)

16 Alla festa, **indossava** un vestito rosso. (*At the party she was wearing a red dress.*)

17 Da bambino **giocava** sempre con il lego, e infatti da grande **ha fatto** l'architetto. (*As a child he always played with Legos; and in fact, when he grew up he became an architect.*)

18 Da giovane, mia nonna **metteva** sempre il cappello quando **usciva**. (*As a young woman, my grandma always wore a hat when she went out.*)

19 **Stavo andando** al mare quando **ha cominciato** a piovere. (*I was going to the beach when it started to rain.*)

20 **Viaggiava** sull'autobus, **leggeva** il giornale e **faceva** la maglia, tutto allo stesso tempo! (*She/He was riding the bus, reading the paper, and knitting, all at the same time.*)

21 Non sembrate sorpresi. **Avevate** già **saputo** la notizia della sua promozione? (*You don't look surprised. Had you already heard of his promotion?*)

22   **Lui era** sempre **stato** un marito modello, ma un bel giorno è sparito. (*He had always been the perfect husband, but one fine day he disappeared.*)

23   Mariella non sapeva che Anna e Luisa **erano nate** in Olanda. (*Mariella didn't know that Anna and Luisa had been born in Holland.*)

24   Me le **avevi date**? Ma io non le trovo più. (*Did you give them to me? I can't find them any longer.*)

25   Gliel'**avevamo detto**, ma non ci hanno creduti. (*We told them, but they didn't believe us.*)

26   **Da bambino/bambina andavo in vacanza al mare ogni anno.**

27   **Andavo in vacanza con i miei genitori e i miei fratelli.**

28   **Ho imparato a nuotare a/quando avevo sette anni.**

29   **Mio padre mi ha insegnato a nuotare.**

30   **Costruivo i castelli di sabbia.**

31   **Avevo molti amici al mare.**

32   **Al mare giocavamo sempre a bocce sulla sabbia.**

33   **Mia madre mi aveva comprato la maschera e le pinne, così io potevo guardare i pesci sott'acqua.**

34   **Non ho mai più incontrato/visto/veduto gli amici che avevo conosciuto al mare.**

35   **Si iscrisse all'Università nel 1924.** (*She enrolled at the University in 1924.*)

36   **Frequentò i corsi di Filosofia, Letteratura francese e Storia dell'arte.** (*She took courses in Philosophy, French Literature, and Art History.*)

37   **Incominciò a dipingere i primi autoritratti.** (*She began painting her first self-portraits.*)

38   **Scrisse dei racconti sulla vita del mondo dell'arte a Torino e continuò ad esporre quadri.** (*She wrote short stories about the art scene in Turin and continued to exhibit her paintings.*)

39   **Nel 1969, pubblicò** *Le parole tra noi leggere.* (*In 1969, she published* Le parole tra noi leggere.)

40   **Nel 1982 incominciò la collaborazione al** *Corriere della Sera*. (*In 1982 she began her collaboration on* Corriere della Sera.)

41   **Continuava a pubblicare saggi e romanzi.** (*She continued to publish essays and novels.*)

42   **I suoi romanzi sono stati tradotti in molte lingue, incluso il giapponese.** (*Her novels have been translated into several languages, including Japanese.*)

43   **Lalla Romano è stata uno degli scrittori/una della scrittrici italiani più importanti del XX secolo.** (*Lalla Romano was one of the most important Italian writers of the twentieth century.*)

Chapter 12

The Future Tense

In This Chapter

▶ Conjugating the future of regular and irregular verbs

▶ Forming and using the future perfect

This is the chapter of the future. The future is a tense you employ to talk about an event that hasn't yet taken place or isn't yet concluded. It has a simple form (**futuro semplice**): **Andrò** (*I will go*); and a compound form called the **futuro anteriore** (*future perfect*): **Sarò andato** (*I will have gone*). You use the future perfect when a future event precedes another future event: **Quando tornerai a casa, Ugo sarà già partito** (*By the time you come home, Ugo will have left*). Here's when you use the future tense:

✔ To describe events happening in the future (usually a far or unspecified future): **Un giorno sarò ricco e famoso.** (*One day I will be rich and famous.*)

✔ To express the intention to do something in the future: **Penso che andrò in California il prossimo anno.** (*I think I'll go to California next year.*)

✔ To express a possibility or probability: **Hanno bussato alla porta, sarà l'UPS che consegna il pacco.** (*Someone knocked on the door; it may be UPS delivering the package.*)

✔ When the first verb of a sentence (either a subordinate or main clause) is in the future: **Quando finirai il liceo, andrai all'università.** (*When you finish high school, you'll go to college.*)

In general, the future is used when talking about unspecified events in time or events that are likely to occur in a distant future. When describing events happening in a near future, use the present tense. Note that in these cases, English often uses the future or the present progressive tense: **Che fai stasera?** (*What are you doing tonight?*); **Io esco con Simona.** (*I'm going out with Simona.*)

Knowing When to Use the Present to Talk about the Future

All languages have rules, and even basic conjugations can be a challenge at first. Not only do Italian verb forms vary more than they do in English, but Italian also takes a few more liberties in using the present tense to describe the future.

Talk about the future with the present in the following cases:

- To mention an event that will happen soon, as in **La vedo domenica** (*I'll see her on Sunday/I'm seeing her on Sunday*).

- To announce a *decision* that's more or less close in time. For example, **Quest'estate vado alle Maldive!** (*This coming summer I'm going to the Maldives!*).

- To refer to an event that's part of a timetable. For instance, **Il semestre autunnale incomincia il 10 ottobre** (*The fall term begins on October 10*).

- To give instructions, such as **Quando arrivi a Londra, va' direttamente alla Stazione Vittoria** (*When you get to London, go straight to Victoria Station*).

Forming the Future Tense

The future is formed by adding the corresponding endings to the infinitive of the verb minus the final **-e.** In **-are** verbs, the **a** of the infinitive changes to **e.** Read on for conjugations of regular and irregular verbs in the future tense.

Many verbs, such as **vivere** (*to live*), are preceded by a prefix, such as **sopra-** in **sopravvivere** (*to survive*). Both regular and irregular verbs formed with prefixes behave like the basic verb without the prefix. Conjugate the verb with the prefix as you'd conjugate the simple verb:

I miei nonni **vivranno** a lungo. (*My grandparents will live a long time*).

Queste piante **sopravvivranno** al freddo. (*The plants will survive the cold.*)

Regular verbs

The future tense in Italian is a thing of beauty: For regular verbs, the conjugation of both **-are** and **-ere** verbs (no matter where the accent is) is exactly the same. And **-ire** verbs follow the same pattern, with an **i** in place of the **e** at the beginning of the ending. In Table 12-1, I list the endings for the three conjugations, followed by a sample conjugation table. Remember that all verbs — regular and irregular — place the accent on the same vowels.

Table 12-1	Endings for Regular Verbs in the Future Tense	
Person	*Ending for -are/-ere Verbs*	*Ending for -ire Verbs*
io	-erò	-irò
tu	-erai	-irai
lui/lei/Lei/esso	-erà	-irà
noi	-eremo	-iremo
voi	-erete	-irete
loro/Loro/essi/esse	-eranno	-iranno

guardare (*to look at*)	
io guard**erò**	noi guard**eremo**
tu guard**erai**	voi guard**erete**
lui/lei/Lei/esso/essa guard**erà**	loro/Loro/essi/esse guard**eranno**
Massimo non mi **guarderà** mai! (*Massimo will never look at me!*)	

The verb **spengere/spegnere** (*to turn off, to extinguish*) forms the simple future regularly but uses only the stem **spegn-.** This is because the infinitive has two forms — **spengere** and **spegnere** — whose meanings don't change. But remember: You hear only **spengere** in Tuscany, whereas the rest of Italy uses **spegnere.**

Verbs that end in **-ciare** and **-giare,** such as **lanciare** (*to throw, to launch*) and **mangiare** (*to eat*), drop the **i** before adding endings because the **-e** of the future ending preserves the soft sound of the infinitive. Verbs that end in **-care** and **-gare,** such as **cercare** (*to look for*) and **pagare** (*to pay*), take **ch** and **gh** before the endings to preserve the hard sound of the infinitive.

Add the verb to the following sentences, choosing among the options in parentheses.

Q. (Pagheremo/Prenderanno/Servirete) noi il conto.

A. **Pagheremo** noi il conto. (*We will pay for the bill.*)

1. Gianni e Piero (balleranno/correranno/visiteranno) la Maratona di New York.

2. Io e i miei fratelli (prenderai/serviranno/daremo) una grande festa.

3. "Marco, (lascerò/partirai/salirai) per Mosca fra un mese?"

4. "Signora, (cambierà/cancelleranno/ricorderò) il suo numero di telefono?"

5. "Signori, (passerà/uscirete/entrerai) dalla porta numero 4."

6. Tu e i tuoi colleghi (finirete/annulleranno/darete) le dimissioni?

Irregular verbs

As usual, some verbs don't follow the rules of the future tense. They conjugate starting from different future stems, depending on the endings of the infinitives (**-are, -ere, -ire**) and on where in the verb the stress falls. Read on for info on these irregular verbs.

Auxiliaries and modal auxiliaries

The verb **essere** (*to be*) is irregular all around when it comes to conjugation, meaning that the conjugated forms don't look anything like the infinitive form. **Avere** (*to have*) is much less irregular; to use **avere** in the future tense, you just drop the **-ere** ending. The following tables show their conjugations.

essere (*to be*)	
io **sarò**	noi **saremo**
tu **sarai**	voi **sarete**
lui/lei/Lei/esso/essa **sarà**	loro/Loro/essi/esse **saranno**
Dove **sarai** tra vent'anni? (*Where will you be in twenty years?*)	

avere (*to have*)	
io **avrò**	noi **avremo**
tu **avrai**	voi a**vrete**
lui/lei/Lei/esso/essa **avrà**	loro/Loro/essi/esse **avranno**
Guarda quei ragazzi: **avranno** vent'anni al massimo. (*Look at those guys: They can't be older than 20.*)	

In conjugating the future tense, the modal auxiliaries **dovere** (*must, shall*), **potere** (*can, may*), and **sapere** (*to know how to*) drop the **-ere** from the infinitive and add an **r** plus the future endings. **Volere** (*will, to want to*) conjugates similarly but also changes the **l** of the stem to **r.** The following tables show the conjugations of these verbs in the future.

dovere (must, shall)	
io **dovrò**	noi **dovremo**
tu **dovrai**	voi **dovrete**
lui/lei/Lei/esso/essa **dovrà**	loro/Loro/essi/esse **dovranno**
Dovrò ridare questo esame. (*I'll have to take this exam again.*)	

potere (*can, may*)	
io **potrò**	noi **potremo**
tu **potrai**	voi **potrete**
lui/lei/Lei/esso/essa **potrà**	loro/Loro/essi/esse **potranno**
Non so quando **potrò** vederti. (*I don't know when I'll be able to see you.*)	

sapere (*to know how to*)	
io **saprò**	noi **sapremo**
tu **saprai**	voi **saprete**
lui/lei/Lei/esso/essa **saprà**	loro/Loro/essi/esse **sapranno**
Non **saprò** mai sciare come te. (*I'll never be able to ski like you.*)	

volere (*will, to want to*)	
io **vorrò**	noi **vorremo**
tu **vorrai**	voi **vorrete**
lui/lei/Lei/esso/essa **vorrà**	loro/Loro/essi/esse **vorranno**
Vorranno conoscerti, prima o poi. (*They'll like to know you, sooner or later.*)	

Irregular verbs of the first conjugation: -are

Some two-syllable verbs ending in **-are** keep the **a** of the infinitive. These verbs are **dare** (*to give*), **fare** (*to do*), and **stare** (*to stay*). They drop the **e** of their endings. The following are their conjugations.

andare (*to go*)	
io **andrò**	noi **andremo**
tu **andrai**	voi **andrete**
lui/lei/Lei/esso/essa **andrà**	loro/Loro/essi/esse **andranno**
Andrete mai in Africa? (*Will you ever go to Africa?*)	

fare (*to do, to make*)	
io **farò**	noi **faremo**
tu **farai**	voi **farete**
lui/lei/Lei/esso/essa **farà**	loro/Loro/essi/esse **faranno**
Cosa **farai** per il tuo compleanno? (*What will you do for your birthday?*)	

stare (*to stay*)	
io **starò**	noi **staremo**
tu **starai**	voi **starete**
lui/lei/Lei/esso/essa **starà**	loro/Loro/essi/esse **staranno**
Stanno imbarcando prendendo l'aereo a quest'ora. (*They may be getting on the plane now.*)	

Add the verb to the following sentences, choosing among the options in parentheses.

Q. "(Vorrai/Farai/Avrà) una torta, tu?"

A. "**Farai** una torta, tu?" ("*Will you make a cake?*")

7. Io (uscirò/sarà/starò) a casa sabato sera.

8. Mamma e papà (staranno/faranno/avrete) le nozze d'oro a dicembre.

9. Noi (potremo/dovremo/vorrete) vendere la barca, purtroppo.

10. "Signore e Signori, (vorremo/potrà/dovrete) lasciare la stanza."

11. "Signore, (andrà/sarai/lascerà) a Mosca il mese prossimo?"

12. Stai tranquillo, domani (starà/farà/saremo) bello.

13. "Tu e tua moglie (farete/saremo/andrete) in vacanza in Messico?"

Irregular verbs of the second conjugation: -ere

To form the future tense, irregular **-ere** verbs follow one of four patterns:

✔ Drop the **-ere** and add **r** plus the ending. Common verbs in this category include **cadere** (*to fall*), **accadere** (*to happen*), **godere** (*to enjoy*), and **vedere** (*to see*).

✔ Drop the **-ere** and replace the **m, n,** or **l** of the stem with an **r**, as in **rimanere** (*to remain*), **tenere** (*to keep*), and **valere** (*to be worth*).

✔ Double the consonant **r,** as in **bere** (*to drink*).

✔ Add the suffix without the **e** to the verbs that have a double **r** in the stem, as in **condurre** (*to lead*), **trarre** (*to pull*), and **porre** (*to put*).

Following are the future conjugation tables for **cadere, rimanere, bere,** and **condurre.**

cadere (*to fall*)	
io cad**rò**	noi cad**remo**
tu cad**rai**	voi cad**rete**
lui/lei/Lei/esso/essa cad**rà**	loro/Loro/essi/esse cad**ranno**
Se sarai prudente, non **cadrai.** (*If you're cautious, you won't fall.*)	

rimanere (*to remain*)	
io rima**rrò**	noi rima**rremo**
tu rima**rrai**	voi rima**rrete**
lui/lei/Lei/esso/essa rima**rrà**	loro/Loro/essi/esse rima**rranno**
Rimarrò qui finché non avrai finito. (*I'll remain here until you're done.*)	

bere (*to drink*)	
io be**rrò**	noi be**rremo**
tu be**rrai**	voi be**rrete**
lui/lei/Lei/esso/essa be**rrà**	loro/Loro/essi/esse be**rranno**
Berremo alla tua salute! (*We'll drink to your health!*)	

condurre (*to lead*)	
io condu**rrò**	noi condu**rremo**
tu condu**rrai**	voi condu**rrete**
lui/lei/Lei/esso/essa condu**rrà**	loro/Loro/essi/esse condu**rranno**
Non ti preoccupare, ci **condurranno** a destinazione. (*Don't worry, they'll take us to our destination.*)	

Irregular verbs of the third conjugation: -ire

Only one of the **-ire** verbs is irregular and important to know: **Venire** drops the **-ire** of the ending and changes the **n** of the stem to a **rr** plus the ending.

venire (*to come*)	
io ve**rrò**	noi ve**rremo**
tu ve**rrai**	voi ve**rrete**
lui/lei/Lei/esso/essa ve**rrà**	loro/Loro/essi/esse ve**rranno**
Verrai alla mia festa di compleanno? (*Will you come to my birthday party?*)	

Add the verb to the following sentences, choosing among the options in parentheses.

Q. State attenti, (resteranno/rimarrete/rischierete) senza benzina!

A. State attenti, **rimarrete** senza benzina! (*Be careful, you'll run out of gas!*)

14. (Accadrà/Accadranno/Verranno) cose terribili il giorno dell'Apocalisse.

15. Al matrimonio io (godrò/berrà/berrò) alla salute degli sposi.

16. Noi (rimarremo/verrete/andranno) in campagna per l'estate.

17. "State attente voi due, (cadrete/terrete/verrete) dalla scala!"

18. Voi (vedrete/vedremo/rimarrete) la partita a casa sua.

19. (Porrà/Condurrà/Trarrà) lui le conclusioni dal tuo rapporto.

20. "(Andrai/Verrai/Andrà) da noi a cena, Luciano?"

Practice writing in the future tense by answering a questionnaire from the University of Utrecht in the Netherlands, where you'll go for a study-abroad program. Follow the clues in the question to decide which tense to use in your answers. Use full sentences, even when it's possible to answer *yes* or *no*. Answer in the affirmative; the word order is the same as in English.

Q. In che Facoltà si iscriverà?

A. **Sono iscritto/a alla Facoltà di Economia e Commercio con indirizzo "Marketing."**

21. Avrà completato la preparazione in Microeconomia e Macroeconomia prima del periodo di studi all'estero?

_____

22. Quando si laureerà?

_____

23. Nella nostra università, si iscriverà ai corsi "Commercio globale" e "Marketing"?

_____

24. Dopo che avrà finito i corsi universitari, farà domanda per uno *stage* per fare un'esperienza di lavoro?

_____

25. Parteciperà ad attività sportive o ricreative organizzate dall'Università?

_____

26. Diventerà membro del "Club degli studenti stranieri"?

_____

27. Quando arriverà a Utrecht, avrà fatto domanda per una borsa di studio Erasmus?

_____

28. Riceverà la risposta alla domanda per la borsa di studio entro il 31 luglio 2008?

_____

29. Avrà bisogno di una sistemazione nel collegio universitario?

_____

Forming the Future Perfect Tense

The future perfect is a compound tense that describes a future event happening *before* another future event. You form it by adding the simple future of the auxiliary verb **essere** (*to be*) or **avere** (*to have*) to the past participle of the verb. (Earlier in this chapter, in the "Irregular verbs" section, I explain how to form the future tense of **essere** and **avere**. Chapter 10 tells you which auxiliary to choose, how to form the past participle, and how to coordinate the past participle with subjects and objects.) Here are **mangiare** (*to eat*), which uses **avere,** and **tornare** (*to return, to go back*), which uses **essere,** in the future perfect.

mangiare *(to eat)*	
io **avrò mangiato**	noi **avremo mangiato**
tu **avrai mangiato**	voi **avrete mangiato**
lui/lei/Lei/esso/essa **avrà mangiato**	loro/Loro/essi/esse **avranno mangiato**
Il gatto **avrà mangiato** la bistecca. (*The cat will have eaten the steak.*)	

tornare *(to return, to go back)*	
io **sarò tornato/tornata**	noi **saremo tornati/tornate**
tu **sarai tornato/tornata**	voi **sarete tornati/tornate**
lui/lei/Lei/esso/essa **sarà tornato/tornata**	loro/Loro/essi/esse **saranno tornati/tornate**
Sarà tornato in ufficio. (*He'll have gone back to work.*)	

To understand how to use the future perfect, compare the verb tenses in the following example sentences:

✔ **Present:** Quando **arriva** in ufficio, gli telefono. (*When I call him, he arrives at the office.*)

✔ **Future:** Quando **arriverà** in ufficio, gli telefonerò. (*When I call him, he'll arrive at the office.*)

✔ **Future perfect:** Quando, **sarà arrivato** in ufficio, gli telefonerò. (*When I call him, he'll have already arrived at the office.*)

Using the clues in parentheses, decide whether to use the present, the future, or the future perfect to complete the following sentences. Because Italian uses the present tense to describe events that take place in the near future, both the simple future tense and the present may be correct in some cases.

0. Guarda che pozzanghere! _____ tutta la notte. (piovere)

A. Guarda che pozzanghere! **Avrà/Sarà piovuto** tutta la notte.

30. Noi _____ alla partita sabato. (andare)

31. Ha detto con tono deciso: "_____ a lavorare in Australia tra due anni!" (andare)

32. L'aereo per Tokyo _____ alle 12:30. (partire)

33. Carlo, quando _____ a Roma, prendi un taxi per venire da noi. (arrivare)

34. Ragazzi miei, _____ in ordine la vostra stanza prima di cena! (mettere)

35. Dopo che tu _____ di lamentarti, noi _____ della tua richiesta. (smettere; parlare)

36. Io vi _____ al mio ritorno dalla Cina. (vedere)

37. "Chi ha suonato alla porta?" "_____ la nostra vicina di casa." (essere)

Answer Key

1 Gianni e Piero **correranno** la Maratona di New York. (*Gianni and Piero will run the New York Marathon.*)

2 Io e i miei fratelli **daremo** una grande festa. (*My brothers and I will have a big party.*)

3 "Marco, **partirai** per Mosca fra un mese?" (*"Marco, will you leave for Moscow in a month?"*)

4 "Signora, **cambierà** il suo numero di telefono?" (*"Madam, will you change your telephone number?"*)

5 "Signori, **uscirete** dalla porta numero 4." (*"[Ladies and] Gentlemen, you will exit gate number 4."*)

6 Tu e i tuoi colleghi **darete** le dimissioni? (*Will you and your colleagues quit?*)

7 Io **starò** a casa sabato sera. (*Saturday night I'll stay home.*)

8 Mamma e papà **faranno** le nozze d'oro a dicembre. (*Mom and Dad will celebrate their golden wedding [anniversary] in December.*)

9 Noi **dovremo** vendere la barca, purtroppo. (*Unfortunately, we'll have to sell the boat.*)

10 "Signore e Signori, **dovrete** lasciare la stanza." (*"Ladies and gentlemen, you will have to leave the room."*)

11 "Signore, **andrà** a Mosca il mese prossimo?" (*"Sir, will you go to Moscow next month?"*)

12 Stai tranquillo, domani **farà** bello. (*Don't worry, tomorrow the weather will be nice.*)

13 "Tu e tua moglie **andrete** in vacanza in Messico?" (*"Will you and your wife go to Mexico on vacation?"*)

14 **Accadranno** cose terribili il giorno dell'Apocalisse. (*Terrible things will happen on the day of the Apocalypse.*)

15 Al matrimonio io **berrò** alla salute degli sposi. (*At the wedding, I will drink to the newlyweds' health.*)

16 Noi **rimarremo** in campagna per l'estate. (*We'll remain at the country for the summer.*)

17 "State attente voi due, **cadrete** dalla scala!" (*"Be careful you two; you'll fall off the ladder!"*)

18 Voi **vedrete** la partita a casa sua. (*You'll watch the game at his/her place.*)

19 **Trarrà** lui le conclusioni dal tuo rapporto. (*He'll draw the conclusions from your report.*)

20 "**Verrai** da noi a cena, Luciano?" (*"Will you come to dinner at our place, Luciano?"*)

21 **L'avrò completata.** (*I will have completed it.*)

22 **Mi laureerò nel . . .** (*I will graduate in . . .*)

23 **Sì, mi iscriverò ai corsi "Commercio globale" e "Marketing."** (*Yes, I will enroll in the "Global Business" and "Marketing" courses.*)

24 **Farò domanda per uno** *stage*. (*I'll apply for an internship.*)

25 **Parteciperò ad attività sportive e ricreative.** (*I will participate in sports and recreational activities.*)

26 **Diventerò membro del Club.** (*I'll become a member of the Club.*)

27 **Avrò fatto domanda per una borsa di studio Erasmus.** (*I will have applied for an Erasmus bursarship.*)

28 **Riceverò una risposta entro il 31 luglio 2008.** (*I will receive an answer by July 31, 2008.*)

29 **Avrò bisogno di una sistemazione.** (*I will need an accommodation.*)

30 Noi **andiamo/andremo** alla partita sabato. (*We will go to the game on Saturday.*)

31 Ha detto con tono deciso: "**Andrò** a lavorare in Australia tra due anni!" (*He/She said with a firm voice: "I'll go work to Australia in two years!"*)

32 L'aereo per Tokyo **parte/partirà** alle 12:30. (*The flight for Tokyo leaves at 12:30.*)

33 Carlo, quando **arrivi** a Roma, prendi un taxi per venire da noi. (*Carlo, when you arrive in Rome, take a cab to get to our place.*)

34 Ragazzi miei, **metterete** in ordine la vostra stanza prima di cena! (*Kids, you will clean your room before dinner!*)

35 Dopo che tu **avrai smesso** di lamentarti, noi **parleremo** della tua richiesta. (*When you [will have stopped] stop complaining, we'll talk about your request.*)

36 Io vi **vedrò** al mio ritorno dalla Cina. (*I'll see you upon my return from China.*)

37 "Chi ha suonato alla porta?" "**Sarà** la nostra vicina di casa." (*"Who rang the doorbell?" "It may be our neighbor."*)

Part IV
Adding Nuances to Moods and Tenses

The 5th Wave   By Rich Tennant

"Saaay, I have an idea. Why don't we turn down the lights and parse a few chapters on conflict resolution from my latest Italian novel?"

In this part . . .

In Part IV, I discuss how Italian, like any language, is a public good shared with others. In order to communicate, you need words to ask questions, and you need to know how to construct answers. You also use different constructions to say that you're acting in the world, or that you're the object of your own actions, or that you're experiencing something being done to you.

Chapter 13

The Imperative

• •

In This Chapter

▶ Forming the informal and formal imperative of regular and irregular verbs

▶ Issuing affirmative and negative commands

▶ Adding pronouns to commands

• •

With the imperative, you encounter one more mood — different from the indicative, the subjunctive, the conditional, and so on. The imperative is the mood of commands and exhortations, like **Abbi fiducia!** (*Have faith!*) or the less-inspiring **Non tirare la coda al gatto!** (*Don't pull the cat's tail!*).

The imperative always implies a blunt command and is mainly used in conversation. To give generic orders, or in signs, advertisements, recipes, and instructions, Italian uses the infinitive.

> **Sonia, mescola la farina!** (*Sonia, mix the flour!*) (Imperative)
>
> **La ricetta dice: "Mescolare la farina e aggiungere tre uova".** (*The recipe says: "Mix the flour and add three eggs."*) (Infinitive)

A sentence such as **Andiamo! È tardi!** (*Let's go! It's late!*) lies between order and exhortation. You use the imperative when addressing a person directly, as in **Passi prima Lei, Signora!** (*Please, you go first, Madam!*); or **Prendano l'ascensore sulla destra!** (*Take the elevator on the right!*). And the imperative is employed mostly (but not exclusively) in the second-person singular and plural.

The future tense of the imperative is identical to the simple future of the indicative. All that distinguishes the two is the placement after the verb of the person to whom you issue a command (if expressed), the exclamation mark, and, in speech, the tone of voice. For example, **Andrete voi in banca a spiegare perché mancano i soldi!** (*You'll be the ones who go to the bank and explain why the money isn't there!*).

In this chapter, you find out how to form the present and future imperative and how to issue affirmative and negative commands.

The Imperative Form of Regular Verbs

When you form an imperative in Italian, you have a sort of reverse rule for the **tu** and **Lei** forms — the **-are** conjugations are a flip of the **-ere** and **-ire** conjugations. For example, the imperative of the verb **cantare** (*to sing*) is **Canta!** (informal) and **Canti!** (formal). In contrast, the imperative forms of **dormire** (*to sleep*), for example, are **Dormi!** (informal) and **Dorma!** (formal).

Informal usage

The imperative mood is used to give orders, advice, and exhortations. The informal imperative form addresses people with whom you're familiar, or when the degree of formality is low (with classmates, children, and co-workers, for example). The informal imperative forms of **tu, noi,** and **voi** are identical to the corresponding present tense forms with one exception: In the **tu** form of **-are** verbs, the **-i** becomes **-a**. Please note that the imperative form of **noi** corresponds to the English *Let's*. For example, **Andiamo a Parigi!** (*Let's go to Paris!*).

Table 13-1 shows the different conjugations for informal usage.

Table 13-1	Informal Imperatives of Regular Verbs	
Verb	*Informal Singular*	*Informal Plural*
guard**are** (*to look*)	(tu) guard**a**! (*[you] look!*)	(noi) guard**iamo**! (*[we] look!*); (voi) guard**ate**! (*[you] look!*)
prend**ere** (*to take*)	(tu) prend**i**! (*[you] take!*)	(noi) prend**iamo**! (*[we] take!*); (voi) prend**ete**! (*[you] take!*)
dorm**ire** (*to sleep*)	(tu) dorm**i**! (*[you] sleep!*)	(noi) dorm**iamo**! (*[we] sleep!*); (voi) dorm**ite**! (*[you] sleep!*)
fin**ire** (*to finish*)	(tu) fin**isci**! (*[you] finish!*)	(noi) fin**iamo**! (*[we] finish!*); (voi) fin**ite**! (*[you] finish!*)

Formal usage

The formal imperative is used less frequently than the informal command form. You go the formal route as a form of respect in situations where a certain degree of formality is required, such as when addressing your own boss, talking to older people, or talking to people you don't know or whom you've just met.

The best way to construct a formal imperative is to start from the **io** form of the present tense because some verbs base their regular formal imperative on an irregular form of the present. These verbs, whose stem changes in the present tense form, are as follows:

- ✔ **andare** (*to go*)
- ✔ **apparire** (*to appear*)
- ✔ **bere** (*to drink*)
- ✔ **cogliere** (*to pick*)
- ✔ **dire** (*to say*)
- ✔ **fare** (*to do, to make*)

- ✔ **porre** (*to put*)
- ✔ **rimanere** (*to remain*)
- ✔ **salire** (*to climb*)
- ✔ **scegliere** (*to choose*)
- ✔ **sedere** (*to sit*)
- ✔ **tradurre** (*to translate*)

- ✔ **trarre** (*to draw, to pull*)
- ✔ **udire** (*to hear*)
- ✔ **uscire** (*to go out*)
- ✔ **venire** (*to come*)

You create the formal **lei** and **loro** imperative by dropping the final **-o** from the **io** form of the present tense and adding **-i/-ino** to the stem of **-are** verbs, and **-a/-ano** to the stem of **-ere** and **-ire** verbs. Table 13-2 shows some examples.

Although you may hear the formal imperative of **Loro** in very upscale restaurants and hotels, this form is often replaced in everyday spoken Italian by the informal imperative form of **voi**, as in **Signore e signori, ascoltate con attenzione!** (*Ladies and gentlemen, listen carefully!*).

Table 13-2	Formal Imperatives of Regular Verbs	
Verb	*Formal Singular*	*Formal Plural*
guard**are** (*to look*)	(tu) guard**i**! (*[you] look!*)	(voi) guard**ino**! (*[you] look!*)
prend**ere** (*to take*)	(tu) prend**a**! (*[you] take!*)	(voi) prend**ano**! (*[you] take!*)
dorm**ire** (*to sleep*)	(tu) dorm**a**! (*[you] sleep!*)	(voi) dorm**ano**! (*[you] sleep!*)
fin**ire** (*to finish*)	(tu) fin**isca**! (*[you] finish!*)	(voi) fin**iscano**! (*[you] finish!*)

The Imperative Form of Irregular Verbs

Some Italian verbs have an irregular conjugation in the imperative mood. This section walks you through the conjugations of these verbs.

Verbs that are irregular in the informal imperative

The verbs **andare** (*to go*), **dare** (*to give*), **fare** (*to do, to make*), and **stare** (*to stay*) have both regular and irregular **tu** informal imperatives: **va'/vai, fa'/fai, da'/dai,** and **sta'/stai.** When speaking, their irregular imperatives are more common than their regular forms. Consider this example: **Sta' zitto e fa' quel che dico!** (*Be quiet and do as I say!*).

The verb **dire** (*to say*) is irregular only in the **tu** form, as in **Di' la verità!** (*Tell the truth!*).

Verbs that are irregular in the formal imperative

The verbs **avere** (*to have*), **essere** (*to be*), **sapere** (*to know how to*), **dare** (*to give*), and **stare** (*to stay*) are irregular in the formal imperative. The modal auxiliaries **dovere** (*must, shall*) and **potere** (*can, may*) don't have the imperative due to their meaning. But **volere** (*will, to want*) and **sapere** (*to know how to*) do, even though you may not use them often. I break down the conjugations of some of the auxiliaries and modal auxiliaries in the following tables.

avere (*to have*)	
	noi **abbiamo** (present indicative)
tu **abbi**	voi **abbiate** (present subjunctive)
lui/lei/Lei/esso **abbia** (present subjunctive)	loro/Loro/essi/esse **abbiano** (present subjunctive)
Abbi pazienza con lei. (*Have patience with her.*)	

essere (*to be*)	
	noi **siamo** (present indicative)
tu **sii**	voi **siate** (present subjunctive)
lui/lei/Lei/esso **sia** (present subjunctive)	loro/Loro/essi/esse **siano** (present subjunctive)
Sii gentile con lei. (*Be nice to her.*)	

sapere (*to know how to*)	
	noi **sappiamo** (present indicative)
tu **sappi**	voi **sappiate** (present subjunctive)
lui/lei/Lei/esso **sappia** (present subjunctive)	loro/Loro/essi/esse **sappiano** (present subjunctive)
Sappi che io non vengo. (*Know that I won't come.*)	

Use the clues in parentheses to fill in the blanks with the appropriate verbs in the present imperative.

0. _____ a spasso il cane! (tu, portare)

A. **Porta** a spasso il cane! (*Walk the dog!*)

1. _____ il mio consiglio, Signora! (ascoltare)

2. _____ con tuo fratello, Mara! (giocare)

3. _____ il vostro nome e cognome in stampatello, Signori! (voi, scrivere)

4. _____ a me, è meglio rimandare la partenza! (loro, credere)

5. _____ la passeggiata, anche se non siamo stanchi! (noi, finire)

6. _____ avanti, Signore e Signori! (loro, venire)

Negative Commands

You form the negative imperative for **tu** using the infinitive form of the verb preceded by **Non** (*Don't*). For example, **Non spendere troppo!** (*Don't spend too much!*). The forms of **noi** and **voi** imperatives are formed by using their affirmative imperative preceded by **Non**. For example, **Non parlate così in fretta!** (*Don't speak so fast!*). You craft the negative form of the formal imperative by adding **Non** to the formal imperative, as in **Non usi quel telefono, non funziona** (*Don't use that phone, it doesn't work*).

The negative informal imperatives of the irregular verbs follow the rules of the regular imperatives.

The only difference between a verb's conjugations in affirmative and negative commands is that in negative commands you use the infinitive preceded by the particle **non** in the second-person singular. For example, **Non tornare tardi!** (*Don't come back late!*). Following are some more examples:

✔ **essere: Non essere!** (*Don't be!*)

✔ **fare: Non lo fare!** (*Don't do it!*)

✔ **andare: Non andare!** (*Don't go!*)

✔ **uscire: Non uscire!** (*Don't go out!*)

✔ **dire: Non lo dire!** (*Don't say it!*)

✔ **bere: Non bere!** (*Don't drink!*)

Each of the following questions contains a reproduced road sign. Use the clues to tell your driver what he or she should or shouldn't do, depending on the sign. Write short commands in the second-person singular and plural.

Q. (rallentare)

A. **Rallenta! Rallentate!** (*Go slower!*)

7. (dare la precedenza)

_____

8. (entrare)

_____

9. (parcheggiare)

_____

10. (sorpassare)

_____

11. (girare a destra)

_____

12. (superare il limite di velocità)

_____

Adding Pronouns to Commands

When you issue a command, emphasis falls on the verb, which usually comes at the beginning of the sentence, as in **Andate a casa!** (*Go home!*).

When the pronoun follows the imperative

Sometimes a pronoun follows the imperative, like the English command *Listen to me*. In this case, the pronoun is attached to the informal imperative form of the verb, as in **Ascoltami bene prima di parlare** (*Listen to me carefully before speaking*). Here are the unstressed pronouns you can attach to the imperative:

- Direct object pronouns: **mi** (*me*), **ti** (*you*), **lo/la** (*him/her*), **ci** (*us*), **vi** (*you*); also **loro** (*them*) placed after the verb but not attached to it

    Aiutala! (*Help her!*)

- Indirect object pronouns: **mi** (*to/for me*), **ti** (*to/for you*), **gli/le** (*to/for him/her*), **ci** (*to/for us*), **vi** (*to/for you*), **gli** (*to/for him*); also **loro** (*to/for them*) placed after the verb

    Compriamogli un paio di guanti. (*Let's buy him a pair of gloves.*)

- **Ci** (*here, there, about this/that*) and **ne** (*about him/her/them, of this/that*)

    Andateci! (*Go there!*)

    Parlatene! (*Talk about that!*)

- Double pronouns: **me lo** (*that to me*), **te le** (*those to her*), **glielo** (*it/that to him/her*), **gliene** (*about that to him*), **ce ne** (*about that to us*)

    Diteglielo. (*Tell it to him/her.*)

    Parlarmene. (*Tell me everything about it.*)

When using a reflexive verb or a direct or indirect object pronoun, the pronoun follows and is attached to the imperative. For example: **Alzati e lavati!** (*Get up and wash yourself!*)

In negative **tu** commands, the pronoun may precede or follow the infinitive. When attached to the infinitive, the infinitive drops the final **-e** before the pronoun, as in **Non preoccuparti; Non ti preoccupare** (*Don't worry*).

Refer to Table 13-3 for the use of reflexive pronouns with the imperative mood. Note that the negative informal imperatives of the irregular verbs listed in Table 13-3 follow the rules of the regular imperatives.

Table 13-3	Reflexive Imperatives		
Affirmative Commands		**Negative Commands**	
Lavati!	*Wash yourself!*	**Non ti lavare!, Non lavarti!**	*Don't wash yourself!*
Si lavi!	*Let him/her wash himself/ herself! Wash yourself!* (FS)	**Non si lavi!**	*Let him/her not wash himself!/ herself! Don't wash yourself!* (FS)
Laviamoci!	*Let's wash ourselves!*	**Non laviamoci!, Non ci laviamo!**	*Let's not wash ourselves!*
Lavatevi!	*Wash yourselves!*	**Non lavatevi!, Non vi lavate!**	*Don't wash yourselves!*
Si lavino!	*Let them wash themselves! Wash yourselves!* (FP)	**Non si lavino!**	*Let them not wash themselves! Don't wash yourselves!* (FP)

When the pronoun precedes the imperative

When using a formal imperative, the pronoun precedes the imperative and the verb, as in **Mi ascolti bene prima di parlare** (*Listen to me carefully before speaking*).

When attaching a pronoun to the irregular **tu** imperative forms of **andare, dare, fare, stare,** and **dire** (refer to the earlier section "The Imperative Form of Irregular Verbs" for more on this), the apostrophe disappears and the first consonant of the pronoun doubles. For example, **Dimmi che verrai!** (*Tell me that you'll come!*).

An exception to this rule is the indirect object pronoun **gli.** When attaching it to the imperative, the first consonant **g** doesn't double after the imperative. For example, **Dagli il libro** (*Give him the book*).

If you issue a negative command in the second-person singular, which uses the infinitive, you drop the final **-e** of the verb. You can attach the pronoun to the verb or insert the unstressed pronoun between the particle **non** (*not*) and the verb. Here are examples of both options:

> **Non telefonargli!** (*Don't call him on the phone!*)
>
> **Non gli telefonare!** (*Don't call him on the phone!*)

When issuing a negative command expressed in the formal imperative, the pronoun is always placed between **Non** and the imperative, as in **Non si preoccupi, signora** (*Don't worry, Madam*).

Chapter 17 discusses reflexive verbs, such as **addormentarsi** (*to fall asleep*) and **lavarsi** (*to wash oneself*), which employ reflexive pronouns placed before the verb. In the imperative of these verbs, the same rules of the pronouns apply. For example, **Alzati** (*Get up*); **Pettinatevi bene** (*Comb your hair well*).

Rewrite each sentence, replacing the nouns/names with direct objects, indirect objects, and double pronouns. Use the unstressed form attached directly to the verb when possible.

Q. Mandate una cartolina a Marco!

A. **Mandategliela!** (*Let's send it to him!*)

13. Porta le sedie in casa!

_____

14. Non mangiare il gelato!

_____

15. Non comprate la frutta!

_____

16. Porta a noi il libro!

_____

17. Saluti Elisa da parte mia, Signora!

_____

18. Non seguano Mario!

_____

19. Invitate Marco e Gianna a cena!

_____

20. Non facciamo la torta!

_____

21. Non regaliamo la radio a Mario!

_____

22. Offrite un bicchiere di vino a loro!

_____

Answer Key

1 **Ascolti** il mio consiglio, Signora! (*Listen to my advice, Madam!*)

2 **Gioca** con tuo fratello, Mara! (*Play with your brother, Mara!*)

3 **Scrivete** il vostro nome e cognome in stampatello, Signori! (*Print your name and surname, ladies and gentlemen!*)

4 **Credano** a me, è meglio rimandare la partenza! (*Believe me, it's better to postpone your departure!*)

5 **Finiamo** la passeggiata, anche se siamo stanchi! (*Let's finish the walk, even though we're tired!*)

6 **Vengano** avanti, Signore e Signori! (*Come in, ladies and gentlemen!*)

7 **Da' la precedenza! Date la precedenza!** (*Yield the right of way!*)

8 **Non entrare! Non entrate!** (*Don't enter!*)

9 **Non parcheggiare! Non parcheggiate!** (*Don't park!*)

10 **Non sorpassare! Non sorpassate!** (*Don't pass!*)

11 **Gira a destra! Girate a destra!** (*Turn right!*) or **Non girare a sinistra! Non girate a sinistra!** (*Don't turn left!*) or **Non andare dritto! Non andate dritto!** (*Don't go straight!*)

12 **Non superare il limite di velocità! Non superate il limite di velocità!** (*Don't exceed the speed limit!*)

13 **Portale in casa.** (*Bring them home.*)

14 **Non mangiarlo!** (*Don't eat it!*)

15 **Non compratela.** (*Don't buy it.*)

16 **Portacelo!** (*Bring it to us!*)

17 **La saluti da parte mia.** (*Say hello to her for me.*)

18 **Non lo seguano!** (*Don't follow him!*)

19 **Invitateli a cena!** (*Invite them to dinner!*)

20 **Non facciamola.** (*Let's not do it.*)

21 **Non regaliamogliela!** (*Let's not give it to him/her!*)

22 **Offriteglielo!** (*Offer it to them!*)

Chapter 14

Forming Conditional and Subjunctive Verbs

· ·

In This Chapter

▶ Working with the present and the past conditional

▶ Putting the present subjunctive to use

▶ Forming the imperfect subjunctive

▶ Understanding the present perfect and the past perfect subjunctive

· ·

The conditional and the subjunctive are two moods; they're different from the indicative mood and from one another. *Mood* represents the speaker's attitude about whether something is considered factual. Here are explanations of each mood:

✔ The *indicative* is the mood of assertions and descriptions, where you're stating straightforward facts. For example, when you say **Parlo spagnolo** (*I speak Spanish*), you're using the indicative mood.

✔ The *conditional* is the mood of hypothetical situations and of events dependent on something else happening. In English, you're using the conditional mood when you use *would* plus an infinitive, as in this sentence: **Vorrei studiare medicina** (*I'd like to study medicine*).

✔ The *subjunctive* is the mood of possibility, uncertainty, and of hypotheses when used in *if . . . then* statements with the conditional. In Italian, a subjunctive statement you may make is **Accetteri quel lavoro se offrissero uno stipendio migliore** (*I'd accept that job if they offered a better salary*).

In this chapter, I show you how to form the present and past conditional and the present, imperfect, present perfect, and past perfect subjunctive. Also in this chapter, I give you the opportunity to practice conjugations and discover how to form conditionals and subjunctives. Chapter 15 focuses on putting these moods into practice, particularly when using the *if . . . then* statements.

Shaping Verbs into the Present Conditional

The *present conditional* is a simple tense that you form by adding suffixes to the stem of the verb, depending on the verb's ending. You use it when you want to express events occurring under certain circumstances or conditions. It's also used to add politeness to offers, advice, and requests that would otherwise sound too blunt. Read on for the conjugations.

Regular verbs

The conjugations for regular verbs in the present conditional mood have one set of endings attached to the future stem of the verb. The future stem of regular verbs is the infinitive of the verb minus the final **-e**; also, in **-are** verbs, the **a** of the infinitive changes to **e** (see Chapter 12 for more on the future). The present conditional endings are the same for the three conjugations (**-are, -ere,** and **-ire** verbs). See Table 14-1.

Table 14-1	Endings for Regular Verbs in the Present Conditional
Person	*Conditional Endings*
io	**-ei**
tu	**-esti**
lui/lei/Lei/esso/essa	**-ebbe**
noi	**-emmo**
voi	**-este**
loro/Loro/essi/esse	**-ebbero**

Both regular and irregular verbs formed with prefixes behave like the basic verb. For example, if you add the prefix **stra-** to **vincere** (*to win*) to create **stravincere** (*to win by a great margin*), you conjugate these two verbs in the same way:

> **Con molta fortuna vincerei un milione di dollari alla lotteria.** (*With a lot of luck, I would win one million dollars and the lottery.*)

> **Con un buon allenatore stravincerebbe.** (*With a good coach, he would win by a great margin.*)

The following table shows you how to conjugate **guardare** (*to look at*).

guardare (*to look at*)	
io guard**erei**	noi guard**eremmo**
tu guard**eresti**	voi guard**ereste**
lui/lei/Lei/esso/essa guard**erebbe**	loro/Loro/essi/esse guard**erebbero**
Non **guarderemmo** mai quel programma! (*We would never watch that show!*)	

As you see for the various conjugations throughout this book, verbs that end in **-ciare** and **-giare,** such as **lanciare** (*to launch, to throw*) and **mangiare** (*to eat*), drop the **i** before the endings because the **-e** of the **-are, -ere,** and **-ire** preserves the soft sound. Verbs that end in **-care** and **-gare,** such as **cercare** (*to look for*) and **pagare** (*to pay*), take **ch** and **gh** before the endings to preserve the hard sound of the infinitive.

Irregular verbs (Well, sort of)

All verbs that have an irregular future stem use the same stem for the conditional. So though it seems that the conditional has irregular verbs, the situation is sort of misleading; the future has the irregular conjugations, and the conditional is built on the future tense. Technically, the conditional *does* follow a regular pattern — you form it by adding the appropriate endings to the future stems of the verb. Because I cover the future tense at length in Chapter 12, I provide conjugations for only the auxiliaries and the modal auxiliaries here; to find out how to form the conditional tense of all other irregular verbs in the future tense, consult Chapter 12 and apply the conjugation pattern for the conditional, which I explain in the preceding section.

You can use **essere** (*to be*) and **avere** (*to have*) by themselves or as auxiliaries in compound tenses (see Chapters 9 and 10 for details). In the present conditional mood, the stem for **essere** is **sar-**. For **avere,** you drop both **e**'s from the infinitive to get **avr-**. The following tables show the conjugations for both **essere** and **avere**.

essere (*to be*)	
io sar**ei**	noi sar**emmo**
tu sar**esti**	voi sar**este**
lui/lei/Lei/esso/essa sar**ebbe**	loro/Loro/essi/esse sar**ebbero**
Sarei felice di conoscerlo. (*I would be happy to meet him.*)	

avere (*to have*)	
io avr**ei**	noi avr**emmo**
tu avr**esti**	voi avr**este**
lui/lei/Lei/esso/essa avr**ebbe**	loro/Loro/essi/esse avr**ebbero**
Non **avrebbe** della moneta? (*Would you happen to have change?*)	

People often use the conditional of the modal auxiliaries **dovere** (*must, shall*), **potere** (*can, may*), **volere** (*to want to*), and **sapere** (*to know how to*) to soften the impact of requests and demands. **Volere** uses the stem **vorr-**.

dovere (*must, shall*)	
io dovr**ei**	noi dovr**emmo**
tu dovr**esti**	voi dovr**este**
lui/lei/Lei/esso/essa dovr**ebbe**	loro/Loro/essi/esse dovr**ebbero**
Perché **dovremmo** pagare noi? (*Why should we have to pay?*)	

potere (*can, may*)	
io pot**rei**	noi pot**remmo**
tu pot**resti**	voi pot**reste**
lui/lei/Lei/esso/essa pot**rebbe**	loro/Loro/essi/esse pot**rebbero**
Potresti richiamarmi? (*Could you call me back?*)	

sapere (*to know how to*)	
io sap**rei**	noi sap**remmo**
tu sap**resti**	voi sap**reste**
lui/lei/Lei/esso/essa sap**rebbe**	loro/Loro/essi/esse sap**rebbero**
Saprebbe dirmi dove posso trovare un buon ristorante? (*Would you be able to tell me where I can find a good restaurant?*)	

volere (*will, to want to*)	
io vor**rei**	noi vor**remmo**
tu vor**resti**	voi vor**reste**
lui/lei/Lei/esso/essa vor**rebbe**	loro/Loro/essi/esse vor**rebbero**
Vorrei parlarti prima possibile. (*I would like to talk to you as soon as possible.*)	

For each of the following sentences, choose the correct verb among the options in parentheses.

Q. (Verrei/Correrei/Giocherei) volentieri, ma ho un appuntamento.

A. **Verrei** volentieri, ma ho un appuntamento. (*I would gladly come, but I have an appointment.*)

1. Elena odia il mare e (potrebbe/dovrebbe/vorrebbe) vendere la barca di suo marito al più presto.

2. Io (vorrei/farei/mangerei) una torta, ma non ho farina.

3. Lei (vorrebbe/accompagneresti/prenderesti) dare le dimissioni.

4. Maria, la nonna non sta bene: la (lasceresti/accompagneresti/prenderesti) tu dal medico, per favore?

5. Mario e Piero (visiterebbero/partirebbero/andrebbero) per Roma, ma c'è sciopero.

6. Noi (berremmo/mangeremmo/godremmo) volentieri una birra.

7. "Signora, (darebbe/offrirebbe/ascolterebbe) alla segretaria il suo numero di telefono?"

8. "Signori, (passereste/potreste/entrereste) uscire dalla porta numero 4?"

9. Tu (vivresti/lasceresti/passeresti) con lei?

10. Voi (pulireste/lavereste/spazzolereste) questa maglia in acqua?

It's Over Now! Forming the Past Conditional

Although the present conditional describes an option that's still possible, the past conditional expresses the idea that that option is no longer likely to happen; the past conditional also describes an action that's not possible in the future, either.

The *past conditional* is a compound tense that's made of the present conditional of the auxiliaries **essere** (*to be*) and **avere** (*to have*) (see the preceding section) along with the past participle of the main verb. The auxiliary you decide on depends on which main verb you're using. (Chapter 10 shows you how to decide which auxiliary verb to use as well as how to form the past participle and coordinate it with subjects and objects.)

For example, in the following sentence, you form the past conditional mood by using the auxiliary **essere** and the past participle of **venire** (*to go*), which is **venuto:**

> **Sarei venuto al cinema con te, ma ero troppo stanco.** (*I would've gone to the movies with you, but I was too tired.*)

Here are two tables of the past conditional of **leggere** (*to read*), which takes the auxiliary **avere**, and of **andare** (*to go*), which takes the auxiliary **essere.**

leggere (to read)	
io **avrei letto**	noi **avremmo letto**
tu **avresti letto**	voi **avreste letto**
lui/lei/Lei/esso/essa **avrebbe letto**	loro/Loro **avrebbero letto**
Avrei letto il giornale, ma l'hai buttato via. (*I would've read the newspaper, but you tossed it.*)	

andare (to go)	
io **sarei andato/andata**	noi **saremmo andati/andate**
tu **saresti andato/andata**	voi **sareste andati/andate**
lui/lei/Lei/esso/essa **sarebbe andato/andata**	loro/Loro **sarebbero andati/andate**
I ragazzi non **sarebbero** mai **andati** alla festa senza di te. (*The boys would've never gone to the party without you.*)	

Putting Verbs in the Present Subjunctive

The *subjunctive mood* expresses doubt, possibility, uncertainty, or personal opinions of the subject, as opposed to plain facts, which are expressed by the *indicative*. The subjunctive can also express emotion, desire, or suggestions. It's generally preceded by a main clause and introduced by the conjunction **che** (*that*). In this section, you discover the present subjunctive, a simple tense formed by adding suffixes to the stem of the verb, depending on the verb's conjugation type.

Regular verbs

You form the present subjunctive by adding the corresponding suffixes to the stem of the verb. The stem is simply the infinitive minus the **-are, -ere,** or **-ire** ending. I list the subjunctive suffixes Table 14-2.

Table 14-2	Suffixes for Regular Verbs in the Present Subjunctive	
Person	*Suffix for -are Verbs*	*Suffix for -ere and -ire Verbs*
io	-i	-a
tu	-i	-a
lui/lei/Lei/esso/essa	-i	-a
noi	-iamo	-iamo
voi	-iate	-iate
loro/Loro	-ino	-ano

Note that the first-person singular and third-person plural persons of the present subjunctive correspond to the conjugation of the formal imperative mood (see Chapter 13). Check it out:

- ✔ **Formal imperative:** Signorina Rutelli, **venga** avanti! (*Miss, come on in!*)
- ✔ **Present subjunctive:** Penso che la signorina Rutelli **venga** da Roma. (*I think that Ms. Rutelli is from Rome.*)

Also, verbs ending in **-ire** that insert **-isc-** between the stem and the verb endings in the present indicative, such as **finire** (*to finish*), follow the same rule in the subjunctive:

Immagino che il film **finisca** bene. (*I imagine that the film has a happy ending.*)

The following table shows you how to conjugate **sentire** (*to hear*).

sentire (*to hear*)	
io sent**a**	noi sent**iamo**
tu sent**a**	voi sent**iate**
lui/lei/Lei/esso sent**a**	loro/Loro/essi/esse sent**ano**
È possibile che non **sentano** perché sono a un concerto. (*It's possible that they can't hear because they're at a concert.*)	

As usual, verbs ending in **-care** and **-gare** add an **h** before endings beginning with **i**. They do so in order to retain the hard sound of the **c** or **g**.

Irregular verbs

When conjugating irregular verbs in the present subjunctive, you usually modify the stem of the infinitive and apply the same suffixes as you do for regular verbs (refer to Table 14-2 for the suffixes to use). Some verbs use a particular modified stem in all six persons, but others use the regular stem (or another modified stem) in the first- and second-person plural. Table 14-3 shows how the stems change for the most common irregular verbs. (Consult Chapter 9 for a more complete list of verbs that modify their stems.)

In the present subjunctive, when a verb has an unaccented **i** in its stem, you drop it if the verb also has an **i** in the suffix. For example, **incominciare** (*to begin*), whose stem is usually **incominci-**, conjugates as **loro incomincino; fare** (*to make, to do*), whose stem is usually **facci-**, conjugates as **noi facciamo**. However, if the **i** in the stem is accented, keep it; for instance, **sciare** (*to ski*), whose stem is **sci-**, conjugates as **loro sciino**.

Table 14-3	Modified Stems of the Present Subjunctive	
Infinitive	*Usual Present Subjunctive Stem*	*Special Stem in the 1st- and 2nd-Person Plural*
andare (*to go*)	vad-	and-
apparire (*to appear*)	appai-	appar-
avere (*to have*)	abb-	
bere (*to drink*)	bev-	
condurre (*to lead*)	conduc-	
dare (*to give*)	di-	
dire (*to say, to tell*)	dic-	
dovere (*must, shall*)	debb-	dobb-
essere (*to be*)	si-	

(continued)

Table 14-3 (continued)

Infinitive	Usual Present Subjunctive Stem	Special Stem in the 1st- and 2nd-Person Plural
fare (to do, to make)	**facci-**	
finire (to end, to finish)	**finisc-**	**fin-**
piacere (to be pleasing)	**piacc-**	
porre (to put)	**pong-**	**pon-**
potere (can, may)	**poss-**	
sapere (to know how to)	**sappi-**	
scegliere (to choose)	**scelg-**	**scegl-**
spegnere (to turn off)	**speng-**	**spegn-**
stare (to stay)	**sti-**	
tenere (to keep, to hold)	**teng-**	**ten-**
trarre (to pull)	**tragg-**	**tra-**
uscire (to go out)	**esc-**	**usc-**
venire (to come)	**veng-**	**ven-**
volere (to will)	**vogli-**	

Creating the Imperfect Subjunctive

The imperfect subjunctive is a simple tense that you form by adding suffixes to the stem of the verb. Like the present subjunctive, the imperfect subjunctive expresses doubt, possibility, uncertainty, personal opinions, emotion, desire, or suggestions. You use it instead of the present subjunctive when your sentence meets the following conditions:

- The verb in the main clause is in a past tense or in the present conditional.
- The action in the subordinate clause occurred simultaneously or after the action in the main clause.

Regular verbs

The imperfect subjunctive uses the same stem as the imperfect indicative, and it adds the same subjunctive endings to the verbs of all conjugations. In other words, it drops the **-re** from the infinitive and adds the endings in Table 14-4.

Table 14-4	Endings for Regular Verbs in the Imperfect Subjunctive
Person	*Ending*
io	**-ssi**
tu	**-ssi**
lui/lei/Lei/esso/essa	**-sse**
noi	**-ssimo**
voi	**-ste**
loro/Loro	**-ssero**

The table that follows gives you a sample conjugation of **temere** (*to be afraid of*).

temere (*to be afraid of*)	
io teme**ssi**	noi teme**ssimo**
tu teme**ssi**	voi teme**ste**
lui/lei/Lei/esso/essa teme**sse**	loro/Loro/essi/esse teme**ssero**
Non sapevo che mi **temessi**. (*I didn't know you were afraid of me.*)	

Irregular verbs

The verbs **essere** (*to be*), **dare** (*to give*), and **stare** (*to stay*) use a modified stem when conjugated in the imperfect. Here are their conjugations.

essere (*to be*)	
io **fossi**	noi **fossimo**
tu **fossi**	voi **foste**
lui/lei/Lei/esso **fosse**	loro/Loro/essi/esse **fossero**
Pensavo che **fossi** più simpatico. (*I thought you were nicer.*)	

dare (*to give*)	
io **dessi**	noi **dessimo**
tu **dessi**	voi **deste**
lui/lei/Lei/esso/essa **desse**	loro/Loro/essi/esse **dessero**
Sarebbe meglio che mi **deste** una mano. (*It'd be better if you gave me a hand.*)	

stare (*to stay, to be*)	
io **stessi**	noi **stessimo**
tu **stessi**	voi **steste**
lui/lei/Lei/esso/essa **stesse**	loro/Loro/essi/esse **stessero**
Vorrei che **stessero** bene. (*I wish they felt well.*)	

Form the present and the imperfect subjunctive of the following verbs.

0. lei _____; lei _____ (fare)

A. lei **faccia**; lei **facesse**

11. tu _____; tu _____ (essere)

12. noi _____; noi _____ (sostenere)

13. voi _____; voi _____ (pagare)

14. io _____; io _____ (bere)

15. noi _____; noi _____ (piangere)

16. lui _____; lui _____ (cercare)

17. noi _____; noi _____ (dovere)

18. io _____; io _____ (finire)

19. voi _____; voi _____ (trarre)

20. loro _____; loro _____ (sapere)

21. tu _____; tu _____ (venire)

22. lei _____; lei _____ (piacere)

23. io _____; io _____ (dire)

24. voi _____; voi _____ (dare)

25. noi _____; noi _____ (essere)

26. tu _____; tu _____ (avere)

Constructing the Subjunctive Mood of the Present Perfect and Past Perfect

The *present perfect subjunctive* and the *past perfect subjunctive* are compound tenses. To put the present perfect and past perfect tenses in the subjunctive mood, you use a subjunctive form of the auxiliary **essere** or **avere** along with the past participle of the main verb. (For rules about forming the past participle, choosing between **essere** and **avere,** and coordinating subjects and past participles, consult Chapter 10.)

The present perfect corresponds to the simple past in English. You use the present perfect subjunctive to describe a past action when the verb in the main clause is in the present tense and requires a subjunctive. Form the subjunctive mood of this tense with

- ✔ The present subjunctive of the auxiliary **essere** or **avere**
- ✔ The past participle of the main verb

The past perfect subjunctive corresponds to the present perfect and preterit of the indicative. It's used whenever one of these tenses is in the indicative mood. Use the past perfect subjunctive in a subordinate clause when the verb in the main clause is in any form of past tense or in the conditional and when the action in the subordinate clause occurred before the action in the main clause. The past perfect subjunctive is formed with

- ✔ The imperfect subjunctive of the auxiliaries **essere** and **avere**
- ✔ The past participle of the main verb

Compare these examples of the present perfect and past perfect in the subjunctive:

- ✔ Present perfect subjunctive: **Credo che Luisa gli abbia parlato.** (*I believe Luisa spoke to him.*)

  Past perfect subjunctive: **Speravo che Luisa gli avesse parlato.** (*I hoped Luisa had spoken to him.*)

- ✔ Present perfect subjunctive: **Temo che siano andati via.** (*I'm afraid they left.*)

  Past perfect subjunctive: **Pensavo che fossero andati via.** (*I thought they had left.*)

The following verbal forms are in the present subjunctive and the imperfect subjunctive. Turn the former into the present perfect subjunctive and the latter into the past perfect subjunctive.

Q. lui esca; uscisse

A. **lui sia uscito; fosse uscito**

27. Elena e Giovanna stiano; stessero _____

28. Piero appaia; apparisse _____

29. io dipinga; dipingessi _____

30. lei dia; desse _____

31. loro abbiano; avessero _____

32. voi temiate; temeste _____

33. lui spenga; spegnesse _____

34. noi veniamo; venissimo _____

35. tu, Maria, vada; andassi _____

36. voi siate; foste _____

Answer Key

1 Elena odia il mare e **vorrebbe** vendere la barca di suo marito al più presto. (*Elena hates the sea, and she'd like to sell her husband's boat as soon as possible.*)

2 Io **farei** una torta, ma non ho farina. (*I would bake a cake, but I don't have flour.*)

3 Lei **vorrebbe** dare le dimissioni. (*She would like to quit.*)

4 Maria, la nonna non sta bene: la **accompagneresti** tu dal medico, per favore? (*Maria, Grandma doesn't feel well: Would you please take her to the doctor's, please?*)

5 Mario e Piero **partirebbero** per Roma, ma c'è sciopero. (*Mario and Piero would leave for Rome, but there's a strike.*)

6 Noi **berremmo** volentieri una birra. (*We would gladly drink a beer.*)

7 "Signora, **darebbe** alla segretaria il suo numero di telefono?" (*"Madam, would you give your telephone number to the secretary?"*)

8 "Signori, **potreste** uscire dalla porta numero 4?" (*"Ladies and gentlemen, could you exit gate number 4?"*)

9 Tu **vivresti** con lei? (*Would you live with her?*)

10 Voi **lavereste** questa maglia in acqua? (*Would you wash this sweater in water?*)

11 tu **sia** (*you were*); tu **fossi** (*you were*)

12 noi **sosteniamo** (*we support*); noi **sostenessimo** (*we supported*)

13 voi **paghiate** (*you pay*); voi **pagaste** (*you paid*)

14 io **beva** (*I drink*); io **bevessi** (*I drank*)

15 noi **piangiamo** (*we cry*); noi **piangessimo** (*we cried*)

16 lui **cerchi** (*he looks for*); lui **cercasse** (*he looked for*)

17 noi **dobbiamo** (*we have to*); noi **dovessimo** (*we had to*)

18 io **finisca** (*I finish*); io **finissi** (*I finished*)

19 voi **traiate** (*you pull/draw*); voi **traeste** (*you pulled/drew*)

20 loro **sappiano** (*they know*); loro **sapessero** (*they knew*)

21 tu **venga** (*I come*); tu **venissi** (*I came*)

22 lei **piaccia** (*she like*); lei **piacesse** (*she liked*)

23 io **dica** (*I say*); io **dicessi** (*I said*)

24 voi **diate** (*you give*); voi **deste** (*you gave*)

25 noi **siamo** (*we are*); noi **fossimo** (*we were*)

26 tu **abbia** (*you have*); tu **avessi** (*you had*)

27 **Elena e Giovanna siano state** (*Elena and Giovanna were*); **fossero state** (*had been*)

28 **Piero sia apparso** (*Piero appeared*); **fosse apparso** (*had appeared*)

29 **io abbia dipinto** (*I painted*); **avessi dipinto** (*I had painted*)

30 **lei abbia dato** (*she gave*); **avesse dato** (*she had given*)

31 **loro abbiano avuto** (*they had*); **avessero avuto** (*they had had*)

32 **voi abbiate temuto** (*you were afraid*); **aveste temuto** (*you had been afraid*)

33 **lui abbia spento** (*he turned off*); **avesse spento** (*he had turned off*)

34 **noi siamo venuti** (*we came*); **fossimo venuti** (*we had come*)

35 **tu, Maria, sia andata** (*you, Maria, went*); **fossi andata** (*you had gone*)

36 **voi siate stati** (*you were*); **foste stati** (*you had been*)

Chapter 15

The Conditional and the Subjunctive in Action

● ●

In This Chapter

▶ Expressing your wishes and requests with the conditional

▶ Working with dependent clauses introduced by *that*

▶ Forming *if . . . then* clauses

● ●

This chapter tells you how you can use the conditional and the subjunctive in various settings. If you happened to open this book to this page and have never encountered the conditional, the subjunctive, or their conjugations in Italian, take a step back and read Chapter 14, where I explain the basic meanings of these tenses and how to handle regular and irregular verbs.

You can use the conditional and the subjunctive in two ways:

✔ To build a sentence that stands alone: For example, with the conditional, you can say **Vorrei comprare un vestito** (*I'd like to buy a dress*). With the subjunctive, you can say **Viva l'Italia!** (*Long live Italy!*) or **Che lui possa tornare sano e salvo!** (*I wish that he comes back safe and sound!*). I doubt you'll go around talking in the subjunctive much, but you may find the tense used in writing, so you need to understand it.

✔ To put two sentences together: For example, **Voglio che tu gli parli** (*I want you to talk to him*) or **Se mi telefonasse le spiegherei tutto** (*If she would call me, I'd explain everything to her*). At times, you'll need the subjunctive and the conditional together; at other times, you'll use them with the indicative (refer to Chapters 9 through 11) or the imperative (refer to Chapter 13).

To help you deal with these options, in this chapter I explain how you can use the conditional by itself to express wishes and polite invitations. I tell you how to build a main sentence and then add a dependent clause that contains a declaration, forming a *declarative dependent clause*. I also tell you how to build a main sentence and then add a condition or a hypothesis, as in **Se muovi la regina, lui ti dà scacco matto** (*If you move your queen, he'll give you checkmate*).

Finally, I help you decide what tense you need: the present, the imperfect, the present perfect . . . and the list goes on. Consult the sections devoted to temporal sequences to get a full picture. Temporal sequences aren't easy, in part because you can't always rely on the patterns of the English language to help you decide what to do in Italian. With that in mind, I give you some basic guidelines to follow.

Using the Conditional by Itself

If you want something, you can be very assertive (as children are) and say **Voglio un gelato!** (*I want ice cream!*). If you're talking to yourself, this sort of statement is okay, but if you're engaging in polite conversation, you may want to be a tad less aggressive. The conditional enables you to tone down your demands, as in **Sposteresti la macchina, per favore?** (*Would you mind moving the car, please?*); and to express surprise and uncertainty, as in **Ci crederesti?** (*Can you believe that?*). In such cases, you build independent sentences with the verb in the conditional.

The conditional has a present and past tense.

- ✔ You use the present conditional when you're talking about something that someone is requesting or wishing right now, as in **La Signora Rossi ti vorrebbe parlare** (*Mrs. Rossi would like to talk to you*).

- ✔ You use the past conditional to convey that something would have been desirable or appropriate, even though it's too late now to do anything about it, as in **Avrei visto volentieri quel film una seconda volta** (*I would like to have seen that movie a second time*).

In both Italian and English, it's often the case that you use some verbs to modify the meaning of another verb. These modal verbs are **dovere** (*must, shall*), **potere** (*can, may*), and **volere** (*will, want to*). They're called **verbi servili** (*modal auxiliaries*) because they provide help.

Italian also uses **sapere** (*to know how to*) as a modal auxiliary, as in **Sapresti aprire la cassaforte?** (*Could/Would you be able to open the safe?*).

Rewrite the following sentences, adding a diplomatic nuance. Change only the verb.

Q. Comprate del pane anche per me.

A. **Comprereste** del pane anche per me? (*Would you buy some bread for me too?*)

1. Cristina e Mara, portate la valigia del nonno?

_____

2. Signora, mi prepara il pacco per oggi pomeriggio?

_____

3. Signori, giocano a bridge con noi?

_____

4. Devi restituirgli i soldi.

_____

5. Vogliono passare per Madrid.

---

6. Possiamo comprare quella casa.

---

7. Lei vuole andarsene, mentre lui vuole rimanere.

Constructing Declarative Clauses

Leaving the world of self-sufficient clauses, this section walks you through the world of dependency, where you build an independent or main clause and then you build another one that can't stand on its own legs. If you start a sentence with the words **Ti dico . . .** (*I'm telling you . . .*), the sentence that follows, introduced by **che** (*that*) — **. . . che lui sta bene** (*. . . that he's well*) is a dependent declarative clause, the most common dependent clause in English and Italian. It's dependent because the sentence is incomplete without the introduction provided by the main clause. It's declarative in the sense that you're declaring or asserting something.

This section tells you how to put together a main clause and a dependent declarative clause in Italian, starting with the simplest case in which both clauses are in the present tense (of the indicative, or of the indicative plus the subjunctive). Then I tell how to handle different tenses.

The relative pronoun **che** means *who, whom, that,* and *which*. It introduces relative clauses, as in **La ragazza che ha telefonato è la zia di Lia** (*The girl who called is Lia's aunt*). (Chapter 8 covers relative pronouns.)

To add a declarative clause in Italian, you have two possible constructions:

- ✔ When you convey certainty in the main clause, you use the present indicative in both clauses, as in **La UPS ci informa che il pacco è in transito** (*UPS informs us that the package is in transit*).

- ✔ When you convey uncertainty or preference, you use the present indicative in the main clause and the present subjunctive in the dependent clause, as in **Spero che tua figlia guarisca** (*I hope that she recovers*).

English often omits the conjunction *that,* but it's something you may not do in Italian when you use the present indicative in the dependent clause.

To help you make the correct construction decision, Table 15-1 provides a list of verbs that require the indicative, and Table 15-2 a list of verbs that require the subjunctive. By no means do these lists include all the verbs at your disposal, but they give you a good idea of the kinds of verbs you can use.

Table 15-1	Verbs in the Main Clause that Need the Indicative in the Dependent Clause	
Assertions	*Perceptions*	
affermare (*to affirm*)	**sentire** (*to listen*)	
dimenticare (*to forget*)	**vedere** (*to see*)	
dire (*to say, to tell*)	**udire** (*to hear*)	
essere certo/sicuro (*to be certain/sure*)		
informare (*to inform*)		
raccontare (*to tell*)		
ricordare/ricordarsi (*to remember*)		
riferire (*to report*)		
rispondere (*to answer*)		
scrivere (*to write*)		
sapere (*to know*)		

Table 15-2	Verbs in the Main Clause that Need the Subjunctive in the Dependent Clause	
Preferences	*Opinions*	*Feelings*
chiedere/domandare (*to ask*)	**credere** (*to believe*)	**essere contento** (*to be glad*)
desiderare (*to wish*)	**dubitare** (*to doubt*)	**essere stupito** (*to be amazed*)
ordinare (*to order*)	**pensare** (*to think*)	**lamentarsi** (*to complain*)
permettere (*to allow, to permit*)	**ritenere** (*to hold*)	**meravigliarsi** (*to wonder*)
preferire (*to prefer*)	**supporre** (*to suppose*)	**temere/aver paura** (*to fear, to be afraid*)
proibire (*to prohibit, to forbid*)	**sospettare** (*to suspect*)	
sperare (*to hope*)		
volere (*to want*)		

In colloquial Italian it's now acceptable to use the indicative even after verbs expressing opinion. For example, you may encounter the sentence **Penso che arriva domani** (*I think he'll arrive tomorrow*). Moreover, at times you may choose the indicative or the subjunctive depending on what you want to say. For example, you can say **Ammetto che hai ragione tu** (*I admit that you're right*), but also **Ammette che sia vero, ma non ne è davvero convinto** (*He admits it's true, but he isn't really convinced*).

Using the subjunctive after a verb that conveys certainty signals that the feelings are ambivalent. In other words, when you reach this level of proficiency in a foreign language, inflexible rules don't make much sense. However, you won't hear people say **Spero che tu hai ragione** (*I hope that you're right*) because the condition of **sperare** (*hoping*) is too subjective to be followed by a verb in the indicative.

Using the verbs in parentheses, fill in the blanks in the following sentences with the verbs in the present indicative or subjunctive, whichever is more appropriate.

Q. Temo che Maria _____ scontenta del nostro lavoro. (essere)

A. Temo che Maria **sia** scontenta del nostro lavoro. (*I'm afraid that Maria is unhappy with our job performance.*)

8. Chiedono che loro _____ la data della firma del contratto. (spostare)

9. Credo che lei _____ _____ dal medico. (andare)

10. Il Signor Poretti dichiara che sua moglie _____ il presidente della società. (essere)

11. L'avvocato afferma che il suo cliente _____ la verità. (dire)

12. Pensi che Mario _____ le dimissioni? (dare)

13. Preferiscono che tu _____ domani. (partire)

Managing Time in Declarative Clauses

In addition to declarative clauses in the present tense, you also can build them to talk about the future, the past, or a combination of tenses. For example, you can say **So** [present] **che è partita** [present perfect] (*I know she has left/she left*). Therefore, this section gives you some guidelines on how to shift from the present to other tenses and how to put together sentences with different tenses. I can't by any means cover all the options you have, so consider this section an introduction to handling temporal sequences in Italian.

The mood and tense of the main clause dictates your choice of mood and tense in the declarative dependent clause. Then you need to consider two more issues:

✔ What temporal relation exists between the main and the dependent clause? You can have a situation where the action in the dependent clause

• Happens at the same time as the action in the main clause, as in **Ti dico che Anna è dal medico** (*I'm telling you that Anna is at the doctor*)

• Happens after the action in the main clause, as in **So che lui verrà** (*I know he'll come*)

• Happens before the action in the main clause, as in **So che Carlo è arrivato** (*I know Carlo has arrived/arrived*)

> ✔ What kind of verb are you using in the main clause? You have two broad categories:
>
> • A verb that conveys certainty, which requires a verb in the indicative in the declarative clause, as in **Io dico che lei ha sonno** (*I'm telling you that she's tired*)
>
> • A verb that conveys opinion or uncertainty, which requires a verb in the subjunctive in the declarative clause, as in **Penso che Mia lasci il lavoro** (*I think Mia is about to leave her job*)

Tables 15-3 and 15-4 summarize your options for declarative clauses in different tenses.

Table 15-3	Tenses in Declarative Clauses with Verbs Conveying Certainty in the Main Clause	
If the tense of the independent clause is in the . . .	**. . . and the action in the dependent clause is . . .**	**. . . then you use the following tense in the dependent clause**
Present: **Dico che . . .** (*I say that . . .*)	Happening at the same time	Present or present progressive: . . . **lui arriva/sta arrivando** (*. . . he's coming*)
Present: **Dico che . . .** (*I say that . . .*)	Happening in the future	Present (near future): **lui arriva** (*. . . he will arrive*) Or future: **lui arriverà** (*. . . he'll arrive*)
Present: **Dico che . . .** (*I say that . . .*)	Happening in the past	Present perfect: . . . **lui è arrivato** (*. . . he arrived*)
Present perfect: **Ho detto che . . .** (*I've said that . . .*) Imperfect: **Dicevo che . . .** (*I said that . . .*) Preterit: **Dissi che . . .** (*I said that . . .*)	Happening at the same time	Imperfect and imperfect progressive: . . . **lui arrivava/stava arrivando** (*. . . he arrived/he would arrive/he was arriving*) Present perfect: . . . **lui è arrivato** (*. . . he arrived/has arrived*)
Present perfect: **Ho detto che . . .** (*I've said that . . .*) Imperfect: **Dicevo che . . .** (*I said that . . .*) Preterit: **Dissi che . . .** (*I said that . . .*)	Happening in the future	Past conditional: . . . **lui sarebbe arrivato** (*. . . he would come*)
Present perfect: **Ho detto che . . .** (*I've said that . . .*) Imperfect: **Dicevo che . . .** (*I said that . . .*) Preterit: **Dissi che . . .** (*I said that . . .*)	Happening in the past	Past perfect: . . . **era arrivato** (*. . . he had arrived*)

Note the use of the past conditional as pointing to the future when you have a past tense in the main clause. Because in English you use the present conditional in this situation, learning to shift to the past conditional in Italian takes some work. My suggestion: lots of practice.

Table 15-4 Temporal Sequence in Declarative Clauses: Subjective State

If the tense of the independent clause is in the ...	... and the action in the dependent clause is ...	... then you use the following tense in the dependent clause
Present: **Penso che** ... (*I think that ...*)	Happening at the same time	Present subjunctive: ... **lui arrivi/stia arrivando** (*... he's arriving*)
Present: **Penso che** ... (*I think that ...*)	Happening in the future	Future: ... **lui arriverà** (*... he'll arrive*)
Present: **Penso che** ... (*I think that ...*)	Happening in the past	Present perfect subjunctive: ... **sia arrivato** (*... he has arrived/ he arrived*)
Present perfect: **Ho pensato che** ... (*I've thought that ...*) Imperfect: **Pensavo che** ... (*I thought that ...*) Preterit: **Pensai che** ... (*I thought that ...*)	Happening at the same time	Imperfect subjunctive: ... **lui arrivasse/stesse arrivando** (*... he would arrive/he would be arriving*) Colloquial: ... **lui arrivava/stava arrivando** (*... he arrived/he was arriving*)
Present perfect: **Ho pensato che** ... (*I've thought that ...*) Imperfect: **Pensavo che** ... (*I thought that ...*) Preterit: **Pensai che** ... (*I thought that ...*)	Happening in the future	Past conditional: ... **lui sarebbe arrivato** (*... he would arrive*)
Present perfect: **Ho pensato che** ... (*I've thought that ...*) Imperfect: **Pensavo che** ... (*I thought that ...*) Preterit: **Pensai che** ... (*I thought that ...*)	Happening in the past	Past perfect subjunctive: ... **fosse arrivato** (*... he had arrived*)

When you use verbs such as **desiderare** (*to wish*), **preferire** (*to prefer*), and **volere** (*to want*) in addressing other people, you use the present conditional in the main clause and the imperfect subjunctive in the declarative clause. For example, **Vorrei che tu venissi al mercato** (*I would like it if you would come to the farmers' market*). The action in question can happen now or in the future. If you're talking about the past, you can use the imperfect indicative or past conditional in the main clause and the past perfect subjunctive in the declarative clause, as in **Preferirei /Avrei preferito che Sandra fosse partita** (*I would prefer/I would have preferred that Sandra had left*).

Using the verbs in parentheses, add the verb in the indicative or the subjunctive to the following declarative clauses.

Q. Afferma che un anno fa al processo _____ la verità. (dire)

A. Afferma che un anno fa al processo **ha detto** la verità. (*He/She says that he/she told the truth at the trial a year ago.*)

14. Laura stava dicendo che Luca _____ da noi domani. (passare)

15. "Signora, desidera che le _____ il pacco a casa?" (consegnare)

16. Lisa temeva che il dottore le _____ brutte notizie. (dare)

17. Speravi che il professore _____ la lezione dopo il tuo ritorno? (ripetere)

18. Nicoletta mi ha scritto che suo marito _____ a Mosca. (arrivare)

19. Mi informano che il senatore _____ le dimissioni ieri sera. (dare)

20. Credo che Ugo _____ da noi ieri sera solo per vedere Carla. (venire)

Setting Conditions: Building If . . . Then Clauses

When you set a condition for an event to happen, you build an *if . . . then* clause. With this construction, you deal both with the time when the action is taking place *and* the feeling you have about it. Here are some of the possible questions that can arise:

✔ Is the consequence of that condition something that will surely happen?

> **Se dai scacco matto all'avversario, vinci la partita.** (*If you checkmate your rival, you win the game.*)

✔ Are you merely considering a possibility?

> **Se avessi tanti soldi comprerei una BMW.** (*If I had a lot of money I'd buy a BMW.*)

✔ Are you saying that something is impossible?

> **Se avessi studiato, avresti passato l'esame.** (*If you had studied, you would have passed the exam.*)

When you build these kinds of sentences, you choose moods and tenses so as to convey both the time when something happens (or doesn't) and its real, possible, or unreal aspect. So in order to build *if . . . then* clauses, you need to be able to handle mood — that is, the feeling or impression you convey about a situation — as well as the temporal sequence.

In the following sections, I start with two different moods you convey with *if . . . then* clauses and their basic temporal sequence. Then I move into variations on that temporal sequence.

Real, possible, and unreal if . . . then clauses

In both Italian and English you often start an *if . . . then* clause with the dependent clause followed by the main clause, as in **Se vieni anche tu** [dependent clause], **vado a vedere la partita** [main clause] (*If you come too, I'll go to the soccer game*). You need to identify the main clause correctly because it's the clause that dictates mood and tense of the dependent clause, even if it comes second when you speak or write. (By the way, it's perfectly acceptable to invert the order of the clauses.)

When you talk about conditions and hypotheses in Italian, you use four moods: the indicative, the imperative, the conditional, and the subjunctive.

In the *if* clause, you never use the conditional after the word **se**, as in **se sarei** (*if I would be*). Other than that rule, you'll find the array of possible combinations in the following list. I introduce the various options with examples because it's easier to explain what's going on (and what you need to do) if I refer to a concrete case.

✔ You can assert that, given a certain condition, a consequence will follow: **Se prendi la medicina, guarisci/ guarirai** (*If you take the medication, you'll recover*). In this case, you use the present or future tense of the indicative **guarisci/guarirai** (*you will recover*) in the main clause and **prendi/prenderai** (*you take/you'll take*) in the dependent clause. The tense you choose depends on whether you're talking about the present, the near future, or the distant future.

✔ You can say that something is merely possible or even unreal:

• You may talk about the present: **Se prendessi la medicina, guariresti** (*If you would take/If you took your medication, you would recover*). Here you use the present conditional **guariresti** (*you would recover*) in the main clause, and the imperfect subjunctive **prendessi** (*you would take/took*) in the dependent clause. That person may take the medication (possible situation), or you know that he won't (unreal situation). You just want to tell him what would happen if he did something. So in this case the present conditional conveys that you're talking about the present, whereas the imperfect subjunctive doesn't convey so much time as mood — a mood of possibility and uncertainty.

• You may talk about the past: **Se avessi preso la medicina, saresti guarito** (*If you had taken your medication, you would have recovered*). This is an unreal situation because you do know what happened: The person in question didn't take his medication and didn't recover, but you believe that the medication would have helped. So in this case the past perfect subjunctive **avessi preso** (*you had taken*) and the past conditional **saresti guarito** (*you would have recovered*) convey both time and mood.

Nowadays it's acceptable to use the imperfect indicative to convey impossibility: **Se mi avvertivate prima, portavo io la pizza** [**Se mi aveste avvertito prima, avrei portato io la pizza**] (*If you [had] told me before, I would have brought pizza*). It's also acceptable to use the imperfect indicative together with the past subjunctive: **Se venivi** [**fossi venuto**] **con noi, ti saresti divertito** (*If you had come with us, you would have had fun*).

Table 15-5 summarizes the sequence of moods and tenses for the three cases.

Table 15-5	*If . . . Then* Clauses: Sequence of Moods and Tenses	
Type of Condition or Hypothesis	**Tense and Mood of the Condition (Dependent Clause)**	**Tense and Mood of the Consequence (Main Clause)**
Certain or real	**se parto** (*I leave*)	**arrivo/arriverò** (*I'll arrive/ I'll be arriving*)
	se partirò (*I'll leave*)	**arriverò** (*I'll arrive/I'll be arriving*)
Possible or unreal in the present	**se partissi** (*I left/I would leave*)	**arriverei** (*I would arrive*)
Unreal in the past	**se fossi partito** (*I had left*)	**sarei arrivato** (*I would have arrived*)

Using the verbs in parentheses, add the appropriate verbal forms to each dependent clause. Keep the same subject in both sentences. When the *if . . . then* clause is of the real type, use the same mood and tense you find in the main clause.

Q. Se la _____, le restituisco il suo libro. (vedere)

A. Se la **vedo**, le restituisco il suo libro. (*If I see her, I'll give her back her book.*)

21. Se _____ una macchina ibrida, risparmieremmo benzina. (comprare)

22. Se Umberto _____ tra due ore, arriva stasera. (partire)

23. Se _____ il corso di latino, avrà mia zia come professore. (prendere)

24. Se _____ in India, farei un corso di yoga. (andare)

25. Se _____ me, avreste risparmiato molti soldi. (ascoltare)

26. Se lo _____, lo avrebbero invitato a cena. (vedere)

Handling variations of temporal sequences of if . . . then clauses

It's important to note that when you have an *if . . . then* clause of the possible or unreal type, the sequence of tenses is fixed. But when you build *if . . . then* clauses of the real type, you have more options, depending on what you want to say. Here's a rundown: If you use *if . . . then* clauses

✔ To talk about rules of a game, you use the present indicative in both sentences. For example, **Se vuoi giocare a tennis, hai bisogno di una racchetta e una pallina** (*If you want to play tennis, you need a tennis racquet and a tennis ball*).

✔ To describe a hypothetical situation in the present or the near future, you can use the present or future indicative. For example, **Se compri/comprerai una barca, vengo/verrò a fare vela con te** (*If you buy a boat, I'll come sailing with you*). You choose the present indicative when you talk about the present or the near future, and you choose the simple future when you refer to a moment farther away in time.

✔ To describe a hypothetical situation in the present or the future, you can also use the imperative (see Chapter 13) in the main clause when you want to issue an invitation or a warning. For example, **Se passi da Roma, vieni a trovarmi** (*If you come to Rome, come see me*); **Se leggi il libro, non dirmi come va a finire!** (*If you read the book, don't tell me how it ends!*).

In English, you don't use the future in the *if* component of *if . . . then* clauses, whereas in Italian you do.

✔ To talk about the past, you use the present perfect. For example, **Se hai letto il libro, hai visto che è a lieto fine** (*If you [have] read the book, you saw/have seen it has a happy ending*).

Keep in mind that you can combine different tenses, because you may have an *if* clause about a situation that precedes the one in the *then* clause. For example, **Se sono partiti ieri, arriveranno fra tre giorni** (*If they left yesterday, they'll arrive in three days*).

You also can use the preterit (see Chapter 11) when writing fiction or history. For example, **Se il generale comprese di aver perso, non lo diede a vedere** (*If the general understood he had lost, he didn't show it*).

Choose the appropriate conclusions to the sentences from the options provided, and write them in the blanks.

andremmo alla Scala	~~avrei portato Ada~~	va a correre tutti i giorni	possiamo fare la torta
lavorerà per l'ONU	sarebbero morti molti pesci	devi denunciarlo alla polizia	risolveresti questa equazione

Q. Se avessi saputo che veniva suo figlio, _____.

A. Se avessi saputo che veniva suo figlio, **avrei portato Ada**. (*If I had known that his/her son was coming, I would have brought Ada.*)

27. Se a mia sorella piacesse l'opera, _____.

28. Se Dora ha comprato lo zucchero, _____.

29. Se la petroliera fosse affondata, _____.

30. Se si laureerà in Legge, _____.

31. Se perdi il passaporto, _____.

32. Se tu fossi Einstein, _____.

33. Se vuoi giocare meglio a tennis, _____.

Answer Key

1. Cristina e Mara, **portereste** la valigia del nonno? (*Cristina and Mara, would you mind carrying Grandpa's suitcase?*)

2. Signora, mi **preparerebbe** il pacco per oggi pomeriggio? (*Madam, would you prepare my packet by this afternoon?*)

3. Signori, **giocherebbero** a bridge con noi? (*Gentlemen, would you play bridge with us?*)

4. **Dovresti** restituirgli i soldi. (*You should give him back his money.*)

5. **Vorrebbero** passare per Madrid. (*They'd like to visit Madrid.*)

6. **Potremmo** comprare quella casa. (*We could buy that house.*)

7. Lei **vorrebbe** andarsene, mentre lui **vorrebbe** rimanere. (*She'd like to leave, whereas he'd like to stay.*)

8. Chiedono che loro **spostino** la data della firma del contratto. (*They're asking them to move the date to sign the contract.*)

9. Credo che lei **vada/stia andando** dal medico. (*I think she's going to her physician.*)

10. Il Signor Poretti dichiara che sua moglie **è** il presidente della società. (*Mr. Poretti states that his wife is the firm's president.*)

11. L'avvocato afferma che il suo cliente **dice** la verità. (*The lawyer says that his client is telling the truth.*)

12. Pensi che Mario **dia** le dimissioni? (*Do you think that Mario will resign?*)

13. Preferiscono che tu **parta** domani. (*They prefer that you leave tomorrow.*)

14. Laura stava dicendo che Luca **sarebbe passato** da noi domani. (*Laura was saying that Luca would stop by tomorrow.*)

15. "Signora, desidera che le **consegniamo** il pacco a casa?" (*"Madam, do you want us to deliver the package to your place?"*)

16. Lisa temeva che il dottore le **desse** brutte notizie. (*Lisa was afraid that the doctor would give her bad news.*)

17. Speravi che il professore **avrebbe ripetuto/ripetesse** la lezione dopo il tuo ritorno? (*Did you hope that the professor would repeat his lecture after your return?*)

18. Nicoletta mi ha scritto che suo marito **è arrivato** a Mosca. (*Nicoletta wrote to me that her husband arrived in Moscow.*)

19. Mi informano che il senatore **dà/darà** le dimissioni ieri sera. (*They inform me that the senator will resign this evening.*)

20 Credo che Ugo **sia venuto** da noi ieri sera solo per vedere Carla. (*I think Ugo came to our place last night only to see Carla.*)

21 Se **comprassimo** una macchina ibrida, risparmieremmo benzina. (*If we bought/would buy a hybrid car, we would save on gas.*)

22 Se Umberto **parte** tra due ore, arriva stasera. (*If Umberto leaves in two hours, he'll arrive this evening.*)

23 Se **prendi** il corso di latino, avrai mia zia come professore. (*If you take the Latin course, you'll have my aunt as your teacher.*)

24 Se **andassi** in India, farei un corso di yoga. (*If I went/would go to India, I'd take a yoga class.*)

25 Se **aveste ascoltato** me, avreste risparmiato molti soldi. (*If you had listened to me, you would have saved a lot of money.*)

26 Se lo **avessero visto**, lo avrebbero invitato a cena. (*If they had seen him, they would have invited him to dinner.*)

27 Se a mia sorella piacesse l'opera, **andremmo alla Scala**. (*If my sister liked opera, we would go to La Scala.*)

28 Se Dora ha comprato lo zucchero, **possiamo fare la torta**. (*If Dora has bought sugar, we can make the cake.*)

29 Se la petroliera fosse affondata, **sarebbero morti molti pesci**. (*If the oil tanker had sunk, a lot of fish would have died.*)

30 Se si laureerà in Legge, **lavorerà per l'ONU**. (*If he/she gets a Law degree, he/she will work for the U.N.*)

31 Se perdi il passaporto, **devi denunciarlo alla polizia**. (*If you lose your passport, you must report it to the police.*)

32 Se tu fossi Einstein, **risolveresti questa equazione**. (*If you were Einstein, you'd solve this equation.*)

33 Se vuoi giocare meglio a tennis, **va a correre tutti i giorni**. (*If you want to play tennis better, run every day.*)

Chapter 16

Satisfying Your Curiosity with Questions and Answers

In This Chapter
▶ Trying different ways of asking questions
▶ Asking (and answering) negative questions
▶ Playing with more ways of answering questions

Constructing questions and answers is one of the easiest things you can do in Italian. You don't need an auxiliary verb, and you don't need to change the word order. You can turn any sentence into a question by simply adding a question mark at the end. For example:

> **Laura studia il russo.** (*Laura studies Russian.*) → **Laura studia il russo?** (*Does Laura study Russian?*)

You can also begin your question with question words, such as **come** (*how*) or **dove** (*where*). In this chapter, I tell you what those words are in Italian and how you can use them. You also can use interrogative adjectives and pronouns, such as **quanto, quanta, quanti, quante** (*how much, how many*); for example, **Quante ciliegie hai mangiato?** (*How many cherries did you eat?*). These words vary in gender and number. With words such as **quale** (*which, what*) and **chi** (*who*), you use interrogative pronouns. (You also encounter them in Chapter 8 as relative pronouns.)

Despite the fact that asking questions in Italian is so easy, I do have some things to explain to you. First of all, I clarify how you can provide positive answers, as in **Laura studia il russo** (*Laura does study Russian*); or negative answers, as in **Laura non studia il russo** (*Laura doesn't study Russian*). I also tell you how to ask interrogative-negative questions, as in **Laura non studia il russo?** (*Doesn't Laura study Russian?*). Finally, I talk about words you use in answers, especially when you give negative answers, and the use of multiple negatives, as in **"È venuto qualcuno alla festa?" "Non è venuto nessuno"** (*"Did anyone come to the party?" "No one came"*).

The Three Ways of Asking a Question

You can ask questions in three ways (depending on what you want to say, of course):

✔ Add a question mark to an affirmative or negative sentence.

> **Vai al mercato?** (*Are you going to the market?*)
>
> **Non vai al mercato?** (*Aren't you going to the market?*)

✔ Use question words, such as **quando** (*when*), **dove** (*where*), **come** (*how*), **perché** (*why*), or **che/che cosa** (*what*).

> **Dove vai in vacanza?** (*Where will you go on vacation?*)

✔ Use interrogative adjectives and pronouns, such as **quale** (*what, which*) or **chi** (*who*).

> **Quale borsa prendi?** (*What purse are you taking?*)
>
> **Chi compra il latte?** (*Who will buy milk?*)

Adding a question mark to a sentence

Asking questions by adding a question mark to an affirmative or negative sentence is pretty straightforward. I don't have much to say about that because it's so easy, but I can spare a few words about the position of the subject in the sentence when you do express it with a specific word, noun, name, or pronoun — something that may or may not happen, especially when it comes to pronouns.

As you know from Chapter 9 (and if you haven't looked at it, check it out), in Italian you don't use subject pronouns very much because the verb's ending takes care of conveying who's performing the action. For example, in the sentence **Dove stai andando?** (*Where are you going?*), the subject is implied by the verb (which is conjugated to *you* singular) and the question is perfectly clear. But when you want to use a name, noun, or pronoun, you can place any of these in different positions in the sentence, depending on what you mean. Mind, you're entering the realm of nuances here because the fundamental meaning of your question (or answer) isn't affected. Here are your options:

✔ You can use a name or a noun. If you ask a direct, non-emphatic question, you place the subject after the verb, as in **Dove sono i ragazzi?** (*Where are the boys?*). If you invert the word order and ask **I ragazzi dove sono?** (*The boys, where are they?*), you add emphasis, perhaps because you're slightly worried. The same happens if you use a name.

✔ You may want to add a pronoun, for two reasons:

  • To avoid misunderstandings. You place the pronoun before the verb, as in **Lei accetterà quel lavoro?** (*Will she accept that job?*).

  • To add emphasis. You place the pronoun after the verb, as in **Pagano loro le tasse?** (*Do they pay taxes?*). As you can see from the translation, in English your question doesn't really convey the nuance you find in Italian. You'd probably construct your sentence differently in English, perhaps saying *They will pay the taxes, won't they?*

Employing the obvious: Question words

Another classic way of asking questions is by introducing the sentence with a question word. Question words are adverbs, which are all invariable. You don't have to change the word order of the sentence; you merely add the question word at the beginning. Here are the Italian question words with some examples of usage:

✔ **Quando** (*when*): **Quando parti?** (*When are you leaving?*)

✔ **Come** (*how*): **Come stai?** (*How are you?*)

✔ **Dove** (*where*): **Dove andate?** (*Where are you going?*)

✔ **Perché** (*why*): **Perché vendi la bici?** (*Why are you selling your bike?*)

In Italian, the interrogative adverb **perché** (*why*) is the same as the conjunction **perché** (*because*) with which you introduce subordinate clauses that explain the reasons or causes of an event. Compare the following examples: **Perché mi hai telefonato?** (*Why did you call me?*); **Ti ho telefonato perché avevo bisogno del tuo parere** (*I called you because I need your opinion*).

You use **come** and **perché** by themselves, but you can add a preposition to **quando** and **dove,** depending on the question you're asking. For example, you say **Dove vai?** (*Where are you going?*) but **Per quale città devi passare per andare a Roma?** (*Through what city are you going to go to Rome?*). Because **quando** enables you to ask questions about time and **dove** about place, you employ some of the prepositions that have to do with time and place. Table 16-1 lists only the simple prepositions you can use in this context, their meanings, and some examples of how to use them with **quando** and **dove.** (Chapter 6 has full coverage of prepositions.)

Table 16-1 Prepositions of Time and Place for Use with Quando and Dove

Preposition	Translation	Examples Using Quando and Dove
di	*of* (time); *from* (place)	**Di quando è quel quadro?** (*When was that painting done?*); **Di dove sei?** (*Where are you from?*)
a	*to* (time)	**A quando rimandiamo l'incontro?** (*To when are we moving the meeting?*)
da	*from, since* (time); *from* (place)	**Da quando non lo vedi?** (literally, *Since when haven't you seen him?*); **Da dove venite?** (*Where are you coming from?*)
per	*by* (time or place)	**Per quando sarà pronto il libro?** (literally, *By when will the book be ready?*); **Per dove sono passati?** (*Where did they travel/go through?*)

Add the appropriate question word to the following sentences.

Q. _____ hai giocato l'asse di cuori?

A. **Perché** hai giocato l'asse di cuori? (*Why did you play the ace of hearts?*)

1. _____ sono i bambini?

2. _____ vai in vacanza, tra una settimana o tra due?

3. _____ hai accettato quel lavoro?

4. _____ spieghi quello che è successo?

Using interrogative pronouns to ask about specifics

You can also ask questions starting with interrogative pronouns, which enable you to ask something specific about people, things, and situations. You place an interrogative pronoun at the beginning of a question. As you probably already know at this point, this rule isn't iron-clad because Italian is pretty flexible with word order. But at this stage of your knowledge of the language, I recommend that you follow that suggestion when you build an interrogative sentence.

The following interrogative pronouns are invariable (they don't take masculine or feminine, singular or plural endings):

✔ **chi** (*who, whom*): Used as a subject (*who*) or direct object (*whom*) *only* with people (and some animals) to inquire about

- The identity of people and some animals, with the verb **essere** (*to be*) conjugated in the person you're inquiring about, as in **Chi sono le tue amiche?** (*Who are your girlfriends?*)

- Who's performing the action, with the verb always in the third-person singular, as in **Chi va al mare?** (*Who's going to the beach of all your sisters?*)

✔ **che cosa, cosa** (*what*): Used as a subject or direct object *only* with things or situations to inquire about

- What action is being performed, as in **Che cosa ti preoccupa?** (*What's worrying you?*); **Che cosa fate?** (*What are you doing?*)

- What's happening, with verbs such as **succedere** and **accadere** (*to happen*), followed by the verb in the third-person singular, as in **Che cosa succede?** (*What's happening?*)

TIP

Instead of **cosa** or **che cosa** you can use **che**. It's more colloquial and a bit more aggressive, as in **Ma che dici?** (*What are you saying?*).

Table 16-2 lists interrogative adjectives/pronouns, which vary in gender and number or only in number.

Table 16-2   **Interrogative Adjectives/Pronouns Used with People and Things**

Translation	Masculine Singular	Feminine Singular	Masculine Plural	Feminine Plural
what, which	quale	quale	quali	quali
Used as adjective	Quale CD vuoi sentire? (*What CD do you want to listen to?*)	Quale gonna ti piace? (*What skirt do you like?*)	Quali libri hai letto? (*What books did you read?*)	Quali rose hai piantato? (*What roses did you plant?*)
Used as pronoun	Ho tre CD. Quale vuoi? (*I have three CDs. Which [one] do you want?*)	Ho due gonne. Quale ti piace? (*I have two skirts. Which [one] do you like?*)	Hanno libri di storia e romanzi, Quali vuoi? (*They have history books and novels. Which [ones] do you want?*)	Hanno rose bianche e rosse. Quali vuoi piantare? (*They have white and red roses. Which [ones] do you want to plant?*)
how much, how many	quanto	quanta	quanti	quante
Used as adjective	Quanto zucchero hai messo nella torta? (*How much sugar did you put in the cake?*)	Quanta frutta hai comprato? (*How much fruit did you buy?*)	Quanti fichi hai mangiato? (*How many figs did you eat?*)	Quante rose hai piantato? (*How many roses did you plant?*)
Used as pronoun	Ho molto miele. Quanto ne vuoi? (*I have a lot of honey. How much do you want?*)	Ho un mucchio di frutta. Quanta ne vuoi? (*I have a lot of fruit. How much do you want?*)	Ho molti fichi. Quanti ne vuoi? (*I have a lot of figs. How many do you want?*)	Ho molte rose. Quante ne vuoi? (*I have many roses. How many do you want?*)

To convey the English pronoun *whose,* you add the preposition **di** to the pronoun **chi,** as in **Di chi sono questi guanti?** (*Whose gloves are these?*).

As you can see in the table, **quale** varies in number but not gender. It drops the **-e** before the third-person singular of the verb **essere** (*to be*) but doesn't take an apostrophe, so it becomes **qual era** (*what, which was*). You use it

✔ To inquire about the identity of a person or thing, as in **Qual è il loro numero di telefono?** (*What's their telephone number?*)

✔ To select one or more items in a group, as in **Quali gonne ti interessano?** (*Which skirts interest you?*)

Quanto varies in gender and number. You use it to inquire about quantities regarding persons or things, coordinating it with the noun to which it refers if that noun is expressed. Otherwise, use the default masculine singular or plural (see Table 16-2), as in **Quanto costa il vestito?** (*How much does that dress cost?*); **"Avevamo cento membri." "Quanti si sono iscritti di nuovo?"** (*"We had 100 members." "How many reenrolled?"*).

You can also use **che** (which is invariable) as an interrogative adjective before nouns referring to people and things, as in **Che lavoro fa?** (*What's his/her job?*).

When you use the interrogative adjective or pronoun as the subject of a sentence, you need to decide what person the verb will take. And if the verb is in a compound form (such as the present perfect, as in **sono andato** [*I have gone*]), you also need to decide the ending of the past participle. When you use any interrogative adjective or pronoun as direct object with a transitive verb, which takes **avere** (*to have*) as its auxiliary, in compound tenses you leave the past participle in the default masculine singular. For example, **Quali libri hai comprato?** (*Which books did you buy?*).

You also can add prepositions to interrogative adjectives/pronouns, as in **Di quante pere hai bisogno per la torta?** (*How many pears do you need for the cake?*). With **quali** (*what, which*) and **quanto** (*how much*) (but not **quanta**), and **quanti/quante** (*how many*), you also can use the preposition **fra/tra** (*by, between, among*). Consider these examples:

Fra quanto tornate? (*How long before you come back?*)

Tra quanti appartamenti potete scegliere? (*Among how many apartments can you choose?*)

Add the appropriate question word or interrogative adjective or pronoun to the following sentences, choosing among the options in parentheses.

0. (Chi/Che cosa/Quale) è capitato?

A. **Che cosa** è capitato? (*What happened?*)

5. (Chi/Quale/Quanto) bussa alla porta?

6. (A chi/Di chi/Qual) è quell'ombrello?

7. (Con quale/Con chi/Chi) giochi a pallone?

8. (Quali/Quante/Quanti) giorni ci sono in una settimana?

9. Mamma, (a chi/a quale/a che cosa) devo dare questo pacchetto?

10. (Quanta/Quanti/Quale) giornali hai comprato?

The Nuances of Negative Adjectives and Pronouns: Q & A

To ask a negative question, you use any of the three formulas I outline for asking positive questions and simply add **non** (*not*) to the sentence, placing it right before the verbal form, simple or compound. Consider these examples:

> **Laura non ha studiato il russo?** (*Hasn't Laura studied Russian?*)
>
> **Perché non ci avete risposto?** (*Why didn't you answer us?*)
>
> **Chi non mangia la carne?** (*Who doesn't eat meat?*)

However, you need to be aware of one important difference between Italian and English: Italian doesn't have the English allergy to piling up negations in negative questions (and answers). Check out this example: **Non gli ha mai più detto nulla nessuno?** (*No one ever told him anything ever again?*). This sentence has five negative words — four if you count the adverbial phrase **mai più** (*ever again*) as one. The rule of thumb is to not look at your English sentence as a complete statement in which you can keep only one word in the negative. Instead look at it as a collection of negative words. For example, in the example sentence, besides the pronoun *No one*, *ever again* and *anything* are non-negative versions of negative words (*never again* and *nothing*). When you need them in Italian, choose their negative forms.

When you ask a negative question you often use negative adjectives and pronouns. Here are the few things you need to know about using them:

✔ **Nessuno, nessuna** (*no, no one, nobody, not any*) is only singular. As an adjective, you use it before a masculine or a feminine noun, as in **Non hanno visto nessuna amica** (*They saw no friend/They didn't see any friend*). As a pronoun, you use it with verbs in the singular and you choose the default singular masculine form for the past participle in a compound verbal form, as in **Non è partito nessuno** (*No one left*).

✔ **Niente/Nulla** (*nothing, not anything*) refers only to things. It's only singular and takes the default singular masculine form for the past participle in a compound verbal form, as in **Non è successo niente** (*Nothing happened*). There is no difference in meaning between **niente** and **nulla.**

Besides indefinite pronouns such as **nessuno** and **niente** used in questions and answers, you have an array of words at your disposal, mostly adverbs, to convey negative situations. You can use the adverbs

✔ **nemmeno/neanche/neppure** (*not even*), followed by a noun, a pronoun, or a name, as in **Non lo sapevi neanche tu?** (*Not even you knew that?*) You can choose any of those three words according to your taste.

✔ **né . . . né** (*neither . . . nor*), as in **Non lo hanno comprato né lui né lei?** (*Neither he nor she bought it?*)

Then you can use the following adverbial phrases:

✔ **non . . . ancora** (*not yet*), as in **Non l'hanno ancora vista?** (*Haven't they seen her yet?*).

✔ **non . . . mai** (*never, not ever*), as in **Non l'avete mai vista?** (*Did you ever see her?*)

✔ **non . . . più** (*no longer, not any longer, no more, not any more*), as in **Non la vedi più?** (*Don't you see her any longer?*)

With these adverbial phrases you place **non** before the verb (simple or compound) and the other component after a simple verbal form, or right after the auxiliary in a compound form, as in the preceding examples. (For more information about adverbs and their placement, head back to Chapter 5.)

Now, on to the most important exception regarding negations: You drop the adverb **non** (*not*) from the sentence (question or answer) if you begin your sentence with one of the following words:

✔ **nessuno**

✔ **nemmeno/neanche/neppure** (followed by a noun, a pronoun, or a name)

✔ **niente**

✔ **né . . . né**

Nessuno ha mangiato niente? (*No one ate anything?*)

Né Laura né Piero sono d'accordo? (*Neither Laura nor Piero agree?*)

Mind, I said *if* you start a sentence with those words. You don't have to. The sentence **Non ha mangiato niente nessuno** (*No one ate anything*) is perfectly all right. It's your choice whether to use one construction or the other.

Responding to Questions

What kind of answer you give to a question depends on the question being asked. When you answer an information question in the negative, you have an array of negative words to add to your answer. You can choose any of the negative adjectives and pronouns or adverbs that I list in the earlier section "Using interrogative pronouns to ask about specifics." All you have to do is to take out the question mark. So a question such as **Non l'hanno ancora vista?** (*Haven't they seen her yet?*) can become an answer: **Non l'hanno ancora vista** (*They haven't seen her yet*). Similarly, **Nessuno ha mangiato niente?** (*No one ate anything?*) becomes **Nessuno ha mangiato niente** (*No one ate anything*).

Simple responses

Even when you answer **sì** or **no,** you have more words to choose from than just those two. Following are lists of expressions that convey various reactions, from absolute agreement to absolute disagreement as well as the nuances in between.

Positive and Tentative Answers	*Negative Answers*
assolutamente (*absolutely*)	**assolutamente no** (*absolutely not*)
certo/certamente (*sure*)	**certo che no/certamente no** (*certainly not*)
di sicuro (*surely*)	**forse no** (*maybe not*)
forse/può darsi (*perhaps*)	**mai** (*never*)
forse sì, forse no (*maybe yes, maybe no*)	**mai più** (*never again*)
grazie (*thank you*)	**nemmeno/neppure/neanche** + name, noun, or pronoun (*not even*)
Penso di sì. (*I think yes.*)	**nessuno** (*no one, nobody*)
Perché no? (*why not? meaning yes*)	**niente/nulla** (*nothing*)
probabilmente (*probably*)	**Penso di no.** (*I think not.*)
senza dubbio (*without any doubt*)	**per niente/niente affatto** (*not at all*)
senz'altro (*no doubt*)	

Using a pronoun in a response

When you engage in a conversation involving questions and answers, pronouns come in handy. If someone asks you **"Conosci Mauro?"** (*"Do you know Mauro?"*), instead of answering **"Conosco Mauro/Non conosco Mauro"** (*"I know Mauro/I don't know Mauro"*), you can say **"Lo conosco/Non lo conosco"** (*"I know him/I don't know him"*). (You can find more on pronouns in Chapter 4.)

You can use personal pronouns in your answers when the word you don't want to repeat is a specific person or thing. But many times your answer will regard the entire situation mentioned in the question. If someone asks you **"Sapevi che i ghiacciai della Groenlandia si stanno sciogliendo a un ritmo che prepoccupa persino gli scienziati più pessimisti?"** (*"Did you know that the glaciers in Greenland are melting at a rate that's alarming even the most pessimistic scientists?"*), you can answer **"Lo sapevo/Non lo sapevo"** (*"I knew it/I didn't know it"*). The pronoun **lo** (*it, that*), which you don't need in English, refers to the entire argument conveyed by the questions. In Italian you can use some set phrases that employ three pronouns: **lo, ci** (*here, there, about this, about that*), and **ne** (*of this, of that, of him, of her, of them*). (See Chapter 4 for more on these pronouns.)

> **"Sapevi che Marta si sposa?"** (*"Did you know Marta is getting married?"*); **"Lo/Non lo sapevo."** (*"I did/I didn't know."*)

"Andate al concerto?" (*"Are you going to the concert?"*); **"Ci/Non ci andiamo."** (*"We are/We aren't going."*)

"Lei ha parlato della tesi?" (*"Did she talk about her dissertation?"*); **"Ne ha/Non ne ha parlato."** (*"She did/She didn't talk about it."*)

"Ti ricordi di comprare le medicine?" (*"Will you remember to buy the medications?"*); **"Me ne/Non me ne ricordo."** (*"I will/I won't remember."*)

"Si sono dimenticati di darle la lettera?" (*"Did they forget to give her the letter?"*); **"Se ne sono/Non se ne sono dimenticati."** (*"They did/They didn't forget."*)

Answer the following questions using full sentences. If you can correctly answer both in the affirmative and the negative, do so to practice both types of answers.

Q. Nel Capitolo 15, hai imparato a porre delle domande e a dare delle risposte?

A. **No, ho imparato a usare il condizionale e il congiuntivo.** (*No, I learned how to use the conditional and the subjunctive.*)

11. Vorresti che ci fossere più esempi in questo capitolo?

_____

12. Vorresti che ci fossero più esercizi?

_____

13. Aggiungeresti degli esercizi con delle figure?

_____

14. Vuoi fare un test delle tue conoscenze riguardo al materiale presentato in questo capitolo?

_____

15. Devi cambiare l'ordine delle parole per fare una domanda in italiano?

_____

16. Se qualcuno ti domanda, "Ti piace leggere?", basta rispondere "sì" o "no"?

_____

17. Se qualcuno ti domanda, "Quante ore ci sono in un giorno?", basta rispondere "sì" o "no"?

_____

18. Qual è la risposta corretta alla domanda 17?

_____

19. In italiano, si può usare più di una negazione in una domanda o una risposta negativa?

_____

20. La frase "Nessuno non può partire" è corretta?

_____

21. Qual è la frase corretta nella domanda 20?

_____

Answer Key

1 **Dove** sono i bambini? (*Where are the children?*)

2 **Quando** vai in vacanza, tra una settimana o tra due? (*When are you going on vacation, in a week or two?*)

3 **Perché** hai accettato quel lavoro? (*Why did you accept that job?*)

4 **Come** spieghi quello che è successo? (*How do you explain what happened?*)

5 **Chi** bussa alla porta? (*Who is knocking at the door?*)

6 **Di chi** è quell'ombrello? (*Whose umbrella is that?*)

7 **Con chi** giochi a pallone? (*With whom do you play soccer?*)

8 **Quanti** giorni ci sono in una settimana? (*How many days are there in a week?*)

9 Mamma, **a chi** devo dare questo pacchetto? (*Mom, whom should I give this package to?*)

10 **Quanti** giornali hai comprato? (*How many newspapers did you buy?*)

11 **Sì, vorrei che ci fossero più esempi.** (*Yes, I'd like more examples.*) or **No, non vorrei che ci fossero più esempi.** (*No, I wouldn't like more examples.*)

12 **Sì, vorrei che ci fossero più esercizi.** (*Yes, I'd like more exercises.*) or **No, non vorrei che ci fossero più esercizi.** (*No, I wouldn't like more exercises.*)

13 **Sì, aggiungerei degli esercizi con delle figure.** (*Yes, I'd add more exercises with pictures.*) or **Non, non aggiungerei degli esercizi con delle figure.** (*No, I wouldn't add more exercises with pictures.*)

14 **Sì, voglio fare un test delle mie conoscenze [riguardo al materiale presentato in questo capitolo].** (*Yes, I want to take a test of what I've learned [about the material presented in this chapter].*) or **No, non voglio fare un test delle mie conoscenze.** (*No, I don't want to take a test of what I've learned.*)

15 **No, non devo cambiare l'ordine delle parole per fare una domanda in italiano.** (*No, I don't have to change word order to ask a question in Italian.*)

16 **Sì, basta rispondere "sì" o "no."** (*Yes, it's sufficient to answer "yes" or "no."*)

17 **No, non basta rispondere "sì" o "no."** (*No, it's not sufficient to answer "yes" or "no."*)

18 **In un giorno ci sono ventiquattro ore.** (*There are 24 hours in a day.*)

19 **Sì, in italiano si può usare più di una negazione in una domanda o una risposta negativa.** (*Yes, in Italian you can use more than one negation in a negative question or answer.*)

20 **No, la frase "Nessuno non può partire" non è corretta.** (*No, the phrase "No one cannot leave" isn't correct.*)

21 **"Nessuno può partire."** or **"Non può partire nessuno."** (*"No one can leave."*)

Chapter 17

The Reflexive, Passive, and Impersonal Constructions

• •

In This Chapter

▶ Being the object of your own actions

▶ Changing active statements into passive ones

▶ Conveying that someone (you don't know exactly who) is doing something

• •

Most of the time you build sentences in which a known agent performs an action that may or may not have an impact on an object. But that scenario doesn't always apply; in this chapter, I discuss situations where you need to use a special verb form because

✔ The subject is the object of its own action, in which case you use the reflexive form.

✔ The subject of the sentence is the passive recipient of an *action performed by an agent* (note the passive voice in italics here — smooth, aren't I?), in which case you need the passive form.

✔ An anonymous someone is doing something, in which case you need the impersonal form.

This chapter explains how you can build those constructions in Italian and helps you understand when it's appropriate to use them.

Turning Yourself into the Object of Your Own Actions

In both Italian and English, a reflexive verb allows you to say that an action is directed at the subject who's performing it. Italian uses reflexive verbs more than English, employing them to convey that

✔ The subject is performing an action on himself or herself: **Io mi lavo** (*I'm washing myself*).

✔ Something is happening to the subject himself or herself, even though it's not something the person is really doing: **Io mi sveglio** (*I'm waking up*).

✔ The action is directed at the subject and a part of himself or herself: **Io mi lavo le mani** (*I wash my hands*).

✔ The subject is doing something for himself or herself: **Io mi faccio gli spaghetti** (*I'm cooking spaghetti for myself*).

✔ Two or more people engage in a reciprocal action: **Noi ci scriviamo** (*We write to one another*).

Forming reflexive verbs

In order to tell a reflexive verb from a regular transitive or intransitive verb, look for the ending **-si** attached to the stem of the infinitive without the final **-e**: **lavare** (*to wash*) → **lavarsi** (*to wash oneself*). Then conjugate a reflexive verb in the desired mood and tense by following these steps:

1. Conjugate the verb as usual (see Parts III and IV), adding the auxiliary **essere** in compound tenses: **I bambini si sono addormentati.** (*The children have fallen asleep.*) Turn to Chapter 9 for coverage of compound tenses.

   But, when you attach the pronoun to an infinitive that follows a modal auxiliary, instead of **essere** (*to be*), you use **avere** (*to have*) as the auxiliary because the verb you're conjugating is the modal auxiliary rather than the reflexive verb.

2. Coordinate the past participle with the subject in compound tenses: **Le bambine si sono addormentate.** (*The little girls have fallen asleep.*) Turn to Chapter 9 to find out about past participles and coordination.

3. Place the reflexive pronouns **mi** (*myself*), **ti** (*yourself*), **si** (*himself, herself, itself, oneself*), **ci** (*ourselves*), **vi** (*yourselves*), **si** (*themselves*) before the verb: **I bambini si addormentano.** (*The children are falling asleep.*) I cover reflexive pronouns in Chapter 4.

Here's an example of a verb conjugated in the reflexive form.

lavarsi (*to wash oneself*): Present Indicative	
io **mi lavo** (*I wash myself*)	noi **ci laviamo** (*we wash ourselves*)
tu **ti lavi** (*you wash yourself*)	voi **vi lavate** (*you wash yourselves*)
lui/lei/Lei/esso **si lava** (*he/she/it/one washes himself/herself/itself/oneself*)	loro/Loro/essi/esse **si lavano** (*they wash themselves*)
Ci laviamo le mani prima di mangiare. (*We wash our hands before eating.*)	

You place the reflexive pronouns before the verb in all moods and tenses, as illustrated in Table 17-1, except for verbal forms that use the gerund or the infinitive. For example, **Lavarsi le mani prima di mangiare è importante** (*To wash one's hands before eating is important*). (I cover gerunds and modal auxiliaries in Chapters 9 and 10.)

Table 17-1 Position of Reflexive Pronouns with the Gerund and Infinitive

Gerund		Modal Auxiliary + Infinitive	
Before the Verbal Form	*OR Attached to the Gerund*	*Before the Verbal Form*	*OR Attached to the Infinitive*
Si sta lavando. (*She's washing herself.*)	**Sta lavandosi.** (*She's washing herself.*)	**Si è voluta lavare.** (*She wanted to wash herself.*)	**Ha voluto lavarsi.** (*She wanted to wash herself.*)

Transforming a transitive verb into a reflexive verb

In Italian you can make most transitive verbs — verbs that require both a subject and an object — reflexive by adding the ending **-si** to the infinitive of the verb. You do this when you need the action of a regular transitive verb to fall on the speaker. For example, **Io mi guardo allo specchio** (*I'm looking at myself in the mirror*); **La neve si è sciolta** (*The snow thawed*). For more information on transitive verbs, turn to Chapter 9. Most transitive verbs can be turned into reflexive verbs; as a rule of thumb, use discernment: You can certainly wash an apple *and* yourself, but you can't drink a beer *and* yourself, right? If you aren't sure whether a verb you just turned into its reflexive form exists, check the dictionary.

Some reflexive verbs have a passive meaning, such as **rompersi** (*to break*). For example, in the sentence **Il bicchiere si è rotto** (*The glass was/got broken*), you're technically saying that the glass was damaged, but the verb used to express that idea is reflexive even though the glass didn't really do anything to itself.

The transitive and reflexive meanings of a verb may not differ much. **Quel film mi ha annoiata** (*That movie bored me*) means more or less the same as **Mi sono annoiata a vedere quel film** (*I got bored watching that movie*). But **Si è ucciso** (*He killed himself*) is very different from **L'hanno ucciso** (*They killed him*). A dictionary will always tell you a verb's transitive and reflexive meanings.

Table 17-2 shows the meanings that common transitive verbs acquire when becoming reflexive.

Table 17-2 Transitive Verbs Used Reflexively

Transitive Verb	Reflexive Verb	Transitive Verb	Reflexive Verb
accomodare (*to accommodate*)	**accomodarsi** (*to take a seat*)	**ricordare** (*to remember someone or something*)	**ricordarsi** (*to remember*)
addormentare (*to put someone to sleep*)	**addormentarsi** (*to fall asleep*)	**rilassare** (*to relax someone or something*)	**rilassarsi** (*to relax*)
affaticare, stancare (*to tire*)	**affaticarsi, stancarsi** (*to get tired*)	**sentire** (*to hear*)	**sentirsi** (*to feel like*)

(continued)

Table 17-2 *(continued)*

Transitive Verb	Reflexive Verb	Transitive Verb	Reflexive Verb
affrettare (*to rush someone or something*)	**affrettarsi** (*to hurry up*)	**scusare** (*to forgive*)	**scusarsi** (*to apologize*)
alzare (*to lift*)	**alzarsi** (*to get up, to stand up*)	**separare** (*to separate*)	**separarsi** (*to separate*)
annoiare (*to bore*)	**annoiarsi** (*to get bored*)	**spaventare** (*to scare*)	**spaventarsi** (*to get scared*)
chiamare (*to call*)	**chiamarsi** (*for one's name to be called*)	**spogliare** (*to undress*)	**spogliarsi** (*to get undressed*)
curare (*to take care of*)	**curarsi** (*to take care of oneself*)	**sposare** (*to wed*)	**sposarsi [con]** (*to get married*)
dimenticare (*to forget someone or something*)	**dimenticarsi** (*to forget*)	**stupire** (*to surprise*)	**stupirsi** (*to be amazed*)
divertire (*to amuse*)	**divertirsi** (*to enjoy oneself*)	**svegliare** (*to wake someone*)	**svegliarsi** (*to wake up*)
fare male (*to hurt someone*)	**farsi male** (*to get hurt*)	**svestire** (*to undress*)	**svestirsi** (*to get undressed*)
fermare (*to stop*)	**fermarsi** (*to stop*)	**tagliare** (*to cut*)	**tagliarsi** (*to cut oneself*)
offendere (*to offend*)	**offendersi** (*to get/be offended*)	**trasferire** (*to transfer*)	**trasferirsi** (*to move one's residence*)
rendere conto (*to report to someone*)	**rendersi conto di** (*to become aware of*)	**vestire** (*to dress someone*)	**vestirsi** (*to get dressed*)

Rewrite the following sentences so that the verbs are reflexive, and use the present perfect. In your sentences, skip the words in brackets.

Q. Bianca ha offeso Marisa.

A. **Marisa si è offesa.** (*Maria got/was offended.*)

1. [La sveglia] ha svegliato Pietro.

_____

2. [Il clown] ha divertito i bambini.

_____

3. Nicola è diventato il marito di Fulvia.

_____

4. I miei genitori hanno dimenticato le chiavi di casa.

_____

5. I signori Bernini sono andati a vivere a Napoli. (trasferire)

_____

6. Mi meraviglia molto che tu non abbia protestato.

_____

Verbs that are pretty much purely reflexive

Some Italian verbs are used mainly in their reflexive sense. If used transitively, they just wouldn't make sense. English has such verbs as well, although they're definitely less common. Consider _to enjoy oneself:_ You wouldn't say "I enjoyed at the party," would you?

The following list shows verbs used mostly, if not only, in the reflexive form:

- **arrabbiarsi**, **adirarsi** (_to get angry_)
- **arrendersi** (_to surrender_)
- **coricarsi** (_to lie down_)
- **fidanzarsi** (_to get engaged_)
- **inchinarsi** (_to bow_)
- **innamorarsi** (_to fall in love_)
- **lamentarsi** (_to complain_)
- **ostinarsi** (_to persist_)
- **pentirsi** (_to repent_)
- **sedersi** (_to sit_)
- **suicidarsi** (_to commit suicide_)
- **vergognarsi** (_to be ashamed of_)

Acting on the body (or parts of it): Reflexive pronoun + transitive verb + direct object

When you talk about someone doing something to his or her body or parts of it, you can "build" a reflexive meaning by using a transitive verb followed by a direct object and preceded by a reflexive pronoun conveying that the action falls onto the subject. In fact, the reflexive pronouns **mi, ti, si,** and so on mean, in this sense, **a/per me** (_to/for me_), **te** (_to/for you_), **lui** (_to/for him_), and so on (see Chapter 4). The subject isn't the direct object of the action — as is the case with real reflexive verbs — but rather it's an indirect object: You're doing things _for_ yourself.

This construction adds emphasis and avoids confusion about the recipient of the action. If you say **Io lavo i capelli** (_I'm washing hair_), you aren't saying whether you're washing your own hair or someone else's. But if you add a reflexive pronoun and say **Io mi lavo i capelli,** you can only be washing your own hair.

Similarly, if the Italian verb you're using is followed by the prepositions **a/per,** as in **insegnare a** (*to teach*), **dire a** (*to say, to tell*), or **raccontare a qualcuno** (*to tell*), you use the reflexive form. For example, **Mi insegno l'inglese da sola** (*I'm teaching English to myself*).

Following are some common verbs used in talking about yourself:

- ✔ **depilarsi** (*to shave*)
- ✔ **lavarsi** (*to wash oneself*)
- ✔ **mettersi** (*to put on*)
- ✔ **pettinarsi** (*to comb one's hair*)
- ✔ **prepararsi** (*to prepare*)
- ✔ **pulirsi** (*to clean oneself*)
- ✔ **radersi, farsi la barba** (*to shave*)

- ✔ **rompersi** (*to break [a limb]*)
- ✔ **spazzolarsi** (*to brush one's hair*)
- ✔ **struccarsi** (*to take off make-up*)
- ✔ **tagliarsi** (*to cut oneself*)
- ✔ **tingersi** (*to dye [one's hair]*)
- ✔ **togliersi** (*to take off*)
- ✔ **truccarsi** (*to put on make-up*)

When speaking about yourself, you can use the reflexive form to emphasize the action that would normally require a simple transitive verb. This use of the reflexive accentuates the fact that you're doing something to pamper yourself. For example, **Adesso bevo un bicchiere di vino** (*I am drinking a glass of wine now*) is transitive; **Adesso mi bevo un bel bicchiere di vino!** (*Now I am going to drink a nice glass of wine!*) is reflexive. The following list shows the most common transitive verbs used in a reflexive form in order to convey this idea.

- ✔ **ascoltarsi** (to listen to)
- ✔ **bersi** (to drink)
- ✔ **comprarsi** (to buy)
- ✔ **cucinarsi** (to cook)

- ✔ **farsi** (to do)
- ✔ **giocarsi** (to gamble away)
- ✔ **mangiarsi** (to eat)
- ✔ **vedersi** (to see, to watch)

If you use a compound with a past participle, you coordinate it with the subject if the object follows the verb, and you coordinate it with the object pronoun preceding the verbs (see Chapter 4 on pronouns). For example, **"Lia si è lavata le mani?" "Se le è lavate."** (*"Did Lia wash her hands?" "She did."*).

Translate the following sentences from English into Italian.

Q. A man is shaving.

A. **Un uomo si rade.**

7. A woman combs her hair.

_____

8. A boy brushes his teeth.

_____

9. A girl puts make-up on her eyes.

_____

10. A cat licks its fur.

_____

11. A man takes off his shirt.

_____

12. Three men cook fish on the barbecue.

_____

Engaging in reciprocal actions

People often engage in activities characterized by reciprocity: They speak to one another, write to one another, and so on. You convey this action in English with the verb in the active form accompanied by the phrases _each other/one another,_ or by using the verb _to get_ + a past participle. In Italian, you use a reflexive verb in the plural because the subject will include at least two people (the section "Forming reflexive verbs," earlier in this chapter, shows you how to form the plural reflexive verb). Consider these examples:

> **Si conoscono da molti anni.** (_They've know each other for many years._)

> **Marina e Pietro si sono fidanzati.** (_Marina and Pietro got engaged._)

Following is a list of some verbs with which you can convey reciprocity. Of course, you can also use some of these verbs to convey an emotion or a state of mind, saying that the subject is feeling something about himself or herself, as in **Nadia si conosce bene** (_Nadia knows herself very well_) as opposed to **Nadia e Maria si conoscono da due anni** (_Nadia and Maria have known each other for two years_).

- **amarsi** (_to love each other_)
- **baciarsi** (_to kiss each other_)
- **chiamarsi, telefonarsi** (_to call/ telephone/talk on the phone to each other_)
- **conoscersi** (_to know each other, to meet_)
- **fidanzarsi** (_to get engaged_)
- **incontrarsi** (_to meet_)
- **odiarsi** (_to hate each other_)
- **parlarsi** (_to speak/talk to each other_)
- **presentarsi** (_to introduce oneself to each other_)
- **salutarsi** (_to greet each other_)
- **scriversi** (_to write each other_)
- **separarsi** (_to get separated from each other_)
- **sposarsi** (_to get married_)
- **stringersi la mano** (_to shake hands_)
- **vedersi** (_to see each other_)
- **volersi bene** (_to care for each other_)

Translate the following sentences from English into Italian.

Q. Giulio and Barbara are calling each other.

A. **Giulio e Barbara si telefonano.**

13. A man and a woman shake hands.

_____

14. Vincenzo and Daria get married.

_____

15. Francesco and Elisabetta love each other.

_____

16. A man and a woman say hello to each other.

_____

17. Two men hate each other.

_____

Moving from the Active to the Passive Form

In the most common sentence construction, the *active* form, you line up a subject, a verb, and an object. Sometimes, though, you may want or need to flip the order of the subject and object, producing the *passive* form. When the recipient is a direct object, you can take that object and turn it into the subject, making the subject the agent responsible for that action. The passive form is useful when you don't know or aren't sure who's performing the action. In Italian, journalists and the news media often use the passive as a means of delivering information as objectively as possible. For example, you may read **"Il corpo di una donna è stato trovato privo di vita ieri mattina in Piazza Statuto"** (*"The body of a woman was found dead yesterday morning in Piazza Statuto"*).

You can only turn verbs that take a direct object from active to passive because the object becomes the subject of a passive sentence.

Passive verbal forms are always compound forms because you need both an auxiliary verb to convey mood and tense and a past participle to convey that something is being done. To turn an active sentence into a passive one, such as **L'inquinamento causa l'effetto serra** (*Pollution causes the greenhouse effect*), follow these steps:

1. Conjugate the auxiliary **essere** in the tense and mood you need, choosing the person and number that matches the object (which is now the subject of the sentence).

   > **L'effetto serra è . . .** (*The greenhouse effect is . . .*)

2. Add the past participle of the main verb coordinated with the subject.

   > **causato . . .** (*caused . . .*)

3. Add the agent, person, or thing responsible for the action, introduced by the preposition **da** (*by*) (if an agent is expressed).

   > **. . . dall'inquinamento** (*. . . by pollution*)

Table 17-3 gives you some examples of tenses in the active and passive forms. You can find complete verb charts in the active, passive, and reflexive forms in Appendix A.

Table 17-3	From Active to Passive Verbal Forms					
Mood and Tense	**Present Indicative**	**Present Perfect Indicative**	**Imperfect Indicative**	**Simple Future Indicative**	**Present Conditional**	**Past Conditional**
Active	io **lodo**	io **ho lodato**	io **lodavo**	io **loderò**	io **loderei**	io **avrei lodato**
Passive	io sono **lodato**	io sono **stato lodato**	io **ero lodato**	io **sarò lodato**	io **sarei lodato**	io **sarei stato lodato**
Mood and Tense	**Present Subjunctive**	**Present Perfect Subjunctive**	**Imperfect Subjunctive**	**Present Imperative**	**Present Infinitive**	**Past Infinitive**
Active	che io **lodi**	che io **abbia lodato**	che io **lodassi**	**loda!**	**lodare**	**avere lodato**
Passive	che io **sia lodato**	che io **sia stato lodato**	che io **fossi stato lodato**	**sii lodato!**	**essere lodato**	**essere stato lodato**

If you use a compound tense, you need two past participles in the passive form: that of the main verb and that of the auxiliary **essere** (**stato, stata, stati, state** [*been*]), both coordinated with the subject. The following example progresses from an active sentence in the present tense (1) to a passive in the present tense (2), and then from an active sentence in the past (3) to a passive in the past (4):

   (1) **Loro mangiano la torta.** (*They're eating the cake.*)

   (2) **La torta è mangiata da loro.** (*The cake is being eaten by them.*)

   (3) **Loro hanno mangiato la torta.** (*They've eaten the cake.*)

   (4) **La torta è stata mangiata da loro.** (*The cake has been eaten by them.*)

Rewrite the following sentences, changing them from the active to the passive form.

Q. I bambini hanno rotto il vetro della finestra.

A. **Il vetro della finestra è stato rotto dai bambini.** (*The window glass was broken by the children.*)

18. Maria ha vinto la gara di sci.

_____

19. Mia sorella venderà la casa.

_____

20. La maestra aveva lodato mio figlio.

_____

21. Costruirono questa casa nel 1927.

_____

22. Nel 1960 Kennedy vinse le elezioni.

_____

23. La casa editrice Mondadori pubblicherà le sue poesie.

_____

24. Diceva che noi avremmo vinto la partita.

_____

Referring to the Anonymous "Someone"

In English, when you aren't sure who's performing an action, or when you want to convey a generic subject, you say that *people, we, you, they,* or *one do/does* something (or you use the passive voice; refer to the earlier section "Moving from the Active to the Passive Form"). To refer to this type of anonymous someone, Italian employs the pronoun **si** followed by a third-person verb. For example, **In questo ristorante si beve dell'ottimo vino** (*In this restaurant we/you/one drink[s] excellent wine*).

When the construction **si** + verb is followed by a plural noun, the verb is in the third-person plural, as in **Si mangiano le pesche d'estate** (*You can eat peaches in summer/Peaches are eaten in summer*).

When using the impersonal **si** in a present perfect tense, **essere** (*to be*) is the auxiliary verb (see Chapter 8 for more on working with compound tenses), followed by the past participle of the verb. For example, **Si è mangiato** (*We ate*).

Note: The same rule of agreement is applied when the construction **si** + verb is followed by a plural noun in the past, as in **Si sono mangiate delle pere squisite** (*We ate [one ate] some delicious pears*).

When **si** is followed by the verb **essere** and an adjective, the adjective agrees in gender and number with the subject. For example, **Si è belle** (*We [women] are beautiful*).

You can use most verbs — transitive and intransitive — impersonally; for example, **Si va** (*we go*), **si parte** (*we leave*), **si beve** (*we drink*), **si impara** (*we learn*), and **si dice** (*people say*). Only the context tells you what subject you want to use in English.

> **Si va al cinema stasera?** (*Are we going to the movies tonight?*)

> **Si dice che la tregua non durerà.** (*People say that the truce won't hold.*)

If you use a reflexive verb impersonally, which you do when the action is expressed by a reflexive verb but the subject isn't stated, you add the pronoun **ci** to the impersonal **si: Ci si lava ogni mattina** (*One washes oneself every morning*).

Translate the following sentences into Italian using the construction with **si**. Consult Chapter 15 for instructions on building declarative dependent clauses.

Q. You can apply for a fellowship online.

A. **Si può fare domanda per una borsa di studio on line.**

25. People say that the princess was killed.

_____

26. Shall we go to the soccer game?

_____

27. People eat more vegetables in summer.

_____

28. You eat well in that restaurant.

_____

29. One can drive through Bologna to go to Rome.

_____

30. A lot of languages are spoken in India.

_____

Answer Key

1 **Pietro si è svegliato.** (*Pietro woke up.*)

2 **I bambini si sono divertiti.** (*The children enjoyed themselves.*)

3 **Nicola si è sposato con Fulvia.** (*Nicola married Fulvia.*)

4 **I miei genitori si sono dimenticati le chiavi di casa.** (*My parents forgot their house keys.*)

5 **I signori Bernini si sono trasferiti a Napoli.** (*Mrs. and Mr. Bernini moved to Naples.*)

6 **Mi sono meravigliato/a molto che tu non abbia protestato.** (*I was very surprised that you didn't protest.*)

7 **Una donna si pettina i capelli.**

8 **Un bambino si lava i denti.**

9 **Una ragazza si trucca gli occhi.**

10 **Un gatto si lecca il pelo.**

11 **Un uomo si toglie la camicia.**

12 **Tre uomini si cucinano il pesce alla griglia.**

13 **Un uomo e una donna si stringono/darsi la mano.**

14 **Vincenzo e Daria si sposano.**

15 **Francesco e Elisabetta si amano.**

16 **Un uomo e una donna si salutano.** or **Un signore e una signora si salutano.**

17 **Due uomini si odiano.**

18 **La gara di sci è stata vinta da Maria.** (*The ski race was won by Maria.*)

19 **La casa sarà venduta da mia sorella.** (*The house will be sold by my sister.*)

20 **Mio figlio era stato lodato dalla maestra.** (*My son was praised by his teacher.*)

21 **Questa casa fu costruita nel 1927.** (*This house was built in 1927.*)

22 **Nel 1960 le elezioni furono vinte da Kennedy.** (*In 1960 the election was won by Kennedy.*)

23 **Le sue poesie saranno pubblicate dalla casa editrice Mondadori.** (*His/Her poems will be published by Mondadori Press.*)

24 **Diceva che la partita sarebbe stata vinta da noi.** (*He said that the game would have been won by us.*)

25 **Si dice che la principessa sia stata uccisa.**

26 **Si va alla partita di calcio?**

27 **Si mangia/mangiano più verdura/verdure in estate/d'estate.**

28 **Si mangia bene in quel ristorante.**

29 **Si può passare da Bologna per andare a Roma.**

30 **Si parlano molte lingue in India.**

Part V
The Part of Tens

The 5th Wave   By Rich Tennant

Sheila finds out her daughter picks up other languages with effortless ease.

"It had an interesting emotional arc and some nice plot twists, but the heroine and subsidiary characters were unconvincing within the historical context."

In this part . . .

*W*hen you're talking with someone in Italian, you always have the option of clarifying what you're saying, or the other person may give you a useful suggestion about how to express yourself better. But if you're writing in Italian, you're on your own — with the help of the chapters in this part, of course. In this part, I warn you about some *false friends,* or words that look similar in Italian and English but mean different things. I share advice on different ways to express yourself and handle nuances of the language, and I also bring your attention to subtle differences in meaning of ten important verb pairs.

Chapter 18

Ten Facts to Remember about Italian Grammar

In This Chapter
▶ Watching out for words that sound or look alike but have different meanings
▶ Getting more out of verbs
▶ Exploring other ways to express the passive voice
▶ Giving voice to strong emotions

This chapter is a mix of Italian grammar tips intended to help you avoid some simple mistakes as well as enrich your Italian speaking and writing skills. I start with what are called in language-learning jargon *false friends* — words that look similar in Italian and English but have different meanings — and move on to other tricky things like verbs used as adjectives or nouns, different ways of expressing the passive voice, and idiomatic constructions. I also tell you how to convey strong emotions and elicit someone's agreement with what you're saying. In other words, this chapter is devoted to nuances of the language that should help you move toward greater fluency.

False Friends: Similar Italian and English Words Don't Necessarily Share Meanings

Italian and English share a lot of words derived from Latin. In several cases, the shared words have similar meanings, like **fortunatamente,** which means *fortunately.* In other cases, their meanings are different: *Catholic* can translate to the Italian **universale** or **cattolico,** depending on the context.

You'll also encounter Italian and English words that resemble one another in spelling but that don't share the same linguistic origin. Words like these trick you into believing you can guess their meanings when you actually can't. These are *false friends.* I list the most common of these false friends in Table 18-1; note how the Italian words in the first column are spelled similar to the English words in the third column.

Table 18-1		False Friends in Italian and English	
Italian	*English Translation*	*English*	*Italian Translation*
affluenza	participation	affluence	ricchezza
agenda	notebook	agenda	ordine del giorno (now also agenda)
annoiare	to bore	to annoy	infastidire
assumere	to hire	to assume	presumere
batteria	drums	battery	pila
conferenza	lecture	conference	convegno
confidenza	familiarity	confidence	sicurezza
conveniente	cheap	convenient	comodo
domandare	to ask	to demand	esigere
dottore	college graduate	doctor	medico
educato	well-mannered	educated	colto
eventualmente	possibly	eventually	finalmente
fabbrica	factory	fabric	tessuto
fattoria	farm	factory	fabbrica
football, calcio	soccer	football	football americano
fresco	cool	fresh	fresco
graduato	non-commissioned officer	graduate	laureato
grosso	big	gross	lordo
incidente	accident	incident	episodio
incosciente	irresponsible	unconscious	non cosciente, inconscio
influenza	flu	influence	influsso, che influirà la situazione
investire	to run over	to invest (money)	investire
istruzione	education	(user's) instruction	istruzione
libreria	bookstore	library	biblioteca
lingua	tongue	language	lingua
magazzino	warehouse	magazine	rivista
minuto	tiny	minute (as in time)	minuto
mutuo	mortgage	mutual	reciproco
occasione	good deal	occasion	opportunità

Italian	English Translation	English	Italian Translation
ordinario	*cheap*	*ordinary*	**medio, normale**
patente	*license*	*patent*	**brevetto**
periodo	*paragraph, chunk of time*	*period (as in punctuation)*	**punto**
personale	*staff*	*personal*	**personale**
piacere	*favor*	*pleasure*	**piacere**
preoccupato	*worried*	*preoccupied*	**pensieroso**
prescrizione	*rule*	*prescription*	**ricetta medica**
pretendere	*to claim*	*to pretend*	**fingere, pretendere**
rappresentazione	*(artistic) representation*	*(political) representation*	**rappresentanza**
ricordo	*recollection*	*record*	**disco, documento**
ricoverare	*to hospitalize*	*to recover*	**guarire**
rumore	*noise*	*rumor*	**diceria**
salario	*wages*	*salary*	**stiipendio**
scolaro	*pupil, student*	*scholar*	**studioso**
sensibile	*sensitive*	*sensible*	**sensato**
simpatico	*nice*	*sympathetic*	**partecipe**
straniero	*foreigner*	*stranger*	**estraneo**
triviale	*vulgar*	*trivial*	**banale**
vocabolario	*dictionary*	*vocabulary*	**lessico**

Italian Verbs Can Have Multiple Functions

You can turn the infinitive of Italian verbs into nouns by adding the singular masculine article **il** (or **l'** or **lo,** depending on the verb's first letters) to the infinitive. This use of the infinitive corresponds to the gerund in English. For example, **il bere** (*drinking*).

You also can turn the present and past participles of verbs into adjectives or nouns.

✔ **Present participle:** You form the present participle by adding **-ante** or **-ente** to the stem of the verb, so that **cantare** becomes **cantante** (*singing*) and **attrarre** becomes **attraente** (*attractive*). Here the distinction between present participle and gerund (see the moods and tense table on the Cheat Sheet) comes in handy: While the past participle ends in **-ante** or **-ente** (plural **-anti** or **-enti**), the gerund ends in **-ando** or **-endo,** as in **andando** (*going*), **dormendo** (*sleeping*), and **finendo** (*finishing*). It's invariable and it can only function as a verbal form.

You can use the present participle as an adjective, as in **La ragazza era attraente** (*The girl was attractive*) or as a noun, as in **Il cantante venne applaudito** (*The singer was applauded*).

✔ **Past participle:** You can use the past participle as a noun. Past participles that become nouns can be masculine, as in **il passato** (*the past*), or feminine, as in **la veduta** (*view*). Past participles also can become adjectives, but because they end in **-o**, they can take four forms: **-o**, **-a**, **-i**, or **-e**. For example, the past participle **amato** becomes **amata, amati, amate,** as in **Petrarca scrisse molte poesie alla donna amata** (*Petrarch wrote many poems to his beloved*).

Some Verbs Turn the Object into the Subject

The verb **piacere** literally means *to be pleasing to* even though it corresponds to the verb *to like*. In English, you can use *to like* to say, *I like ice cream,* but you also could say, *Ice cream is pleasing to me.* The latter may sound awkward, but it's still grammatically correct. The construction is similar to the Italian verb **piacere: Il gelato piace a me,** or more fluently, **Mi piace il gelato.** You coordinate the verb with the thing that's liked, and you convey the person who likes something with an indirect object pronoun, mostly conjugated in third-person singular and plural, placed before the verb (see Chapter 4 for more information about pronouns). (Remember that the opposite of **piacere** is **non piacere.**)

You use the same construction you use for **piacere** with several other verbs, which I show in the following list:

✔ **accadere, capitare, succedere** (*to happen to someone*)

✔ **bastare** (*to be sufficient to, to be enough for someone, to suffice to someone*)

✔ **dispiacere** (*to be sorry about [used for feelings and mental states rather than things]*)

✔ **far(e) piacere** (*to please someone, to be pleasing to someone*)

✔ **far(e) dispiacere** (*to displease someone*)

✔ **importare** (*to matter to someone*)

✔ **interessare** (*to be interested in, to interest someone*)

✔ **mancare** (*to lack, to miss*)

✔ **parere, sembrare** (*to appear to someone, to seem to someone*)

You can use these verbs in two ways: You can turn the person who's the subject into the receiver of the action; or you can use the verb with the person or thing performing the action as the subject. Beware that the two constructions aren't interchangeable and that you'll be saying two different things. Consider these examples: **Non mi interessa se tu vieni o no** (*I don't care whether you're coming or not*), and **I problemi di Paolo non interessano a nessuno** (*Paolo's problems don't matter to anyone*).

Some Verbs Can't Live Without Pronouns

The following widely used verbs are completely idiomatic in the sense that you can't make out their meanings by understanding the meanings of their components. Each of these verbs adds both a reflexive pronoun matched to the person who's performing the action (expressed in the infinitive with **si,** which becomes **se** to ease pronunciation) and another pronoun, at times **ne** (*of this, of that, from this/that place*) and at times **la** (*this thing, this situation*). Neither of these pronouns points to something real; they solely play an idiomatic function.

- **andarsene** (*to go away, to leave*): **È tardi. Me ne vado a casa.** (*It's late. I'll go home.*)

- **cavarsela** (*to make it*): **La tormenta ci ha sorpreso, ma ce la siamo cavata.** (*The snowstorm was suddenly upon us, but we made it.*)

- **farcela** (*to be able to make it*): **Non preoccuparti della valigia, ce la faccio da sola.** (*Don't worry about the suitcase, I can carry it by myself.*)

- **tornarsene** (*to come back, to return from, to go back*): **È meglio che ce ne torniamo a casa.** (*It's better to go home.*)

- **vedersela** (*to see to it oneself*): **Ma le vedo io per le tasse.** (*I'll see to the taxes myself.*)

- **venirsene** (*to come, to walk*): **Se ne veniva piano piano.** (*He was walking slowly.*)

Fare Is the Jack of All Trades

The verb **fare** is as common in Italian as *to do* or *to make* is in English. It means both *to do* and *to make,* and colloquially (and a bit lazily), it replaces a lot of other verbs. For example, **fare da mangiare** (*to make food*) is the same as **cucinare** (*to cook*); **fare una festa** (*to make a party*) is the same as **dare una festa** (*to give a party*); and so on.

You also use the verb **fare** followed by an infinitive to convey the expressions *to have something done, to get something done, to cause something to happen, to make something happen.* You can use it to express two different ideas:

- You have something done on your behalf: **Faccio pitturare la casa.** (*I'll have the house painted.*)

- Someone has caused something to happen: **Il gatto ha fatto cadere il vaso.** (*The cat made the vase fall.*)

You can even use **fare** followed by **fare,** as in **Faccio fare il pacco** (*I'll have them make the package*). And you can use it reflexively: **Farsi fare qualcosa** means *to have something done to/for oneself.* For example, **Mi faccio tagliare i capelli** (*I'll have my hair cut*).

Fare is a transitive verb which takes **avere** (*to have*) as its auxiliary in compound tenses. But when it's used reflexively, as **farsi,** it needs the auxiliary **essere** (*to be*).

da + Verb = Four Possible Meanings

You use **da** (*from, by*) followed by an infinitive to say that something *is to be done* or *can be done*, with four different nuances.

- Something is available for us to do: "**Hai dei libri da leggere?**" "**Ne ho troppi!**" ("*Do you have any books to read?*" "*I have too many!*")

- Something must be done: **Il professore ci ha dato da leggere tre libri.** (*The professor assigned three books to read.*)

- Something needs to be done: **La mia automobile è da lavare.** (*My car needs washing.*)

- Something is worth doing: **È un posto da vedere.** (*It's a place worth seeing.*)

Convey the Passive Voice in More than One Way

You can say that things have been done by someone using verbs other than **essere** (*to be*). Unlike **essere,** which conveys a static condition, these verbs convey motion and are helpful when you wish to emphasize the process that has led to a certain result. Their use is governed by idiomatic patterns rather than rules, which you'll pick up by reading or listening to native speakers. For example, you may say **Il lavoro andrà finito entro domani** (*The job will have to be finished by tomorrow*) but not **Sono rimasta assunta** (*I remained hired*). You conjugate the verb that functions as the auxiliary just as you would conjugate the verb **essere,** and you add the past participle of the main verb. In the case of **venire** and **andare,** you can say **vengono/vanno fatte** (*they must be done, they are done*), but not **sono venute fatte** (literally, *they have come done*). Here are the alternatives to **essere:**

- **venire** (*to come*) can mean *to be* or *to get:* You can only use **venire** in the simple tenses of the active voice, as in **Le porte vengono chiuse** (*The doors are being/closed*).

- **andare** (*to go*) can mean *to get:* It's used only in the third-person singular or plural, as in **La casa andò distrutta** (*The house was destroyed*). It also can mean *to have to,* or *must;* you can use it with the subject in any person, as in **Le tasse vanno pagate subito** (*The taxes have to be paid at once*).

- **rimanere** (*to remain*) can mean *to get:* You use it to emphasize the consequences of an event, as in **Il conducente è rimasto bloccato sull'autostrada** (*The driver was stuck in traffic on the highway*).

You convey constructions such as *I was told* or *We were reminded* by using **essere** or **venire** impersonally, in the third-person singular:

- **essere** (*to be*) in the present perfect + past participle of the main verb: **È stato detto loro di parlare col medico.** (*They were told to talk to their physician.*)

- **venire** (*to be, to get*) in the present indicative or other simple tense followed by the past participle of the main verb: **Le verrà consigliato di cambiare lavoro.** (*She'll be advised to look for another job.*)

Convey Strong Emotion with Exclamatory Words

When you feel something strongly, you can use several different short phrases that convey your emotion and draw the listener's attention to it. Here's a rundown of your options:

- **Che!** (*What!, What a!*): Followed by an adjective or a noun, without any article:

    Che disgrazia! (*What a terrible accident!*)

    Che bei bambini! (*What beautiful children!*)

- **Come!** (*How!*): Followed by a verb with the subject placed after it: **Com'è pesante quella valigia!** (*How heavy that suitcase is!*)

- **Quanto!** (*How much!, How many!*): Matched in gender and number to the noun that follows. You also can use **quanto** as an indefinite pronoun (see Chapter 7). In this case, you can use it with a noun; or you can add any verb conveying quantity, or the verb **essere** (*to be*) and an adjective. The verb and the adjective are matched to the subject of the sentence (at times expressed and at times conveyed by the verb):

    Quanta gente! (*So many people!*)

    Quanto hai speso! (*You spent so much!*)

    Quanto sono stati gentili! (*How kind they were!*)

- **Ecco!** (*Here/There he/she/they is/are!*): Used if someone you've been waiting for has finally arrived, or if you want to draw someone's attention to something. If you use a pronoun to refer to that person, you attach it it to **Ecco**:

    "Dov'è Maria?" "Eccola!" (*"Where is Maria?" "Here/There she is!"*)

    "Hai visto i miei occhiali?" "Eccoli!" (*"Have you seen my glasses?" "Here/There they are!"*)

Lasciare Grants (Or Requests) Permission

Your daughter wants to go to a sleepover, and you give her permission by telling her, *I'll let you go, but you need to finish your homework first.* In Italian, you use the verb **lasciare** followed by a verb in the infinitive to grant or request permission, as in **Ti lascio andare ma prima devi finire i compiti.**

If you use a pronoun to express the person to whom you're giving permission, you have two options for constructing your sentences:

- **If the person is the only direct object in the sentence,** you use the direct object pronouns, usually in their weak form, placed before the verbal form, as in **La lascia andare al centro commerciale?** (*Will you let her go to the superstore?*).

✔ **If you have both a person to whom you're giving permission and a direct object,** you represent the person with an indirect object pronoun. If you use a double pronoun, you represent the person with an indirect object pronoun and the thing you're letting her do with a direct object pronoun. For example, **Lascio che Mario ascolti il CD!** → **Glielo lascio ascoltare** (*I let him listen to the CD*). (Turn to Chapter 4 for more on pronouns.)

You place pronouns before the verbal form **lasciare** + infinitive, or attached to **lasciare** when it's in the infinitive, the imperative, or the gerund (see Chapter 9).

When you use **lasciare** followed by a sentence introduced by **che**, you need the verb in the subjunctive, as in **Hanno lasciato che lui passasse per primo** (*They let him go first*). (Chapters 15 and 16 cover the subjunctive and use of **che**.)

If You Want Someone to Agree with You, Add Non è vero?

You may want to make sure that you understand what someone just told you, or you may want someone to agree to what you just said. In English, you take the auxiliary of the verb (or the verb *to do* if there's no auxiliary) and add a question to the end. In Italian, you always use **È vero** (*Is it true?*) or **Non è vero?** (*Isn't it true?*) regardless of whether you're using an auxiliary and which one it is. For example, **Possiamo andare tutti con la tua macchina, non è vero?** (*We can all go with your car, can't we?*).

Chapter 19

Ten Subtle Verb Distinctions

In This Chapter

▶ Understanding slight differences in verb meanings

▶ Choosing the right verbs for specific actions

*T*he meanings of some Italian verbs have very subtle but very important differences even though their English translations are nearly identical. In this chapter, I cover the most common nuances between ten pairs of verbs, clarifying the range of meanings that each verb lays claim to.

Abitare (To Live, To Reside) versus Vivere (To Live, To Reside)

You use **abitare** (*to live, to reside*) to talk about your address, as in **Abito in Italia, a Milano, in Via Sarpi 18** (*I live in Italy, in Milan, at 18 Via Sarpi*). You also can say **Vivo in Italia, a Milano** (*I live in Italy, in Milan*). But even though everyone would understand you, you're less likely to say, **Vivo in Via Sarpi** (*I live on Via Sarpi*). **Vivere** conveys more than just having a dwelling: It refers to your entire life, which is likely to have a larger context. **Vivere,** therefore, refers to one's *life,* not just to one's residence; for example, you may say, **Ha vissuto a lungo** (*He had a long life*).

When speaking of a residence, you also can use **stare** (*to reside*); for example, **"Dove stai?" "Sto in Via Sarpi."** (*"Where do you live? What is your address?" "I live on Via Sarpi."*).

Andare (To Go) versus Partire (To Leave)

Andare describes the action of going to the movies, the office, the moon, and so on, or the action of going from one place to another, like from room to room, or from city to city. When using **andare,** you add **da** (*from*) to the place you're leaving and **a, in,** or **su** to the place you're going to. For example, **Andiamo da Roma a Napoli** (*We're going from Rome to Naples*).

Partire describes going on a trip, but it points to the organizational and physical activities required to reach your destination. You can say: **Parto per Shanghai** (*I'm leaving for Shanghai*) or **Parto per le vacanze** (*I'm leaving for my vacation*), both of which mean *I've loaded my car, I've got my maps, my tank is full of gas,* and so on. You add **da** if you mention where you're leaving from, and add **per** to your destination. But you don't use **partire** and say, **Parto per l'ufficio** (*I'm leaving for the office*), even if you have an hour-long commute. Instead, you say, **Vado in ufficio** (*I'm going to the office*). And if you're going on vacation and you wish to emphasize that instead of working you'll be having fun, you say **Vado in vacanza** (*I'm going on vacation*).

Sapere (To Know) versus Conoscere (To Be Acquainted With)

Sapere conveys knowledge, whereas **conoscere** means *to be acquainted with, be aware of, to recognize*. So, you say, **Sai a che ora parte il treno?** (*Do you know what time the train leaves?*) but, **Conosci mia sorella?** (*Do you know my sister?*). The Socratic injunction *Know thyself!* therefore translates to **Conosci te stesso!**

Fare (To Do) versus Essere (To Be)

You can use **fare** to talk about people's jobs, as in **Laura fa il medico** (*Laura is a physician*). You use it especially when you ask questions such as **Che cosa fai? Che lavoro fai?** (*What do you do? What's your job?*). You also can use the verb **essere** (*to be*), saying **Ida è avvocato** (*Ida is a lawyer*). But with the verb **essere,** you imply that a person's profession defines his or her identity. When the role you play becomes your identity, you use **essere** instead of **fare**. For example, you don't say **Ratzinger fa il papa** (*Ratzinger is a Pope*), but rather **Ratzinger è il papa** (*Ratzinger is the Pope*).

Essere (To Be) versus Stare (To Stay)

You use **essere** to express situations that last over time and indicate not just physical being but also emotions and feelings; for example, **Sei contenta?** (*Are you happy?*). As I explain in the preceding section, **essere** has to do with identity, as in **È una donna coraggiosa** (*She's a courageous woman*). However, when it comes to talking about *how you are,* you use **stare**. For example, **Stai bene?** (*Are you all right?*) may regard your health or your feelings. Americans use the set phrase *How are you?* (**Come stai?, Come sta?**) as a form of salutation, to which people answer rhetorically *I'm fine,* usually regardless of how they actually feel. In Italy, if you ask **Come stai?,** you're likely to get a report on the person's health and state of mind. Use **Buon giorno** (*Good morning*) or **Buona sera** (*Good evening*) when meeting someone and **Ciao** (*hello*) only with people you address informally.

Suonare (To Play an Instrument) versus Giocare (To Play a Game or a Sport)

If you're referring to playing an instrument, you use **suonare** (*to play*). For example, if you're a pianist, you say **Suono il piano** (*I play the piano*). If you're engaged in a game or a sport, you use **giocare** (*to play*) and say **Gioco a tennis** (*I play tennis*) or **Gioco a bridge** (*I play bridge*), for example, adding **a** to the game or sport you're playing. You also can add a direct object with **giocare** in order to be more specific, like **Hanno giocato tre partite a/di calcio** (*They played three soccer matches*). **Giocare/giocarsi** also means *to gamble,* as in **Ha giocato tutti i suoi soldi a baccarat** (*He gambled all his money at baccarat*).

Partire (To Leave) versus Uscire (To Go Out) or Lasciare (To Leave)

Because **partire** means *to go on a trip,* you don't say **Parto dalla stanza** (*I'm leaving the room*), but rather **Esco dalla stanza** (*I'm walking out of the room*), **Lascio la stanza** (*I'm leaving the room*), or **Io ho lasciato il telefonino a casa** (*I left my cellphone at home*). But **uscire** points only to physical motion, whereas **lasciare** can imply your reasons for leaving. For example, you use **lasciare** to explain why you're walking out of the room: **A che ora dobbiamo lasciare la camera?** (*What time do we have to be out of the room?*). However, you can also use **uscire** metaphorically, meaning *to go out with* or *to date:* **Escono insieme da tre mesi** (*They've been dating for three months*).

Prendere (To Take, To Have) versus Bere (To Drink) or Mangiare (To Eat)

Instead of saying that you're *drinking* a beverage or *eating* a hamburger, you may want to say that you're *having* them, like *I'm having a hamburger.* You can use **prendere** (*to have*) to order food or to convey that you're deciding what to eat or drink, whereas with **bere** (*to drink*) or **mangiare** (*to eat*) you point to physical activities. For example, **Non prendo il caffè dopo cena** (*I don't have coffee after dinner*).

Potere (Can, May) Versus Riuscire (Can, To Be Able To)

In English, you use *can* to express power and ability, including success, and *may* to convey permission. In Italian, you use **potere** to convey power and permission, and **riuscire** to convey success. See the difference in these examples: **Posso fumare qui?** (*May I smoke here?*); **Non sono riuscita a finire il lavoro in tempo** (*I wasn't able to finish the assignment on time*).

Udire/Sentire (To Hear) versus Ascoltare (To Listen To)

The distinction between the verbs **udire** or **sentire** (*to hear*) and **ascoltare** (*to listen to*) parallels the distinction in English. *To hear* means that you're exposed to sounds, whether you like it or not, and **udire** is used more often in literature. *To listen to* means that you've decided to pay attention to those sounds. For example, you say **Ho sentito il campanello** (*I heard the bell ring*), but **Ascolto la sinfonia "Dal nuovo mondo"** (*I'm listening to the symphony "From the New World"*).

Part VI
Appendixes

The 5th Wave   By Rich Tennant

"If you're having trouble with irregular verbs, try using flash cards and taking more fiber."

In this part . . .

The appendixes in this part are helpful quick-reference resources. For regular and irregular conjugations of the most important simple tenses of verbs, head to Appendix A. You may find it helpful to see all the possible verb variations and similarities in one place. Appendixes B and C are dictionaries to provide fast and easy support when you're stumped, although they can't replace full and complete Italian dictionaries. (One suggestion when it comes to dictionaries: Try to use a monolingual dictionary as much as possible and a bilingual one only as support.)

Appendix A

Verb Charts

• •

*T*hese charts summarize regular conjugations patterns and provide full lists of irregular conjugations for commonly used verbs in the most important simple tenses. Then I list conjugations of irregular verbs. I conjugate the verb only in its irregular moods and tenses, except for **essere** (which is almost completely irregular) and **avere,** because you really need all their forms at your fingertips. When you look at the irregular verb and don't find a tense listed, you can assume that particular verb is regular in that tense, even though it's irregular in many others. **Fare** (*to do, to make*) is a good example of one of these quirky verbs.

Here are some suggestions to help you use the charts. I list a verb that "establishes" a pattern of irregularity (so to speak), for example dipin**gere** (*to paint*). I bold the letters that you'll have to drop when the verb takes irregular forms. Then I give you those irregular forms. So you find io dipin**si** (*I painted*). When I tell you that another verb, let's say pian**gere** (*to weep*), behaves like dipin**gere**, I mean that in the same moods and tenses, piangere drops the same letters that dipingere does and takes the same suffixes: io pian**si** (*I wept.*) This setup also gives you a nice way to practice your conjugations and memorize them.

Note: In this appendix, I list conjugations in the order of the six persons to which correspond six forms of the verb: **io** (*I*), **tu** (*you*), **lui** (*he*) which also stands for **lei, esso, essa** (*she, it*), **noi** (*we*), **voi** (*you*), and **loro** (*they*) which also stands for **essi, esse** (*they*).

Regular Verbs

Tables A-1, A-2, and A-3 report the endings for regular verbs in each of the three conjugations.

Table A-1	Verb Endings, Various Tenses, First Conjugation in -are						
Subject	Present Indicative	Imperfect Indicative	Preterit Indicative	Simple Future Indicative	Present Conditional	Present Subjunctive	Imperfect Subjunctive
io	-o	-avo	-ai	-erò	-erei	-i	-assi
tu	-i	-avi	-asti	-erai	-eresti	-i	-assi
lui	-a	-ava	-ò	-erà	-erebbe	-i	-asse

(continued)

Table A-1 *(continued)*

Subject	Present Indicative	Imperfect Indicative	Preterit Indicative	Simple Future Indicative	Present Conditional	Present Subjunctive	Imperfect Subjunctive
noi	-iamo	-avamo	-ammo	-eremo	-eremmo	-iamo	-assimo
voi	-ate	-avate	-aste	-erete	-ereste	-iate	-aste
loro	-ano	-avano	-arono	-eranno	-erebbero	-ino	-assero

Table A-2   Verb Endings, Various Tenses, Second Conjugation in -ere

Subject	Present Indicative	Imperfect Indicative	Preterit Indicative	Simple Future Indicative	Present Conditional	Present Subjunctive	Imperfect Subjunctive
io	-o	-evo	-ei (-etti)	-erò	-erei	-a	-essi
tu	-i	-evi	-esti	-erai	-eresti	-a	-essi
lui	-e	-eva	-é (-ette)	-erà	-erebbe	-a	-esse
noi	-iamo	-evamo	-emmo	-eremo	-eremmo	-iamo	-essimo
voi	-ete	-evate	-este	-erete	-ereste	-iate	-este
loro	-ono	-evano	-erono (-ettero)	-eranno	-erebbero	-ano	-essero

Table A-3   Verb Endings, Various Tenses, Third Conjugation in -ire

Subject	Present Indicative	Imperfect Indicative	Preterit Indicative	Simple Future Indicative	Present Conditional	Present Subjunctive	Imperfect Subjunctive
io	-o	-ivo	-ii	-irò	-irei	-a	-issi
tu	-i	-ivi	-isti	-irai	-iresti	-a	-issi
lui	-e	-iva	-ì	-irà	-irebbe	-a	-isse
noi	-iamo	-ivamo	-immo	-iremo	-iremmo	-iamo	-issimo
voi	-ite	-ivate	-iste	-irete	-ireste	-iate	-iste
loro	-ono	-ivano	-irono	-iranno	-irebbero	-ano	-issero

Regular Verbs with a Twist: Simple Spelling Changes

Verbs that change spelling aren't really irregular because they modify *only* the spelling to maintain the same pronunciation throughout some tenses.

-care/-gare verbs

giocare (to play)

Present Indicative: gioco, giochi, gioca, giochiamo, giocate, giocano

Simple Future Indicative: giocherò, giocherai, giocherà, giocheremo, giocherete, giocheranno

Present Conditional: giocherei, giocheresti, giocherebbe, giocheremmo, giochereste, giocherebbero

Present Subjunctive: giochi, giochi, giochi, giochiamo, giochiate, giochino

pagare (to pay)

Present Indicative: pago, paghi, paga, paghiamo, pagate, pagano

Simple Future Indicative: pagherò, pagherai, pagherà, pagheremo, pagherete, pagheranno

Present Conditional: pagherei, pagheresti, pagherebbe, pagheremmo, paghereste, pagherebbero

Present Subjunctive: paghi, paghi, paghi, paghiamo, paghiate, paghino

-ciare/-giare verbs

falciare (to mow)

Present Indicative: falcio, falci, falcia, falciamo, falciate, falciano

Simple Future Indicative: falcerò, falcerai, falcerà, falceremo, falcerete, falceranno

Present Conditional: falcerei, falceresti, falcerebbe, falceremmo, falcereste, falcerebbero

Present Subjunctive: falci, falci, falci, falciamo, falciate, falcino

mangiare (to eat)

Present Indicative: mangio, mangi, mangia, mangiamo, mangiate, mangiano

Simple Future Indicative: mangerò, mangerai, mangerà, mangeremo, mangerete, mangeranno

Present Conditional: mangerei, mangeresti, mangerebbe, mangeremmo, mangereste, mangerebbero

Present Subjunctive: mangi, mangi, mangi, mangiamo, mangiate, mangino

-gliare verbs

consigliare (to advise)

Present Indicative: consiglio, consigli, consiglia, consigliamo, consigliate, consigliano

Present Subjunctive: consigli, consigli, consigli, consigliamo, consigliate, consiglino

-ìare verbs

sciare (to ski)

Present Indicative: scio, scii, scia, sciamo, sciate, sciano

Present Subjunctive: scii, scii, scii, sciamo, sciate, sciino

-iare verbs

studiare (to study)

Present Indicative: studio, studi, studia, studiamo, studiate, studiano

Present Subjunctive: studi, studi, studi, studiamo, studiate, studino

-ire verbs that add -sc-

finire (to finish)

Present Indicative: finisco, finisci, finisce, finiamo, finite, finiscono

Present Subjunctive: finisca, finisca, finisca, finiamo, finiate, finiscano

Verbs conjugated like finire — which add **-sc-** after the stem and before the conjugated ending — include agire (*to act*), capire (*to understand*), colpire (*to hit*), costruire (*to build*), gestire (*to manage*), guarire (*to recover*), unire (*to unite*), and preferire (*to prefer*).

Irregular Verbs

A verb is irregular when you have to modify its stem, ending, or both. Following are the most common irregular verbs and the tenses in which they're irregular.

Auxiliaries and modal auxiliaries

avere (to have)

Present Indicative: ho, hai, ha, abbiamo, avete, hanno

Imperfect Indicative: avevo, avevi, aveva, avevamo, avevate, avevano

Preterit Indicative: ebbi, avesti, ebbe, avemmo, aveste, ebbero

Simple Future Indicative: avrò, avrai, avrà, avremo, avrete, avranno

Present Conditional: avrei, avresti, avrebbe, avremmo, avreste, avrebbero

Present Subjunctive: abbia, abbia, abbia, abbiamo, abbiate, abbiano

Imperfect Subjunctive: avessi, avessi, avesse, avessimo, aveste, avessero

Present Gerund: avendo

Past Participle: avuto

essere (to be)

Present Indicative: sono, sei, è, siamo, siete, sono

Imperfect Indicative: ero, eri, era, eravamo, eravate, erano

Preterit Indicative: fui, fosti, fu, fummo, foste, furono

Simple Future Indicative: sarò, sarai, sarà, saremo, sarete, saranno

Present Conditional: sarei, saresti, sarebbe, saremmo, sareste, sarebbero

Present Subjunctive: sia, sia, sia, siamo, siate, siano

Imperfect Subjunctive: fossi, fossi, fosse, fossimo, foste, fossero

Present Gerund: essendo

Past Participle: stato

dovere (must, shall)

Present Indicative: devo, devi, deve, dobbiamo, dovete, devono

Simple Future Indicative: dovrò, dovrai, dovrà, dovremo, dovrete, dovranno

Present Conditional: dovrei, dovresti, dovrebbe, dovremmo, dovreste, dovrebbero

Present Subjunctive: debba, debba, debba, dobbiamo, dobbiate, debbano

potere (can, may)

Present Indicative: posso, puoi, può, possiamo, potete, possono

Simple Future Indicative: potrò, potrai, potrà, potremo, potrete, potranno

Present Conditional: potrei, potresti, potrebbe, potremmo, potreste, potrebbero

Present Subjunctive: possa, possa, possa, possiamo, possiate, possano

sapere (to know)

Present Indicative: **so, sai, sa,** sap**piamo**, sapete, sa**nno**

Preterit Indicative: **seppi,** sapesti, **seppe,** sapemmo, sapeste, **seppero**

Simple Future Indicative: saprò, sap**rai**, saprà, sap**remo**, sap**rete**, sap**ranno**

Present Conditional: sap**rei**, sap**resti**, sap**rebbe**, sap**remmo**, sap**reste**, sap**rebbero**

Present Subjunctive: sap**pia**, sap**pia**, sap**pia**, sap**piamo**, sap**piate**, sap**piano**

volere (will, to want)

Present Indicative: vo**glio**, **vuoi**, **vuole**, vo**gliamo**, volete, vo**gliono**

Preterit Indicative: vo**lli**, volesti, vo**lle**, volemmo, voleste, vo**llero**

Simple Future Indicative: vorrò, vo**rrai**, vorrà, vo**rremo**, vo**rrete**, vo**rranno**

Present Conditional: vo**rrei**, vo**rresti**, vo**rrebbe**, vo**rremmo**, vo**rreste**, vo**rrebbero**

Present Subjunctive: vo**glia**, vo**glia**, vo**glia**, vo**gliamo**, vo**gliate**, vo**gliano**

First conjugation in -are

andare (to go)

Present Indicative: **vado, vai, va,** andiamo, andate, **vanno**

Simple Future Indicative: andrò, and**rai**, and**rà**, and**remo**, and**rete**, and**ranno**

Present Conditional: and**rei**, and**resti**, and**rebbe**, and**remmo**, and**reste**, and**rebbero**

Present Subjunctive: **vada, vada, vada,** andiamo, andiate, **vadano**

dare (to give)

Present Indicative: do, d**ai**, d**à**, diamo, date, **danno**

Preterit Indicative: d**etti**, d**esti**, d**ette**, d**emmo**, d**este**, d**ettero**

Present Subjunctive: d**ia**, d**ia**, d**ia**, d**iamo**, d**iate**, d**iano**

Imperfect Subjunctive: d**essi**, d**essi**, d**esse**, d**essimo**, d**este**, d**essero**

fare (to do, to make)

Present Indicative: fa**ccio**, fai, fa, **facciamo**, fate, fanno

Imperfect Indicative: **facevo, facevi, faceva, facevamo, facevate, facevano**

Preterit Indicative: fe**ci**, facesti, fe**ce**, facemmo, faceste, fe**cero**

Present Subjunctive: **faccia, faccia, faccia, facciamo, facciate, facciano**

Imperfect Subjunctive: **facessi, facessi, facesse, facessimo, faceste, facessero**

Present Gerund: **facendo**

Past Participle: **fatto**

stare (to stay)

Present Indicative: sto, **stai**, sta, stiamo, state, **stanno**

Preterit Indicative: stetti, **stesti**, stette, **stemmo**, **steste**, **stettero**

Simple Future Indicative: starò, starai, starà, staremo, starete, staranno

Present Subjunctive: stia, stia, stia, stiamo, stiate, stiano

Second conjugation in -ere

alludere (to hint)

Preterit Indicative: allu**si**, alludesti, allu**se**, alludemmo, alludeste, allu**sero**

Past Participle: allu**so**

Verbs conjugated like allu**dere** include: chiu**dere** (*to close*), deci**dere** (*to decide*), divi**dere** (*to divide*), esplo**dere** (*to explode*), eva**dere** (*to escape*).

accendere (to light up, to turn on)

Preterit Indicative: acce**si**, accendesti, acce**se**, accendemmo, accendeste, acce**sero**

Past Participle: acce**so**

Verbs conjugated like accen**dere** (acces-) that take **-s-** in the simple past and the past participle include compren**dere** (*to understand*), condivi**dere** (*to share*), divi**dere** (*to divide*), emer**gere** (*to come to the surface*), esplo**dere** (*to explode*), eva**dere** (*to escape*), immer**gere** (*to immerse, to dip, to plunge*), mor**dere** (*to bite*), per**dere** (*to lose*), pren**dere** (*to take*), ra**dere** (*to shave*), ri**dere** (*to laugh*), ripren**dere** (*to start again, to take again*), and scen**dere** (*to descend*).

aggiungere (to add)

Preterit Indicative: aggiun**si**, aggiungesti, aggiun**se**, aggiungemmo, aggiungeste, aggiun**sero**

Past Participle: *aggiunto*

Verbs conjugated like aggiun**gere** include dipin**gere** (*to paint*), distin**guere** (*to distinguish*), estin**guere** (*to extinguish*), fin**gere** (*to pretend*), giun**gere** (*to arrive*), mun**gere** (*to milk*), pian**gere** (*to cry*), por**gere** (*to hand to*), pun**gere** (*to sting*), raggiun**gere** (*to join*), spin**gere** (*to push*), and tin**gere** (*to dye*).

cadere (to fall)

Preterit Indicative: cad**di**, cadesti, cad**de**, cademmo, cadeste, cad**dero**

Simple Future Indicative: cad**rò**, cad**rai**, cad**rà**, cad**remo**, cad**rete**, cad**ranno**

Present Conditional: cad**rei**, cad**resti**, cad**rebbe**, cad**remmo**, cad**reste**, cad**rebbero**

cogliere (to pick)

Present Indicative: colgo, cogli, coglie, cogliamo, cogliete, colgono

Preterit Indicative: colsi, cogliesti, colse, cogliemmo, coglieste, colsero

Present Subjunctive: colga, colga, colga, cogliamo, cogliate, colgano

Past Participle: colto

Verbs conjugated like cogliere include scegliere (*to choose*), sciogliere (*to melt*), and togliere (*to take out*).

correre (to run)

Preterit Indicative: corsi, corresti, corse, corremmo, correste, corsero

Past Participle: corso

Verbs conjugated like correre include accorrere (*to run*), discorrere (*to chat*), ricorrere (*to appeal*).

concedere (to grant)

Preterit Indicative: concessi, concedesti, concesse, concedemmo, concedeste, concessero

Past Participle: concesso

conoscere (to be acquainted with)

Preterit Indicative: conobbi, conoscesti, conobbe, conoscemmo, conosceste, conobbero

Past Participle: conosciuto

Verbs that modify one or more consonants of the stem and/or then double it like cadere include dirigere (diress-) (*to direct*), discutere (discuss-) (*to discuss*), leggere (less-) (*to read*), proteggere (protess-) (*to protect*), redigere (redass-) (*to redact*), reggere (ress-) (*to hold*), rompere (rupp-) (*to break*), scrivere (scriss-) (*to write*), and riconoscere (riconobb-) (*to recognize*).

cuocere (to cook)

Present Indicative: cuocio, cuoci, cuoce, c[u]ociamo, c[u]ocete, cuociono

Preterit Indicative: cossi, c[u]ocesti, cosse, c[u]ocemmo, c[u]oceste, cossero

Present Subjunctive: cuocia, cuocia, cuocia, cuociamo, cuociate, cuociano

Past Participle: cotto

crescere (to grow)

Present Indicative: cresco, cresci, cresce, cresciamo, crescete, crescono

Preterit Indicative: crebbi, crescesti, crebbe, crescemmo, cresceste, crebbero

Present Subjunctive: cresca, cresca, cresca, cresciamo, cresciate, crescano

Past Participle: cresciuto

Verbs conjugated like crescere include accrescere (*to increase*) and decrescere (*to decrease*).

dipingere (to paint)

Preterit Indicative: dipin**si**, dipingesti, dipin**se**, dipingemmo, dipingeste, dipin**sero**

Past Participle: dipin**to**

Verbs conjugated like dipin**gere** are fin**gere** (*to pretend*), mun**gere** (*to milk*), and pian**gere** (*to weep*).

flettere (to flex)

Preterit Indicative: fle**ssi,** flettesti, fle**sse**, flettemmo, fletteste, fle**ssero**

Past Participle: fle**sso**

Verbs conjugated like fle**ttere** (fle-) include rifle**ttere** (*to reflect*).

fondere (to thaw)

Preterit Indicative: fusi, fondesti, **fuse**, fondemmo, fondeste, **fusero**

Past Participle: **fuso**

Verbs conjugated like fondere include con**fondere** (*to confuse*) and dif**fondere** (*to spread*).

friggere (to fry)

Preterit Indicative: fri**ssi**, friggesti, fri**sse**, friggemmo, friggeste, fri**ssero**

Past Participle: fri**tto**

leggere (to read)

Preterit Indicative: le**ssi**, leggesti, le**sse**, leggemmo, leggeste, le**ssero**

Past Participle: le**tto**

Verbs conjugated like le**ggere** include ele**ggere** (*to elect*) and rile**ggere** (*to reread*).

mettere (to put)

Preterit Indicative: **misi**, mettesti, **mise**, mettemmo, metteste, **misero**

Past Participle: me**sso**

Verbs conjugated like me**ttere** include amme**ttere** (*to admit*), perme**ttere** (*to permit*), prome**ttere** (*to promise*), and trasme**ttere** (*to transmit*).

muovere (to move)

Preterit Indicative: **mossi, m[u]ovesti, mosse, m[u]ovemmo, m[u]oveste, mossero**

Past Participle: **mosso**

Verbs conjugated like m**uovere** include comm**uovere** (*to move emotionally*), prom**uovere** (*to promote*), and rim**uovere** (*to take away*).

nascere *(to be born)*

Preterit Indicative: na**cqui**, nascesti, na**cque**, nascemmo, nasceste, na**cquero**

Past Participle: **nato**

nascondere *(to hide)*

Preterit Indicative: nasco**si**, nascondesti, nasco**se**, nascondemmo, nascondeste, nasco**sero**

Past Participle: nasco**sto**

You conjugate rispo**ndere** *(to reply)* as you do nasc**ondere**.

piacere *(to like)*

Present Indicative: piac**cio**, piaci, piace, piac**ciamo**, piacete, piac**ciono**

Preterit Indicative: piac**qui**, piacesti, piac**que**, piacemmo, piaceste, piac**quero**

Present Subjunctive: piac**cia**, piac**cia**, piac**cia**, piac**ciamo**, piac**ciate**, piac**ciano**

Past Participle: piac**iuto**

Verbs conjugated like piac**ere** include dispiac**ere** *(to dislike, to feel sorry)*, tac**ere** *(to be silent)*, and giac**ere** *(to lie)*.

piovere *(to rain)*

Preterit Indicative: piov**vi**, piovesti, piov**ve**, piovemmo, pioveste, piov**vero**

prendere *(to take, to catch)*

Preterit Indicative: pre**si**, prendesti, pre**se**, prendemmo, prendeste, pre**sero**

Past Participle: **pre**so

Verbs conjugated like prend**ere** (pre**s-**) include scend**ere** *(to descend)*.

proteggere *(to protect)*

Preterit Indicative: prote**ssi**, proteggesti, prote**sse**, proteggemmo, proteggeste, prote**ssero**

Past Participle: prote**tto**

rimanere *(to remain)*

Present Indicative: riman**go**, rimani, rimane, rimaniamo, rimanete, riman**gono**

Preterit Indicative: rima**si**, rimanesti, rima**se**, rimanemmo, rimaneste, rima**sero**

Simple Future Indicative: rima**rrò**, rima**rrai**, rima**rrà**, rima**rremo**, rima**rrete**, rima**rranno**

Present Conditional: rima**rrei**, rima**rresti**, rima**rrebbe**, rima**rremmo**, rima**rreste**, rima**rrebbero**

Present Subjunctive: rima**nga**, rima**nga**, rima**nga**, rimaniamo, rimaniate, rima**ngano**

Past Participle: rima**sto**

rompere (to break)

Preterit Indicative: ruppi, rompesti, **ruppe**, rompemmo, rompeste, **ruppero**

Past Participle: rotto

Verbs conjugated like **r**ompere (**r-**) include cor**r**ompere (*to corrupt*).

sconfiggere (to defeat)

Preterit Indicative: sconfi**ssi**, sconfiggesti, sconfi**sse**, sconfiggemmo, sconfiggeste, sconfi**ssero**

Past Participle: sconfi**tto**

scrivere (to write)

Preterit Indicative: scri**ssi**, scrivesti, scri**sse**, scrivemmo, scriveste, scri**ssero**

Past Participle: scri**tto**

Verbs conjugated like scri**vere** include sottoscri**vere** (*to subscribe*) and trascri**vere** (*to transcribe*).

scuotere (to shake)

Preterit Indicative: sc**ossi**, sc[u]otesti, sc**osse**, sc[u]otemmo, sc[u]oteste, sc**ossero**

Past Participle: sc**osso**

Verbs conjugated like sc**uotere** include perc**uotere** (*to hit*) and risc**uotere** (*to cash*).

sedere (to sit)

Present Indicative: siedo (seggo), siedi, siede, sediamo, sedete, **siedono (seggono)**

You conjugate **possedere** (*to own*) as you do **sedere**.

stringere (to tighten)

Preterit Indicative: strinsi, stringesti, strinse, stringemmo, stringeste, strinsero

Past Participle: stretto

spegnere (and less common spengere) (to turn off)

Preterit Indicative: spe**nsi**, spegnesti, spe**nse**, spegnemmo, spegneste, spen**sero**

Past Participle: spe**nto**

succedere (to happen, to succeed)

Preterit Indicative: succe**ssi**, succcedesti, succe**sse**, succedemmo, succedeste, **succe**ssero

Past Participle: succe**sso**

tenere (to keep)

Present Indicative: ten**go**, **tieni, tiene**, teniamo, tenete, ten**gono**

Preterit Indicative: ten**ni**, tenesti, ten**ne**, tenemmo, teneste, ten**nero**

Simple Future Indicative: ter**rò**, ter**rai**, ter**rà**, ter**remo**, ter**rete**, ter**ranno**

Present Conditional: ter**rei**. ter**resti**, ter**rebbe**, ter**remmo**, ter**reste**, ter**rebbero**

Present Subjunctive: ten**ga**, ten**ga**, ten**ga**, teniamo, teniate, ten**gano**

Verbs conjugated like te**nere** include soste**nere** (sost**en-**) (*to maintain*).

vedere (to see)

Preterit Indicative: vi**di**, vedesti, vi**de**, vedemmo, vedeste, vi**dero**

Simple Future Indicative: ved**rò**, ved**rai**, ved**rà**, ved**remo**, ved**rete**, ved**ranno**

Present Conditional: ved**rei**, ved**resti**, ved**rebbe**, ved**remmo**, ved**rebbe**, ved**rebbero**

Past Participle: veduto, **visto**

Verbs conjugated like **vedere** include ri**vedere** (*to see again*) and stra**vedere** (*to lose one's senses over*).

vincere (to win)

Preterit Indicative: vin**si**, vincesti, vin**se**, vincemmo, vinceste, vin**sero**

Past Participle: vin**to**

Verbs conjugated like vin**cere** include convin**cere** (*to convince*) and stravin**cere** (*to win big*).

vivere (to live)

Preterit Indicative: vi**ssi**, vivesti, vi**sse**, vivemmo, viveste, vi**ssero**

Past Participle: vi**ssuto**

Verbs conjugated like vi**vere** include convi**vere** (*to cohabit*) and sopravvi**vere** (*to survive*).

Third conjugation in -ire

apparire (to appear)

Present Indicative: appa**io** (appari**sco**), appari (appari**sci**), appare (appari**sce**), appariamo, apparite, appa**iono** (appari**scono**)

Preterit Indicative: appar**vi**, apparisti, appar**ve**, apparimmo, appariste, appar**vero**

Present Subjunctive: appa**ia**, appa**ia**, appa**ia**, appariamo, appariate, appa**iano**

Past Participle: appar**so**

Verbs conjugated like appar**ire** include riappar**ire** (*to reappear*) and scompar**ire** (*to disappear*).

aprire (to open)

Preterit Indicative: ap**ersi** (apr**ii**), apristi, ap**erse** (apr**ì**), aprimmo, apriste, ap**ersero** (aprirono)

Past Participle: ap**erto**

Verbs conjugated like ap**rire** include cop**rire** (*to cover*), off**rire** (*to offer*), **riscoprire** (*to rediscover*), scop**rire** (*to uncover, to discover*), and soff**rire** (*to suffer*).

dire (to say, to tell)

Present Indicative: d**ico**, d**ici**, d**ice**, d**iciamo**, d**ite**, d**icono**

Imperfect Indicative: d**icevo**, d**icevi**, d**iceva**, d**icevamo**, d**icevate**, d**icevano**

Present Subjunctive: d**ica**, d**ica**, d**ica**, d**iciamo**, d**iciate**, d**icano**

Imperfect Subjunctive: d**icessi**, d**icessi**, d**icesse**, d**icessimo**, d**iceste**, d**icessero**

Present Gerund: d**icendo**

Past Participle: d**etto**

Verbs conjugated like **dire** include bene**dire** (*to bless*), contrad**dire** (*to contradict*), and dis**dire** (*to cancel*).

morire (to die)

Present Indicative: **muoio**, **muori**, **muore**, moriamo, morite, **muoiono**

Simple Future Indicative: **morrò** (morirò), **morrai** (morirai), **morrà** (morirà), **morremo** (moriremo), **morrete** (morirete), **morranno** (moriranno)

Present Conditional: **morrei** (morirei), **morresti** (moriresti), **morrebbe** (morirebbe), **morremmo** (moriremmo), **morreste** (morireste), **morrebbero** (morirebbero)

Present Subjunctive: **muoia**, **muoia**, **muoia**, moriamo, moriate, **muoiano**

Past Participle: **morto**

offrire (to offer)

Preterit Indicative: **offersi** (offrii), offristi, **offerse** (offrì), offrimmo, offriste, **offersero** (offrirono)

Past Participle: **offerto**

You conjugate **soffrire** (*to suffer*) as you do **offrire**.

salire (to go up)

Present Indicative: sal**go**, sali, sale, saliamo, salite, sal**gono**

Present Subjunctive: sal**ga**, sal**ga**, sal**ga**, saliamo, saliate, sal**gano**

Verbs conjugated like sal**ire** include assal**ire** (*to assault*) and risal**ire** (*to go up again, to resurface*).

udire (to hear)

Present Indicative: odo, odi, ode, udiamo, udite, **odono**

Present Subjunctive: oda, oda, oda, udiamo, udiate, **odano**

uscire (to go out)

Present Indicative: esco, esci, esce, usciamo, uscite, **escono**

Present Subjunctive: esca, esca, esca, usciamo, usciate, **escano**

You conjugate ri**uscire** (*to succeed*) as you do **uscire.**

venire (to come)

Present Indicative: ven**go, vieni, viene,** veniamo, venite, ven**gono**

Simple Future Indicative: verrò, verrai, verrà, verremo, verrete, verranno

Present Conditional: verrei, verresti, verrebbe, verremmo, verreste, verrebbero

Preterit Indicative: venni, venisti, ven**ne,** venimmo, veniste, ven**nero**

Present Subjunctive: ven**ga,** ven**ga,** ven**ga,** veniamo, veniate, ven**gano**

Verbs conjugated like ven**ire** (**ven-**) include avven**ire** (*to happen*), diven**ire** (*to become*), preven**ire** (*to prevent*), proven**ire** (*to derive, to arrive*), and rinven**ire** (*to come to*).

Combining Irregularities: Verbs that Use an Older Stem

A few verbs use an older stem and/or modify the one they have now. **Bere** (*to drink*) comes from **bevere**; it also forms persons from **berr-**; **condurre** (*to lead*) comes from **conducere**; **porre** (*to lay*) comes from **ponere** but it also takes **pong-** in some persons (see its conjugation); and **trarre** (*to draw*) comes from **trahere,** which becomes **tragg-** or **trass-** in some moods and tenses.

bere (to drink)

Present Indicative: be**vo,** be**vi,** be**ve,** be**viamo,** be**vete,** be**vono**

Imperfect Indicative: be**vevo,** be**vevi,** be**veva,** be**vevamo,** be**vevate,** be**vevano**

Preterit Indicative: be**vei,** be**vesti,** be**vve** (be**vé,** be**vette**), be**vemmo,** be**veste,** be**vvero** (be**verono,** be**vettero**)

Simple Future Indicative: ber**rò,** ber**rai,** ber**rà,** ber**remo,** ber**rete,** ber**ranno**

Present Conditional: ber**rei,** ber**resti,** ber**rebbe,** ber**remmo,** ber**reste,** ber**rebbero**

Imperfect Subjunctive: be**vessi,** be**vessi,** be**vesse,** be**vessimo,** be**veste,** be**vessero**

Present Gerund: bevendo

Past Participle: bevuto

condurre (to lead)

Present Indicative: conduco, conduci, conduce, conduciamo, conducete, conducono

Imperfect Indicative: conducevo, conducevi, conduceva, conducevamo, conducevate, conducevano

Preterit Indicative: condussi, conducesti, condusse, conducemmo, conduceste, condussero

Present Subjunctive: conduca, conduca, conduca, conduciamo, conduciate, conducano

Imperfect Subjunctive: conducessi, conducessi, conducesse, conducessimo, conduceste, conducessero

Present Gerund: conducendo

Past Participle: condotto

All verbs formed with **-durre** (which is the basis for **condurre**) behave like it: de**durre** (*to deduce, to deduct*), intro**durre** (*to introduce*), pro**durre** (*to produce*), ri**durre** (*to reduce*), de**durre** (*to seduce*), and tra**durre** (*to translate*).

porre (to lay)

Present Indicative: pongo, poni, pone, poniamo, ponete, pongono

Preterit Indicative: posi, **ponesti**, pose, ponemmo, poneste, **posero**

Present Subjunctive: ponga, ponga, ponga, poniamo, poniate, pongano

Imperfect Subjunctive: ponessi, ponessi, ponesse, ponessimo, poneste, ponessero

Present Gerund: ponendo

Past Participle: posto

All verbs formed with **porre** behave like it: com**porre** (*to compose*), de**porre** (*to depose*), op**porre** (*to oppose*), and sup**porre** (*to suppose*).

trarre (to draw)

Present Indicative: **traggo**, trai, trae, traiamo, traete, **traggono**

Imperfect Indicative: traevo, traevi, traeva, traevamo, traevate, traevano

Preterit Indicative: **trassi, traesti, trasse, traemmo, traeste, trassero**

Present Subjunctive: **tragga, tragga, tragga,** tra**iamo,** tra**iate, traggano**

Imperfect Subjunctive: tra**essi,** tra**essi,** tra**esse,** tra**essimo,** tra**este,** tra**essero**

Present Gerund: traendo

Past Participle: tra**tto**

All verbs formed with **trarre** behave like it: at**trarre** (*to attract*), con**trarre** (*to contract*), ri**trarre** (*to portray*), and sot**trarre** (*to subtract*).

Appendix B

English-Italian Dictionary

● ●

Here are some of the Italian words used throughout this book, arranged alphabetically in English, to help you when writing or speaking Italian.

a, an: **un, uno** (m.)/**una** (f.)

about, of: **di**

above: **sopra, di sopra**

actually: **effettivamente**

after: **dopo**

again: **di nuovo**

against: **contro**

all: **tutto, tutti**

already: **già**

although: **sebbene**

always: **sempre**

among: **tra**

and: **e**

to answer: **rispondere**

anyone: **chiunque**

anything: **qualcosa, qualsiasi cosa**

any: **alcuno, alcuni**

around: **intorno**

to arrive: **arrivare**

as much, as many: **quanto, quanti; tanto, tanti**

as soon as: **non appena**

at: **a, in**

bad: **cattivo**

badly: **male**

to be: **essere**

to be used to: **essere abituato a**

beautiful: **bello**

because: **perché**

before: **prima**

to begin: **incominciare**

behind: **dietro a**

to believe: **credere**

below: **sotto, di sotto**

best: **ottimo**

better: **meglio, migliore**

between: **tra**

big: **grosso**

bitter: **amaro**

to bore: **annoiare**

to borrow, to loan: **prendere a prestito**

boy: **ragazzo**

to be born: **nascere, essere nato**

both . . . and: **sia . . . sia**

to bring: **portare**

to bring up: **tirare su**

to build: **costruire**

but: **ma**

to buy: **comprare, acquistare**

by: **da, in** (+ means of transportation)

to call: **chiamare, telefonare**

to call back, to recall: **richiamare**

can, to be able to, may: **potere**

to cancel: **annullare, cancellare, disdire**

to change: **cambiare**

cheap: **a buon mercato**

to choose: **scegliere**

to clean: **pulire**

close: **vicino**

to close: **chiudere**

to come: **venire**

to correct: **correggere**

currently: **attualmente**

day: **giorno**

dear: **caro**

to defend: **difendere**

to die: **morire**

difficult: **difficile**

to divorce: **divorziare**

to do: **fare**

down: **giù**

to drink: **bere**

to drive: **guidare**

early: **presto**

easy: **facile**

to eat: **mangiare**

either . . . or: **o . . . o**

to end: **finire**

enough: **abbastanza**

to enter: **entrare**

even though: **sebbene**

ever: **mai**

everyone: **ciascuno, tutti**

everything: **tutto**

everywhere: **dappertutto**

to exit: **uscire**

expensive: **caro, costoso**

to fall: **cadere**

far: **lontano**

fast: **veloce, velocemente, in fretta**

fat: **grasso**

a few: **alcuni**

few: **pochi**

finally: **finalmente**

to find: **trovare**

to finish: **finire**

to fly: **volare**

for: **per**

to forget: **dimenticare, dimenticarsi**

to forgive: **perdonare**

fresh: **fresco**

to frighten: **spaventare**

from: **da, di** (origin)

to get: **ottenere, ricevere**

to get married: **sposarsi**

to give: **dare, donare**

to give back: **restituire**

gladly: **volentieri**

to go: **andare**

to go out: **uscire**

good: **buono**

great: **grande**

to grow: **crescere**

happy: **felice**

to hate: **odiare**

to have: **avere**

he: **lui**

to hear: **sentire**

her: **lei, [il] suo, [la] sua, [i] suoi, [le] sue**

here: **qui, lì**

hers: **[il] suo, [la] sua, [i] suoi, [le] sue**

him: **lui**

his: **[il] suo, [la] sua, [i] suoi, [le] sue**

to hold: **tenere**

to hope: **sperare**

hour: **ora**

how: **come**

how much, how many: **quanto, quanti**

I: **io**

if: **se**

in: **in, a**

in front of, before: **di fronte [a]**

inside: **dentro**

intelligent: **intelligente**

interesting: **interessante**

it: **esso, essa**

its: **[il] suo, [la] sua, [i] suoi, [le] sue**

to keep: **tenere**

kind: **gentile**

to know: **sapere, conoscere**

large: **largo**

late: **tardi**

least: **minimo**

to leave: **lasciare, partire**

to lend: **imprestare**

less, less than: **meno, meno di/che**

to let: **lasciare, permettere**

to like: **piacere**

to listen to: **ascoltare**

a little, a little of: **un po', un po' di**

little: **piccolo**

to live: **vivere, abitare**

to look at: **guardare**

to look for: **cercare**

to lose: **perdere**

a lot: **molto, molti**

to love: **amare**

to make: **fare**

man: **uomo**

to marry: **sposare**

me: **me**

to meet: **incontrare**

meeting: **riunione**

mine: **[il] mio, [la] mia, [i] miei, [le] mie**

more, more than: **più, più di/che**

most: **massimo**

to move: **muovere, muoversi**

must: **dovere**

my: **[il] mio, [la] mia, [i] miei, [le] mie**

near: **vicino**

need: **avere bisogno di**

neither . . . nor: **né . . . né**

never: **non . . . mai**

new: **nuovo**

night: **notte**

no: **no**

no, no one, none: **nessuno**

not: **non**

not yet: **non ancora**

nothing: **niente, nulla**

now: **ora, adesso**

nowhere: **da nessuna parte**

of: **di**

to offer: **offrire**

often: **spesso**

old: **vecchio**

on: **su, sopra**

one: **uno, una, si**

only: **solo, soltanto**

to open: **aprire**

or: **o**

our, ours: **[il] nostro, [la] nostra, [i] nostri, [le] nostre**

outside: **fuori**

over: **sopra**

to own: **possedere**

to pass: **passare**

to pay: **pagare**

to play: **giocare, suonare (uno strumento)**

to prefer: **preferire**

pretty: **carino**

to put: **mettere**

quickly: **rapidamente, in fretta**

to raise: **allevare, aumentare**

to receive: **ricevere**

to remember: **ricordare, ricordarsi**

to remind someone of something: **ricordare qualcosa a qualcuno**

to rent: **affittare (un appartamento), noleggiare (un'automobile)**

to repeat: **ripetere**

to reserve: **prenotare**

to return: **ritornare, restituire**

sad: **triste**

same: **stesso**

to say: **dire**

to see: **vedere**

to sell: **vendere**

to send: **mandare**

serious: **serio**

shall: **dovere**

she: **lei**

to ship: **spedire**

short: **piccolo, basso**

to shut: **chiudere**

since: **da quando, poiché**

to sleep: **dormire**

slowly: **lentamente, piano**

small: **piccolo**

so: **così**

so as: **in modo da/che**

some: **un po' di, del, alcuni**

something: **qualcosa**

somewhere: **da qualche parte**

soon: **presto**

to speak: **parlare**

to spend: **spendere**

to stay: **stare**

still: **ancora**

to stop: **fermare, fermarsi**

stupid: **stupido**

to succeed: **riuscire, succedere**

sweet: **dolce**

to take: **prendere, portare**

to talk: **parlare**

tall: **alto**

to tell: **dire, raccontare**

that: **che** (conj. and relative pron.), **il quale, quello**

the: **il**

their: **[il] loro, [la] loro, [i] loro, [le] loro**

theirs: **[il] loro, [la] loro, [i] loro, [le] loro**

them: **loro**

then: **allora, poi**

there: **là, ci**

they: **loro**

thin: **magro**

to think: **pensare**

this: **questo**

to travel: **viaggiare**

to try: **cercare, provare**

to: **a, in, da**

too much, too many: **troppo, troppi**

toward: **verso**

through: **attraverso, per**

ugly: **brutto**

unless: **a meno di/che**

until: **finché, finché non**

up: **su**

us: **noi**

to use: **usare**

very: **molto**

to wait: **aspettare**

to walk: **camminare**

to want, will: **volere**

to watch: **guardare**

we: **noi**

to wear: **indossare, portare**

well: **bene**

what: **che, che cosa**

when: **quando**

where: **dove**

whereas: **mentre**

whether: **se**

which: **che, il quale, i quali**

while: **mentre**

who, whom: **che, il quale, i quali**

who, whom: **chi**

why: **perché**

to wish: **desiderare**

with: **con**

without: **senza**

woman: **donna**

to work: **lavorare**

worse: **peggio, peggiore**

worst: **pessimo,**

yes: **sì**

yet: **ancora**

you: **tu/te, voi/vi**

young: **giovane**

your, yours: **[il] tuo/vostro, [la] tua/vostra, [i] tuoi/ vostri, [le] tue/vostre**

Appendix C

Italian-English Dictionary

• •

Here are some of the Italian words used throughout this book, arranged alphabetically in Italian, to help you when writing or speaking Italian.

a: *at, in, to*

abbastanza: *enough*

abitare: *to live*

acquistare: *to buy*

adesso: *now*

affittare (un appartamento): *to rent (an apartment)*

alcuno, alcuni: *a few, any, some*

allevare: *to raise*

allora: *then*

alto: *tall*

amare: *to love*

amaro: *bitter*

ancora: *still, yet, more*

andare: *to go*

annoiare: *to bore*

annullare: *to cancel*

aprire: *to open*

arrivare: *to arrive*

ascoltare: *to listen to*

aspettare: *to wait*

attraverso: *through*

attualmente: *currently, now*

avere: *to have*

avere bisogno di: *to need*

basso: *short, low*

bello: *beautiful*

bene: *well*

bere: *to drink*

brutto: *ugly*

a buon mercato: *cheap*

buono: *good*

cadere: *to fall*

cambiare: *to change*

camminare: *to walk*

cancellare: *to cancel*

carino: *pretty*

caro: *dear, expensive*

cattivo: *bad*

cercare: *to look for, to try*

che: *that* (conj. and relative pron.), *who, whom, which*

che, che cosa: *what*

chi: *who, those who*

chiamare: *to call*

chiamarsi: *for one's name to be*

chiudere: *to close, to shut*

chiunque: *anyone, whoever*

ci: *here, there, us*

ciascuno: *everyone*

come: *how*

comprare: *to buy*

con: *with*

conoscere: *to be acquainted with, to know*

contro: *against*

correggere: *to correct*

così: *so*

costoso: *expensive*

costruire: *to build*

credere: *to believe*

crescere: *to grow*

da: *by, from, through*

dappertutto: *everywhere*

dare, donare: *to give*

dei: *some, any*

del: *a little, some, of the*

dentro: *inside*

desiderare: *to wish*

di: *about, of, from*

dietro a: *behind*

difendere: *to defend*

difficile: *difficult*

dimenticare, dimenticarsi: *to forget*

dire: *to say, to tell*

divorziare: *to divorce*

dolce: *sweet*

donna: *woman*

dopo: *after*

dormire: *to sleep*

dove: *where*

dovere: *must, shall, to have to, to be obliged to*

e: *and*

effettivamente: *actually*

entrare: *to enter*

essere: *to be*

essere abituato a: *to be used to*

facile: *easy*

fare: *to do, to make*

felice: *happy*

fermare, fermarsi: *to stop*

finché, fino a quando: *until*

finire: *to end, to finish*

forte: *strong, fast*

fra: *among, between*

fresco: *fresh, cool*

in fretta: *fast, quickly*

di fronte [a]: *in front of, before*

fuori: *out, outside*

gentile: *kind*

già: *already*

giocare: *to play*

giorno: *day*

giovane: *young*

giù: *down*

grande: *great*

grasso: *fat*

grosso: *big*

guardare: *to watch, to look at*

guidare: *to drive*

il: *the*

imprestare: *to lend*

in, in (+ means of transportation): *in, at, to, by*

incominciare: *to begin*

incontrare: *to meet*

indossare, portare: *to wear*

intelligente: *intelligent*

interessante: *interesting*

intorno: *around*

io: *I*

la: *the*

là: *there*

largo: *large*

lasciare: *to leave, to let*

lavorare: *to work*

lei: *she, her*

lentamente: *slowly*

lì: *there*

lontano: *far*

loro: *they, them*

loro, il loro: *their, theirs*

lui: *he, him*

ma: *but*

magro: *thin*

mai: *ever*

male: *badly*

malvolentieri: *unwillingly*

mandare: *to send*

mangiare: *to eat*

massimo: *most*

me: *me*

meglio: *better*

meno, meno di/che: *less, less than*

a meno di/che: *unless*

di meno: *less*

mentre: *while, whereas*

mettere: *to put*

migliore: *better*

minimo: *least*

mio, il mio: *my, mine*

in modo da/che: *so as*

molto, molti: *very, much, many, a lot*

morire: *to die*

muovere, muoversi: *to move*

nascere, essere nato: *to be born*

ne: *of this, of that, of him, of them*

né . . . né: *neither . . . nor*

da nessuna parte: *nowhere*

nessuno: *no, no one, nobody*

niente: *nothing*

no: *no*

noi: *we, us*

noleggiare (un'automobile): *to rent (a car)*

non: *not*

non ancora: *not yet*

non appena: *as soon as*

non . . . mai: *never*

nostro, il nostro: *our, ours*

notte: *night*

nulla: *nothing*

nuovo: *new*

di nuovo: *again*

o: *or*

o . . . o: *either . . . or*

odiare: *to hate*

offrire: *to offer*

ora: *hour, now*

ottenere: *to get*

ottimo: *best*

pagare: *to pay*

parecchio: *a lot, several*

parlare: *to talk, to speak*

partire: *to leave*

passare: *to pass*

peggio: *worse*

peggiore: *worse*

pensare: *to think*

per: *for, through*

perché: *because, why*

perdere: *to lose*

perdonare: *to forgive*

pessimo: *worst*

piacere: *to like*

piano: *slowly*

piccolo: *small, short*

più, più di/che: *more, more than*

di più: *more*

pochi: *few*

poco: *too little, small*

poi: *then*

poiché: *since, as*

portare: *to bring, to take*

possedere: *to own*

potere: *can, may*

preferire: *to prefer*

prendere: *to take*

prendere a prestito: *to borrow, to loan*

prenotare: *to reserve*

presto: *early, soon*

prima: *before*

primo: *first*

prossimo: *next*

provare: *to try*

pulire: *to clean*

da qualche parte: *somewhere*

qualcosa: *anything, something*

qualcuno: *someone, somebody*

quale, il quale, i quali: *which, what, who*

qualsiasi cosa: *anything*

quando: *when*

da quando: *ever since*

quanti: *all those who*

quanto, quanti: *how much, how many, as much, as many*

quello: *that*

questo: *this*

qui: *here*

racontare: *to tell*

ragazzo: *boy*

rapidamente: *quickly, fast*

restituire: *to give back, to return*

ricevere: *to receive, to get*

richiamare: *to call back, recall*

ricordare qualcosa a qualcuno: *to remind someone of something*

ricordare, ricordarsi: *to remember*

ripetere: *to repeat*

rispondere: *to answer*

ritornare: *to return*

riunione: *meeting*

riuscire: *to succeed*

sapere: *to know*

scegliere: *to choose*

se: *if, whether*

sebbene: *although, even though*

sempre: *always*

sentire: *to hear*

senza: *without*

serio: *serious*

si: *one, we, they*

sì: *yes*

sia . . . sia: *both . . . and*

solo, soltanto: *only*

sopra: *over*

sopra, di sopra: *above*

sotto, di sotto: *below*

spaventare: *to frighten*

spedire: *to send, to ship*

spendere: *to spend*

sperare: *to hope*

spesso: *often*

sposare: *to marry*

sposarsi: *to get married*

stare: *to stay*

stesso: *same*

stupido: *stupid*

su: *on, up, over*

suo, il suo: *his, her, hers, its*

suonare: *to play, to ring*

tanto, tanti: *as much, so much, as many, so many*

tardi: *late*

te: *you*

telefonare: *to call, to telephone*

tenere: *to hold, to keep*

tirare su: *to bring up*

tra: *among, between*

triste: *sad*

troppo, troppi: *too much, too many*

trovare: *to find*

tu: *you*

tuo, il tuo: *your, yours*

tutti: *everyone, all*

tutto: *everything, all*

ultimo: *last, latest*

un po', un po' di: *a little, a little of*

un/uno, una: *a, an, one*

uomo: *man*

usare: *to use*

uscire: *to exit, to go out*

vecchio: *old*

vedere: *to see*

veloce: *fast, quick*

velocemente: *fast, quickly*

vendere: *to sell*

venire: *to come*

verso: *toward*

viaggiare: *to travel*

vicino: *near, close*

vivere: *to live*

voi: *you*

volare: *to fly*

volentieri: *gladly*

volere: *to want, will*

vostro, il vostro: *your, yours*

Index

• B •

• C •

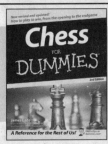
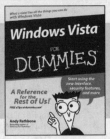

SPORTS, FITNESS, PARENTING, RELIGION & SPIRITUALITY

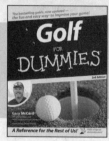

0-471-76871-5

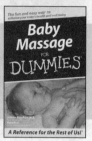

0-7645-7841-3

Also available:
- Catholicism For Dummies
  0-7645-5391-7
- Exercise Balls For Dummies
  0-7645-5623-1
- Fitness For Dummies
  0-7645-7851-0
- Football For Dummies
  0-7645-3936-1
- Judaism For Dummies
  0-7645-5299-6
- Potty Training For Dummies
  0-7645-5417-4
- Buddhism For Dummies
  0-7645-5359-3

- Pregnancy For Dummies
  0-7645-4483-7 †
- Ten Minute Tone-Ups For Dummies
  0-7645-7207-5
- NASCAR For Dummies
  0-7645-7681-X
- Religion For Dummies
  0-7645-5264-3
- Soccer For Dummies
  0-7645-5229-5
- Women in the Bible For Dummies
  0-7645-8475-8

TRAVEL

0-7645-7749-2

0-7645-6945-7

Also available:
- Alaska For Dummies
  0-7645-7746-8
- Cruise Vacations For Dummies
  0-7645-6941-4
- England For Dummies
  0-7645-4276-1
- Europe For Dummies
  0-7645-7529-5
- Germany For Dummies
  0-7645-7823-5
- Hawaii For Dummies
  0-7645-7402-7

- Italy For Dummies
  0-7645-7386-1
- Las Vegas For Dummies
  0-7645-7382-9
- London For Dummies
  0-7645-4277-X
- Paris For Dummies
  0-7645-7630-5
- RV Vacations For Dummies
  0-7645-4442-X
- Walt Disney World & Orlando
  For Dummies
  0-7645-9660-8

GRAPHICS, DESIGN & WEB DEVELOPMENT

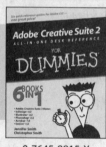

0-7645-8815-X

0-7645-9571-7

Also available:
- 3D Game Animation For Dummies
  0-7645-8789-7
- AutoCAD 2006 For Dummies
  0-7645-8925-3
- Building a Web Site For Dummies
  0-7645-7144-3
- Creating Web Pages For Dummies
  0-470-08030-2
- Creating Web Pages All-in-One Desk
  Reference For Dummies
  0-7645-4345-8
- Dreamweaver 8 For Dummies
  0-7645-9649-7

- InDesign CS2 For Dummies
  0-7645-9572-5
- Macromedia Flash 8 For Dummies
  0-7645-9691-8
- Photoshop CS2 and Digital
  Photography For Dummies
  0-7645-9580-6
- Photoshop Elements 4 For Dummies
  0-471-77483-9
- Syndicating Web Sites with RSS Feeds
  For Dummies
  0-7645-8848-6
- Yahoo! SiteBuilder For Dummies
  0-7645-9800-7

NETWORKING, SECURITY, PROGRAMMING & DATABASES

0-7645-7728-X

0-471-74940-0

Also available:
- Access 2007 For Dummies
  0-470-04612-0
- ASP.NET 2 For Dummies
  0-7645-7907-X
- C# 2005 For Dummies
  0-7645-9704-3
- Hacking For Dummies
  0-470-05235-X
- Hacking Wireless Networks
  For Dummies
  0-7645-9730-2
- Java For Dummies
  0-470-08716-1

- Microsoft SQL Server 2005 For Dummies
  0-7645-7755-7
- Networking All-in-One Desk Reference
  For Dummies
  0-7645-9939-9
- Preventing Identity Theft For Dummies
  0-7645-7336-5
- Telecom For Dummies
  0-471-77085-X
- Visual Studio 2005 All-in-One Desk
  Reference For Dummies
  0-7645-9775-2
- XML For Dummies
  0-7645-8845-1

HEALTH & SELF-HELP

0-7645-8450-2

0-7645-4149-8

Also available:

- Bipolar Disorder For Dummies
  0-7645-8451-0
- Chemotherapy and Radiation
  For Dummies
  0-7645-7832-4
- Controlling Cholesterol For Dummies
  0-7645-5440-9
- Diabetes For Dummies
  0-7645-6820-5* †
- Divorce For Dummies
  0-7645-8417-0 †

- Fibromyalgia For Dummies
  0-7645-5441-7
- Low-Calorie Dieting For Dummies
  0-7645-9905-4
- Meditation For Dummies
  0-471-77774-9
- Osteoporosis For Dummies
  0-7645-7621-6
- Overcoming Anxiety For Dummies
  0-7645-5447-6
- Reiki For Dummies
  0-7645-9907-0
- Stress Management For Dummies
  0-7645-5144-2

EDUCATION, HISTORY, REFERENCE & TEST PREPARATION

0-7645-8381-6

0-7645-9554-7

Also available:

- The ACT For Dummies
  0-7645-9652-7
- Algebra For Dummies
  0-7645-5325-9
- Algebra Workbook For Dummies
  0-7645-8467-7
- Astronomy For Dummies
  0-7645-8465-0
- Calculus For Dummies
  0-7645-2498-4
- Chemistry For Dummies
  0-7645-5430-1
- Forensics For Dummies
  0-7645-5580-4

- Freemasons For Dummies
  0-7645-9796-5
- French For Dummies
  0-7645-5193-0
- Geometry For Dummies
  0-7645-5324-0
- Organic Chemistry I For Dummies
  0-7645-6902-3
- The SAT I For Dummies
  0-7645-7193-1
- Spanish For Dummies
  0-7645-5194-9
- Statistics For Dummies
  0-7645-5423-9

Get smart @ dummies.com®

- **Find a full list of Dummies titles**
- **Look into loads of FREE on-site articles**
- **Sign up for FREE eTips e-mailed to you weekly**
- **See what other products carry the Dummies name**
- **Shop directly from the Dummies bookstore**
- **Enter to win new prizes every month!**

* Separate Canadian edition also available
† Separate U.K. edition also available

Available wherever books are sold. For more information or to order direct: U.S. customers visit www.dummies.com or call 1-877-762-2974.
U.K. customers visit www.wileyeurope.com or call 0800 243407. Canadian customers visit www.wiley.ca or call 1-800-567-4797.